To Cap It All

To Cap It All

The Autobiography of

JOHN RUDGE

With Simon Lowe

Forewords by
Sir Alex Ferguson, Carol Shanahan and Robbie Williams

pitch

First published by Pitch Publishing, 2023
Reprinted, 2023
2

Pitch Publishing
9 Donnington Park,
85 Birdham Road,
Chichester,
West Sussex,
PO20 7AJ
www.pitchpublishing.co.uk
info@pitchpublishing.co.uk

A CIP catalogue record is available for this book from the British Library.

ISBN 978 1 80150 501 7

Typesetting and origination by Pitch Publishing

Printed and bound in Great Britain by TJ Books, Padstow

Contents

Dedication

To my long-suffering wife, Del, who has put up with me for 60-odd years.

I've always said she was my best signing.

Foreword by Sir Alex Ferguson

WHEN I first came to Manchester United in 1986 it was a big challenge to bring our club back to the forefront of football, which meant travelling around the country watching games and, in particular, a lot of interest in reserve games. At almost every game we saw the same faces. My assistant Archie Knox called them 'The Old Soldiers' and amongst them was John Rudge, manager of Port Vale. Every game I went to he was there. Archie and I really admired all these old pros turning up to all these games in all kinds of weather. So, when I got my first call from John, I took it with the enthusiasm of a young boy because I wanted to understand where he got all his energy from.

Well, the conversation didn't go as I thought as, after the pleasantries, John swiftly got to the point of needing a player on loan, which was not a problem as Archie and I had a shared belief that some of the young players needed experience in the tough lower leagues. However, negotiating with John was like robbing a bank. He gave me a sad sob story, crying about lack of money and the chairman not giving him enough financial support. I eventually gave in, completely exhausted.

When you consider the length of time John had been managing Port Vale and how he had the nous to negotiate against other managers all for the good of the club – he was an absolute genius!

It must have been a shock to all the Vale fans when he moved across the road to Stoke City and he served them with the same energy and commitment because John knows only that way.

I know that when people analyse John's career they will nod in unison to a life well spent and a man who sacrificed so much to be the best of himself. If I wander into a reserve game now, I will not be surprised to see that old bonnet on top of that bald head – no identification needed.

Well done John!

Sir Alex Ferguson, CBE

Foreword by Carol Shanahan

FOOTBALL IS made up of legends and heroes and the individuals who are bestowed with these titles have generally contributed much to their clubs and their communities. That word – legend – is used to describe players, managers, staff and supporters at clubs up and down the country and around the world. In some cases this happens far too easily, but clearly in the case of John Rudge there is no debate to be had. Universally, and unequivocally, he is a Port Vale legend.

One of the first things I did when Kevin and I began to consider buying the club was to arrange an introduction to John. I recall our early conversations very well and remember very clearly his exclamations (in an emotional manner that I have come to appreciate is 'very John Rudge') 'Don't do it, under any circumstances, do not do it!' I have since learned he was simply trying to protect me from the pressures of owning a football club. It was an opinion my husband Kevin and I respected, but, as John himself often says, 'You ignored the best advice I ever gave you,' to which I reply that I am grateful that I did.

Meeting with John was less about getting his opinion on purchasing the club – as he has learned over the past few years, when I have my heart set on something, I will generally do it! – but more what Port Vale meant to him. Listening to John talk about the club gave me a clear understanding of not just what we were buying, but what we would be responsible for and custodians of.

John talks so fondly of the club's supporters and how they kept him in a job, while our fans so often talk about the 'Rudgie Years' as the most significant era in the club's history, revelling in the success and memories created during that period. When John talks about those famous FA Cup victories, promotions and the Autoglass Trophy, you see and hear his pride in the achievements. It is now a big motivation of ours to give John and those supporters more of those experiences to recreate the 'Rudgie Years' because there have been so many challenges for the club and its fans since those special days.

We asked John to be the club's life president quite soon after we completed the purchase of the club and were so delighted he said yes. He is a wonderful ambassador for everything about Port Vale and the city of Stoke-on-Trent, not just what happens on the pitch.

John has actually become a really good friend of Kevin's; he comes to all of the matches with us and Kevin and John sit together both at games and in the back of the car on our journeys to away matches. They share a sense of humour that combines taking the mickey out of each other with love and mutual respect. Del (Rudge) and I say they are like Statler and Waldorf from *The Muppet Show*, heckling away together while we look on and quietly shake our heads!

As much as we have fun attending matches together, John has become a good mentor to me and a strong counsel on a variety of matters. I was naïve to the football industry when we purchased the club, so when I have had to make big decisions or solve seemingly insurmountable challenges, I have asked John for his opinion because I know he will always have the best interests of Port Vale plus Kevin and I at heart – not always an easy balancing act to strike.

Wherever you go with John, whether it is an opposition boardroom, an awards ceremony or out to a restaurant, it is like you are with royalty! Everybody knows him; he is so widely respected, carries so much experience and tells so many great stories, as you are about to find out. I've heard a lot of them from the back of the car and even though I will on occasions exclaim 'John, you can't put that in' my guess is that he has!

Rudgie is simply a wonderful man, whom I love to pieces, and he deserves all the plaudits that come his way.

Carol Shanahan
Club Chairperson, Port Vale Football Club

Foreword by Robbie Williams

NOW; NOT name-dropping – although a few will be dropped. There is a reason why I'm about to write what I'm about to write. All will become clear.

I've spent time with Elton John, Princess Diana, Maradona, King Charles, Gianni Versace. The list goes on …

I've never wanted to call them by their titles: Sir Elton, Your Majesty, El Pibe de Oro (look it up), Your Highness etc…

I've never felt the need to.

But I **NEED** to call John Rudge 'Mr Rudge', and he won't let me.

'Please call me, John,' he'll say, so I do. But every time *John* falls out of my mouth it feels gigantically inappropriate.

So, now if I call him John I say *Mr Rudge* to myself in my head.

He is **MY** Sir … and if he decides that I should call him 'Your Highness' I will.

For a small bunch of much forgotten about people that exist somewhere between the North starting and the Midlands ending, during the 80s and 90s Mr Rudge was the glue that brought us much joy, cohesion and a sense of relevancy.

I'm indebted to him for all the glorious memories that remain so close to my heart.

Here's to you, Sir John.

Your fan,

Robbie Williams

Acknowledgements

THIS BOOK has taken a very long time to write, almost 25 years in fact. Not because I was stuck for anything to say, but because I began writing it in the late 1990s with *The Sentinel* newspaper journalist Chris Harper as a celebration of my impending 20th year at Port Vale, but then got the sack.

The fact that I swiftly moved across the Potteries to Stoke City FC to become the director of football meant it wasn't really appropriate to publish an autobiography and, in any case, my career had plenty more years to run, as it turned out.

Life then just overtook me and instead of my book being about a one-club, long-serving manager it has become very much a book of two halves, the first of which details my playing career and time in charge at Vale Park, and the second of which unfolded at the Britannia Stadium (or Bet365 Stadium as it is now known), including promotion to the Premier League, Stoke City's first ever FA Cup Final appearance and European football. From Halifax to Hajduk Split, it's been quite a journey.

There have been fantastic times, relegations, wonderful players, protests and sackings, promotions and great cup victories, joy, heartache and tears. I wouldn't have changed a minute of it.

Thank you to everyone who assisted me, including Jane Camillin at publisher Pitch Publishing, Paul Dalling our editor, Dean Rockett our proofreader and Duncan Olner, our designer. To Port Vale club photographer, Gerard Austin, for access to his fantastic archive and taking photographs of me in my office. Thanks too to all of the players, coaches and staff who I have shared my working life with at all of my clubs, not to mention the irrepressible George Andrews, doyen of Potteries radio, plus fabulous fans like Geoff Wakefield and Mark Porter for helping jog my memory with their own recollections of days gone by.

Also to *The Sentinel* sports editor Rob Cotterill, Stoke City reporter Pete Smith and picture editor Peter Stonier for all their assistance in the archive, and to Reach plc for giving us permission to use them; thanks too to Pete for access to his own personal archive. Also, thanks to Jon Colman, the Carlisle United reporter at the *News and Star* in Cumbria, for access to some great photographs and assistance in publicising the book. I have to give huge thanks to renowned Stoke City author Simon Lowe for setting aside partisan feelings to do such a fantastic job in updating and revising Chris's original draft manuscript and sitting down with me for long reminiscence sessions to help me tell the tale post-1999.

Thanks a million to Sir Alex Ferguson for agreeing to write a foreword for me. Some of what he has written may possibly be true. Also to the incredible Carol Shanahan, chairperson at Port Vale FC, for her own kind words about me, and the legend that is Robbie Williams for finding the time between gigs and touring the world to make such an inimitable contribution.

I am only doing this now because the wonderful Port Vale supporters, who have been so fantastic to me over the years – yes, even despite me joining Stoke City – informed me during the Covid-19 pandemic that they wanted to raise £100,000 to erect a statue of me outside Vale Park. I wouldn't usually be into such aggrandising gestures, but I am so touched by the Vale fans' desire to show their appreciation to me that I wanted to help, so all of my royalties from this book will be going into that fund. Maybe you'll visit the Vale someday and see just how buying this book has helped make that dream a reality. If so, thank you.

Preface
Decision Time

SUMMER 1997; I find myself sitting at my desk in my home office, on which is a contract with my name on it. The job I have verbally agreed to accept would be just the second of my managerial career. The problem? It was as the manager of Stoke City Football Club ... and I was currently the manager of their deadly city rivals.

After 17 years at the club, 13 of those as manager, I was known as 'Mr Port Vale', but I was now about to cross the bitter divide that cleaves Stoke-on-Trent in two football-wise.

My kids were in tears and my wife was worried about the potential repercussions.

How on earth had I got here? Could I lift that pen and sign?

As Sir Alex Ferguson is oft quoted as saying; 'Football, bloody hell!'

Introduction
A Tale of One City

STOKE-ON-TRENT IS a medium-sized city in the north Midlands, not far from the footballers' playground of south Cheshire. At least these days. Back in the 1980s and 90s it was a working-class metropolis split along fervent lines, dependent upon whether you wore red and white for Stoke City, generally in the south of the city, or white and black for Port Vale, more to the north. When I joined Vale in 1980, the sides hadn't played competitively for 23 years and by the time we did face each other it would be over 32 years. It was one of the greatest honours of my career to upset all that history and establish Port Vale as the pre-eminent club in the city for a period in the 1990s, winning four derbies, whilst losing only three, and finishing above Stoke in several seasons. We won classic cup ties against them and sparked a cross-city rivalry back into life which had been forgotten about for more than a generation.

That I should then cross the city to work for the Potters, as Stoke City are known, may have hurt many loyal Vale fans, but I have always had a wonderful reception back at Vale Park and I am now the club president there, supporting the wonderful work of Carol and Kevin Shanahan, who bought the club at a crisis point in May 2019 and have done wonderful work since, by attending on matchdays and meeting with sponsors, etc. So, not only did I once cross the divide, I then went back again.

When I first arrived, the difference between Stoke City and Port Vale was that Stoke were in the top division with several internationals in their team, while Vale were at the foot of the Fourth Division with gates at or below 2,000; very much the poor relations.

The good news in that scenario was that because the clubs were so far apart – quite frankly the board and management at Stoke thought Vale were a non-entity – we could loan or sign players from the Potters, plus play against them in pre-season games, and they wouldn't worry about it. Our fans, however, often did; taking against some players merely because they had, at some point in their career, appeared in the red and white stripes. That's how divided the city was even then.

When, a decade later, Stoke had been relegated to Division Two and I had won two promotions with Vale to get us promoted into that same division, everything changed, escalating to heights that I don't think any of us were ready for.

It became a white-hot rivalry. We were no longer the irrelevant cousins across the city, but, to steal Sir Alex Ferguson's phrase about his relationship with Manchester City once they began their rise to challenge his Manchester United team, we were 'noisy neighbours'. We challenged, annoyed and beat Stoke regularly, finishing above them in the league table and knocking them out of cups on several occasions. So much so, that they wouldn't loan or sell us players and certainly wouldn't play us in pre-season. Our fans loved it. And so did I and the players. We thrived on being the underdogs, the upstarts, the giant-killers. In our eyes, Stoke City and their fans had big pretensions and delusions of grandeur. We loved taking them down.

The Potteries derbies became major events, many of which are talked about even now; Mark Stein's late penalty after 'falling' over Paul Musselwhite, Dave Regis' shot sticking on the line in the Vale Park mud, Martin Foyle's late clinching FA Cup goal, the atmospheres, the build-ups and the aftermaths.

It was wonderful to be involved in and I loved every minute, despite the regular argy-bargy on the terraces and outside the grounds that pockmarked some of those occasions.

Even when I joined Stoke City as director of football in 1999 and saw the rivalry from the other side of the fence, albeit not in the role of manager, I could relish the intensity, which, in my opinion, is equalled by few other same-city rivalries; maybe Glasgow, Manchester and Liverpool can hold a candle to it, but others don't come close. And don't forget I've played in a Bristol derby.

That's the prism within which I worked for 33 years of my footballing life, first on one side of the divide, then on the other. Somehow, I've survived fairly unscathed and now both sets of supporters sing 'John Rudge, he's got no hair, but we don't care' at me when I see them.

It's been a wonderful 40-odd years in this city I now call home, in which my children and grandchildren have grown up with Potteries accents. I wouldn't change it for the world.

Chapter 1

Stepping into Denis Law's Shoes (and Bed)

'I lay there, in Denis Law's bed, wondering if I would ever be sold for £55,000. I don't think I even totalled that amount of transfer fees in my entire career!'

John Rudge

I WAS born in Wolverhampton on 21 October 1944 as the Second World War drew to its bitter close. I lived with my sister Pat, who is six years older than me and so clever I always say she was born with my brains, in a typical three-up, three-down terraced house on the Dudley Road just outside the town centre with our parents, Marie and Jack (although his christened name was Frank Harold Rudge, everyone called him Jack). In keeping with those kinds of properties, the house didn't have an inside toilet at the time. We had to brave the cold to visit the privy in the backyard, which was not only open to the stars, but had no light, which made visits after dusk problematic. My main memory of this contraption isn't during that time, but stems from the first occasion I took my then girlfriend, and now wife, Del, to meet my parents. I had to guide her out into the open air to find the toilet and then stand guard so no one else tried to enter. It wasn't what she was used to, and she came from Huddersfield!

Ours was a warm family environment, although my father was a Jekyll and Hyde character. He was an accomplished capstan operator, setting and operating a capstan lathe at a factory works in Wolverhampton; that is when he fancied going to work, which wasn't that often. His split personality emerged when he'd had a drink, which was most nights. Dad was a complex man, but I know he would have loved to see me succeed in football management. He died in 1972, when I was playing for Bristol Rovers. He did come to watch me play occasionally throughout my career, though.

My mother was a proud, hard-working woman who ran a fruit and veg market stall at Wolverhampton market for over 60 years. I can still remember her shouting in a loud, Black Country voice, 'I weigh bananas; anyone want a nice pound of pears …?' Mum had that stall until she was 80 years old. Remarkable.

We had other relations who worked on the market, so it really did feel like a family down there. My Uncle Jack had an indoor stall that specialised in Asian food. He had served in the Royal Air Force in India and was familiar with its dishes and spices, so found a niche in the market, particularly with the growing Asian population in the area. I helped him for the princely sum of two shillings and sixpence a day, the equivalent of about 12 pence now, but worth considerably more to me. As a result, I can still count in Punjabi to this day. We used to have dozens of old biscuit tins lined up containing goods like black-eyed peas, chilli powder and curry powder. I remember we used to go up to Birmingham to buy rice, which was weighed out in measures and put in brown sugar bags. It was a thriving business. I still remember the occasion when I was twirling a bag of turmeric powder and it burst, showering the customer in a sea of yellow. It took forever to get that out of my hair. Yes, I did have hair back then.

I started on the market very young (it saved mum paying for childcare which she simply couldn't afford, I suppose), helping my mother out, first pushing the little truck full of stock to and from the wholesalers' van to the stall, before graduating to selling to customers. Then on a Saturday afternoon I would go and watch my boyhood team Wolves when they were at home, taking one of the fruit and veg boxes with me to stand on so I could see over the wall of the paddock, which sank down some way beneath pitch level, to admire my heroes. I wasn't particularly tall then, so really needed the box. Some say I haven't grown since!

Mum strove to enable my sister and I to enjoy a loving, close, Catholic upbringing on scant resources and tried to get both of us everything we required. She bought me a leather-cased football that was the talk of the street. Older boys used to knock on our door to see if I was coming out to play and, if I couldn't, could they borrow my ball? I would be out like a flash as often as I could. Playing with older and stronger boys probably helped me being selected for St Mary's and St John's Primary School Under-11 football team when I was just seven years old.

'Can you play with your left foot, Rudge?' asked the teacher who picked the team. 'Of course I can,' I responded. So, I played, despite being three or four years younger. I don't know why, but the older boys called me 'Oscar'.

So now my Saturdays consisted of helping out down the market, playing football for the school, then going to watch the Wolves in the afternoon. Blissful times.

I moved on to St Joseph's secondary modern school, but I was only interested in football, not academic subjects, and was selected to represent Wolverhampton Schoolboys, training with the squad a couple of evenings a week, having been recommended by one of my teachers.

At that time Wolverhampton Wanderers were one of the best clubs in the world, with a team packed full of England internationals, including wizard winger Johnny Hancocks, who was my role model as a small, lithe, quick attacker, Ron Flowers, a teak-tough midfielder, and legendary captain Billy Wright. Under manager Stan Cullis, Wanderers won the league title in 1953/54 and took part in prestigious floodlit, televised friendlies against European clubs such as the Hungarians Honvéd and touring Soviet sides Dynamo and Spartak Moscow, plus Real Madrid. These games were the precursor for the European Cup, which began in 1955, and has now developed into the Champions League. I remember that famous game against Honvéd on 13 December 1954 so well. Wolves won 3-2 and Cullis claimed our heroes to be world champions afterwards, as they had beaten the side which boasted most of the Hungarian team which had thrashed England 6-3 at Wembley just a year before. The thing I particularly recall is the Hungarians going two goals ahead early on, but then Wolves overpowering them in the second half. The equaliser and winning goals were scored in a quick two-minute salvo by Roy Swinbourne, a wonderful centre-forward, both from passes by amateur striker Dennis Wilshaw, who, despite being an England international, was also a schoolteacher.

My fruit and veg box allowed me to see the likes of Puskás, Yashin and Di Stéfano, all of whom were fabulous players, and I also remember an FA Cup tie in January 1957 against Bournemouth in which one of the Cherries' players, Reg Cutler, hit the headlines for breaking a goal post as the third-tier club beat mighty Wolves 0-1, causing a huge shock.

Another hero of mine was the England goalkeeper Bert Williams. Bert used to happily sign autographs as he walked from Molineux out and about into Wolverhampton and would look like the Pied Piper with a stream of youngsters in his wake. There were so many lads keen to get his signature that, by the time it was your turn, you could be a quarter of a mile away from the ground!

I was lucky because I had a wonderful mentor in the shape of my sister's boyfriend and then, later, my brother-in-law, Peter Clark. Peter was playing for the reserves and was understudy to Eddie Clamp, the former Arsenal and England international, who anchored Wolves' midfield. Peter used to take me down to Molineux to watch games, and also into the park to work on my technique, but unlike him, I never realised my ambition to wear the famous gold and black shirt as Wolves declined to sign me on as an apprentice, despite my star turns for the schoolboys team, when I reached the age of 15 in 1959. I always felt that was because they thought I was too small, but even by the age of 15, I was 5ft 7in and would go on to grow to 5ft 10in. I know what you're thinking, he's never that tall!

I was inconsolable, but help was at hand swiftly in the form of Lawrie Kelly, a former player who was scouting for Huddersfield Town, who were in Division Two at the time. Myself and a lad called Graham French, who was a left-winger and went on to have a decent career at Shrewsbury and Luton, had been playing together in the Wolverhampton schoolboys team and, at the end of one game, Lawrie approached us and said, 'How would you fancy going to Huddersfield as apprentices?'

We jumped at the chance.

Luckily, even though I was only 15, my parents said I could go. I looked at my grandson when he was 15 and couldn't believe at that age I was allowed to disappear off to the north to live in a completely unknown Yorkshire town. I can only think my parents knew I had to pursue my dream, having seen my utter devastation at having been told Wolves weren't going to sign me. So, I joined the Huddersfield Town 'ground staff' – the term used in those days for being an apprentice.

To start with I didn't live up in Yorkshire all the time, but caught the train from Wolverhampton on a Monday morning and returned after the Saturday morning youth team game. Quickly, though, I moved into digs full-time.

As it happened, days before I arrived at Leeds Road in March 1960, Huddersfield had sold Denis Law to Manchester City for a British record fee of £55,000. The digs I initially moved into was a big, shared property in Milnsbridge, owned by a Mrs Sobey, which housed a mix of apprentices and established players. In fact, my bed was in a row of three in this room and had recently been vacated by none other than Law himself. Denis was four and a half years older than me, so that gave me something of a target to aim for!

So, here I was sleeping in the Lawman's bed (as he was known) and, as I lay there, finding myself wondering if I would ever be sold for £55,000. The answer turned out to be a resounding 'no'. I don't think I even totalled that amount of transfer fees in my entire career!

On top of that, one of the first things I found in my section of the wardrobe was a pair of Denis's smart, black shoes which he had somehow left behind. It must have been the enormous signing-on fee of around £50 he'd received that caused him to forget them, I'd imagine ...

The other two lads in the room confirmed that I could have these smart size sevens, which was my size, but I thought I'd make a present of them to my father. So, I took them home and gave them to dad, who was over the moon. No sooner had I told him whose shoes they were, than he togged himself up smart and wore them down the pub, telling everyone who'd listen that he was wearing Denis Law's shoes! Dad did this regularly for years.

It was so cold in Mrs Sobey's house that we kept our woollen football socks on in bed and it was so damp that when we put our pyjamas in front of the little gas fire to get them warm, steam rose off them in a cloud. There were frequent fights amongst the lads over playing cards and I learned of one incident when Denis was reported to have punched one lad straight through the window. As for food, everything came with chips and fag ash – so much for a footballer's healthy diet in those days.

There was nothing glamorous about being a ground staff boy at a Second Division club. We did all the menial chores like getting on our hands and knees to scrub the corridor with a brush and soap on Fridays, ready for the match on Saturday. We were spurred on by the hope of finding a bob or two, but we suspected the groundsman had already conducted his search.

The first-teamers would train on the pitch on Mondays and we'd be ready to leap over the perimeter wall to make up the numbers to show the pros how promising we were if their numbers were depleted through injury or illness. Our organised football was restricted to the Northern Intermediate League on Saturday mornings and after the game I would hurry to the station to catch the train home, via Stoke, never realising the Potteries would play such a large part in my life.

I must admit it was tearful at times when, as a young lad, I left my parents' house at 6.30am on a Monday to head back to Huddersfield, taking with me my clean washing that had been aired in front of the living room fire, whilst hoping the train would get me to the ground for a 9am start or I'd be punished with even more chores.

I often wondered while on that train whether I really wanted the heartache of being away from my family, but I desperately wanted to become a professional footballer and was driven on by my determination. My brother-in-law, Peter, was a massive influence in urging me on, himself a professional until a serious knee injury ended his aspiration to be a First Division player. He eventually moved on to Doncaster, Mansfield, Stockport and Crewe in the lower leagues. Sadly, Peter eventually had to retire, a lesson for me in the fragility of footballers' careers.

* * *

I started at Huddersfield at £7 a week as an apprentice. From that, I would have to fund my regular visits home to see my folks. During those trips, I also continued to help out at the market to earn some extra pennies. Even when I turned pro, I carried on working at the market in the summer break to top up my earnings. Buying and selling was part of my upbringing and it stood me in good stead later in my career at Bournemouth when injuries prevented me from playing and also, I believe, in the horse trading that is buying and selling footballers when I became a manager. Can you imagine a modern footballer doing that now?

That work ethic stood me in good stead for life, as did the one proviso my parents gave me when I started as a 15-year-old with Huddersfield Town; I had to get myself a back-up trade.

I hadn't been the Brain of Britain at school, being obsessed with football, as I say, but I started going to college, learning initially to be a radio and television engineer, one day a week on top of my apprentice duties at Huddersfield. I remember the chap taking the course simply putting a television in front of me at the college and just saying, 'right, there's a fault on there, find it'. No other assistance or advice given! I had no chance. All the other students on the course were already working in TV shops and that kind of thing, so they had that background and regular working practice. I was kicking footballs around. So, that didn't last long.

I was still gently nudged regularly by my mother, who was desperate to know I had something to fall back on, so I dabbled in a range of other courses, sometimes on days off, sometimes in the evenings and gained GCE 'O' levels in English, management and accountancy. All that studying meant that I always had something outside football on the go throughout my career. Also, when it came to management, I was ready for the long and lonely evenings driving to watch players, studying form and tactics.

The club didn't push any kind of education agenda. That sort of thing came in much later, with football academies now ensuring their youngsters take and pass exams, as well as learn football skills. My major concern, although not as great as my mother's, was what would I do if I didn't get signed on professionally? In the 1950s and 60s, football clubs didn't give two hoots about that.

More is the pity, perhaps, that I did not study physiotherapy at night school as, even then as a young player, I was struggling with injuries, picking up knocks, strains and stresses all the time. My hamstrings were a big problem and these issues blighted my career. My physique also wasn't the strongest; my legs were like sticks, but that litheness allowed me to flit round defenders, so it worked both ways. At that time, we didn't do weights or anything like that to bulk up. On Fridays, as light preparation for the following day's game, we used to don our spikes and go sprinting, which was my strength as I was quick, but there was very little that made us stronger built into our training. In common with many sprinters, my hamstrings often tweaked. I'd liken myself in that sense to former England striker Michael Owen, who I would later sign for Stoke City, in that sense, but it is the only comparison I can draw between him and me!

As it turned out, though, I never used that education directly to get myself a job outside football, but I firmly believe that having it, and indeed the drive, nous and dedication to achieve all that instead of just sitting back on my laurels and assuming I would continue to have a career in the game, stood me in great stead when it came to being offered coaching and then managerial positions.

* * *

Despite those injury issues, I was taken on when many weren't and turned professional in November 1961 just after my 17th birthday. By then I was 5ft 10in tall, decent with my head and fast as a whippet. At least that's how I tell it.

Not everyone was as lucky. Graham French, the lad I had been spotted alongside, blotted his copybook one day when he was walking from the ground up the road to a nearby cafe in a small group, including me. As we walked, we saw this girl walking towards us and for some reason Graham decided to shout at her, 'Are you dropping 'em tonight?'

Not surprisingly the girl took great offence and, realising that we were young footballers, she went into the mill where she worked next to the ground and told the manager, who then told the owner, who happened to be a director of Huddersfield Town, what had occurred. Graham was sent home after that.

I made my debut the following season, in which we ended up sixth in the Second Division under manager Eddie Boot. But I couldn't make the breakthrough into the first team, appearing mostly for the reserves when I wasn't injured. I also had a slight problem in that, try as I might, I could never get my left foot to be as good as my right. If I'm honest, as good as my right was, and it was very good, my left was as weak. I could never improve it, despite working so hard on it.

At that time, Huddersfield were a good Second Division club that included Raymond Wilson, who would go on to play left-back in England's 1966 World Cup-winning side, Mike O'Grady, an exceptional left-winger, and former England goalkeeper Ray Wood, who had survived the Munich air crash in February 1958. He had played only one more game for Manchester United following the disaster, joining Huddersfield that summer. The manager, Eddie Boot, ran a tyre business on the side and never swore, but had the knack of winding players up, so they often did.

We often used to play in the big car park just outside the ground so we didn't wreck the pitch. Beforehand, Eddie would come into the apprentices' dressing room and tell us not to be overawed by the 'fupping' (his version of the F word) pros or let them kick us about. He would then go and tell the first team not to let the youngsters get the better of them. By the time we got out there we were all spitting blood. There were often fights in that car park, plus a lot of bad grazes from some of the tackles that flew in on the totally inappropriate surface. It was a unique managerial style, I suppose.

My problem as a youngster was displacing the two strikers who were in possession of the first-team shirts as they were both hugely experienced pros who scored fairly regularly. One was Scottish striker Les Massie, who netted over 100 goals for Town in a ten-year career at Leeds Road. He was in his heyday while I was trying to break through, which made my job very difficult.

Alongside Les was senior pro Len White, a stocky, powerful striker who was coming to the end of a wonderful career in which he had become Newcastle United's second-highest scorer, with 153 goals, behind Jackie Milburn, his team-mate in the heady days of the Magpies winning FA Cups in the 1950s. Both were, of course, overtaken by Alan Shearer in the early 2000s. With that pair ahead of me there were few opportunities to make the breakthrough.

Successfully making the first team, however, was Chris Balderstone, who was a little older than me and had risen through the ranks after signing as a 17-year-old from Shrewsbury Town, where he had been a youth player. 'Baldy' was one of those admirable, but annoying, individuals who was good at every sport, eventually making a dual career in both football and as a cricketer, even playing for England, then going on to become an umpire. As a footballer he was a lovely, skilful midfielder who could see a great pass and deliver it, like radar. To be either is fantastic. To be both is exceptional.

I got on very well with Chris and we ended up as big pals. I was amazed at his ability to play both sports to such a high standard and his dedication to mastering the skills of each. Later in his career he would famously play both football and cricket professionally on the same day; turning out for Leicestershire during the day in a County Championship match against Derby at Chesterfield, ending the day 51 not out, and then haring 30-odd miles up the M1 to play for Doncaster Rovers that evening in a 1-1 draw against Brentford. He then returned to complete his century the next morning. Remarkable.

One of my big pals at Huddersfield was a lad called Allan Gilliver, a strapping centre-forward who was the same age as me. We came through the ranks and made our first-team debuts together aged 17. We actually only found out we were going to play against Swansea Town (as they were called then) in the local evening newspaper, the night before the game. The manager never told us. We defeated the Swans 4-1 on Monday, 6 May 1963 and Allan netted two of our goals. We got on so well, that, eventually, I was Allan's best man. We decided to move digs across town so we could live together and lodged with a lady called Mrs Clarke.

As a young man of some standing in Huddersfield, I was also on the lookout for a young lady to sweep off her feet. I didn't really go out drinking as I wanted to give myself the best chance at making it in the Huddersfield first team, but my sprightliness in jinking through defences since the age of seven stood me in good stead on the dance floor and I won the Butlin's dance competition during one holiday when I was 16!

That wasn't how I eventually met my wonderful wife Del, though. Nor was our meeting your typical football romance story. I actually just needed to make a phone call home. The problem was my new digs had no phone line connected, as was fairly common at that time, so I went outside and cast my eye up and down the Bradford Road, spotting a hairdresser's salon almost directly opposite. I knocked on and asked the girl who opened the door if I could use their phone. She said yes, so I rang home and chatted with my parents for a few minutes, giving them updates. Then, after putting the phone down, I said thank you to the girl and left.

That really was my lucky day as, little did I realise it then, but I would end up spending the rest of my life with that young lady, whose name it transpired was Dellice, a name I've never heard of before or since. She really is unique, my Del!

Following that call, every time I left the digs, I could see Del looking out of the salon, hiding a bit behind the curtain, seeing if it was me coming out of the front door. So, I knew she fancied me from the way she looked at me. I reciprocated, watching her while she opened the salon. It was like a little courtship dance at distance across the Bradford Road; the 60s weren't yet swinging in Yorkshire. Del was beautiful. So, I kept phoning home more and more regularly so I could meet her and have a chat with her. My parents weren't used to all this contact from me! Finally, I plucked up the courage and we began stepping out together and have now been married nearly 60 years.

Very simply, for me, meeting Del was the best thing I ever did. We have spent our lives together, through thick and thin, and she has been a huge support and key influence behind the scenes for me, especially during the years I was manager at Port Vale. She was bringing up the children, while I flitted around the country watching players in far-flung glamorous places such as Grimsby, Darlington, Gillingham and Hull.

Actually, at the end of that season we met in, we broke up because I was going home for the summer to work on the market to earn extra cash. After I returned for the start of the following season, there was this Miss Huddersfield Town competition at the Town Hall. Del's friends had realised I'd be there and dared her to enter. Once I saw her on stage, I realised what I'd been missing. Not that she won, but she won me. I asked her out again and that was it.

* * *

Actually, how Del had come to run that salon is something of a tale in itself.

Del's mother died when she was nine. She had grown up in Hull, but her parents had split up and, as her father moved to Huddersfield, she was brought over to live with him. He had no idea how to look after a child and, as he was just living in a room in digs, he didn't have anywhere for her to sleep. Remarkably, when he went to visit a local landlady to ask if she had a spare house he could rent, instead of giving him accommodation, the landlady took Del under her wing as she wouldn't see this young lass living in such conditions. This lovely lady was called Edith Longbottom; who Del, and eventually I, called 'Auntie'. She never formally adopted Del, but she treated her as if she was her own.

Auntie had recently lost her husband, who had made quite a bit of money and invested it in property, mainly terraced houses with no bathrooms which were all rented out, so she was quite wealthy. Del stayed with Auntie and was brought up effectively as the daughter she had never had, while Del's father faded into the background, seemingly relieved to have palmed his daughter off, although to be fair to him, he was slightly disabled as he had a gammy leg having suffered with polio as a youngster.

Del had a much better childhood in that house than she would have done otherwise. There was an old sheepdog called Shep, which looked after Del as much as she looked after him. Auntie also had a hen run and geese. Del had to collect the eggs and the geese often chased her as she tried to take theirs. But best of all Auntie was the owner of a sweet shop, which she leased out, and took part of the rent in sweets, so Del could have them.

When she was 19, Auntie leased the hairdressing shop for Del, who'd trained to be a hairdresser since the age of 15, buying the incumbent business for her for £150 as the lady who ran it was retiring. The salon just so happened to be situated right opposite our digs. How lucky for me.

Influenced by Del, and fed up with TV repairs and the like, I had a go at hairdressing as one of my back-up options. Insert your own joke here … The irony of the terrace chant, 'He's got no hair, but we don't care' which rang out from the Bycars End at Vale Park on a regular basis is not lost on me, especially as even by then I was thinning on top. Del took me to a place in Halifax where I could learn to cut gentlemen's hair. But it was in a unisex salon and I soon got fed up with, what I call 'women's talk' all the time. It used to drive me daft, so I packed that up. Instead, I continued going back to night school and got those five 'O' levels, although that took me until I was 22, passing an exam here and another there.

* * *

In 1964, after failing to win any of the first nine games of the season, Eddie Boot got the boot and Tom Johnston was installed as Huddersfield manager. He arrived after being in charge of Rotherham and Grimsby, but my injuries meant I didn't really feature very much under him. I played two games at the start of the 1966/67 season, but then dropped out of the first-team picture entirely and, as I had been at Huddersfield for six years, but only played five senior matches, I suppose he thought he wasn't going to get many games out of me. The Terriers were a very good side at that point, often challenging for promotion from the Second Division, so, as I wasn't in his plans, the manager allowed me a move to Second Division rivals Carlisle United in December 1966 for the princely fee of £4,000. Not quite Denis Law proportions! I had just turned 22. My replacement in the Huddersfield squad was a young whippersnapper called Frank Worthington, promoted from the youth ranks. I wonder what became of him?

The start of my three-year stay at Carlisle was memorable for the fact that Del and I got married on Sunday, 2 April 1967, back in Huddersfield, with my cousin Gordon Potts as my best man. Sadly, Auntie, who had made the bridesmaids' dresses, wasn't well enough to attend as she was in hospital. Our honeymoon was just one night in a hotel at Scotch Corner, before I returned to training in Carlisle on the Tuesday morning. That's the lot of a footballer during the season.

The day before our wedding, we won 2-1 at Hull City and I was on such a high towards the end of the game that I knocked the ball out of the goalkeeper's hands and smashed it into the Boothferry Park net. It didn't stand and, for my sins, I had my name taken by referee Mr Staveley for the first time in my career for 'ungentlemanly conduct'. My lips remain sealed as to my conduct, gentlemanly or otherwise, on my wedding night.

Chapter 2

More Muscle on a Chip

'Rudge is the only player to pull a muscle while putting on his tracksuit.'

Robin Perry, Bristol Rovers reporter for the *Bristol Evening Post*

FEELING THAT we were starting out on a new adventure, when Del and I moved to Cumbria in December 1966, we moved into our first home together. We were one of a set of four Carlisle United players living all in a row, in two sets of semi-detached club houses. However, in common with most players at my level at that time, owning a house was way out of my reach on the wages I was earning, despite the wage cap for footballers having been lifted in 1961. So, we found ourselves living in a club house, owned and (allegedly) maintained by Carlisle United. It had two bedrooms, a lounge and a kitchen and was heated solely by one coal fire, no central heating at all. Consequently, it was absolutely bloody freezing. I remember the windows getting solid with ice, with icicles hanging off the tap on the basin in the bathroom … yes, bathroom. It had all mod cons.

Having said that, as newly-weds, we felt this was like some kind of palace, although, when my parents came to visit, we actually had to put a mattress in the bath for my dad to sleep on as he couldn't even get forty winks on the lumpy bed in the spare room.

Our 'palace' cost us £2 7s 6d (£2.38) per week in rent; it was actually £2 for the house and 7s 6d for the garage! That was par for the course back then. Young players could simply never dream of being able to afford our own houses. At that time, Carlisle United actually had a policy that all players were on the same wage of £27 10s (£27.50) per week, with a £4 win bonus, so we were all in the same boat, or so we thought. One of my compatriots was striker Hughie McIlmoyle, a Brunton Park legend. Hughie was a good player, who had played for Leicester City in the FA Cup Final in 1961, losing to double-winning Spurs, and had then joined Carlisle in 1963, scoring 47 goals in 77 appearances before being sold to Wolves in October 1964. He returned to Carlisle to join us again in September 1967 and I enjoyed playing alongside him. We dovetailed well.

But, after he arrived as a senior pro, Hughie caused a lot of controversy and resentment in the dressing room when it became apparent that he was an exception to the 'same wage' policy we had all bought into. Instead, he was earning £35 per week, plus win bonus, plus extra for his column in the local newspaper. That did not go down well with the rest of us. Hughie eventually moved on again, being sold to Middlesbrough in October 1969 for a whopping £55,000 … that fee again! He had scored 19 goals in 69 appearances in his second spell at the club. Desperate to cash in on their prize asset, Carlisle pushed through his transfer for a fee that was around 14 times what our semi-detached club house (which we couldn't afford to buy) was worth. It was actually, the second-highest fee in the country that season, which shows you how prized his signature was. It didn't go too well at his new club, though, and stories soon filtered out about how unsettled Hughie and his family were in the North East; he even threatened to quit the game for a new job – delivering milk – before being transferred to Preston North End.

Despite the various challenges, we enjoyed living in Carlisle and loved making the most of access to the Lake District, going for walks and days out. Every so often we would embark on the intrepid journey to see my parents in Wolverhampton in my first car, a Mini, which I bought when I was 19 going on 20 in Huddersfield. It got a few miles on it when we lived in Carlisle, I can tell you.

Del continued to work as a hairdresser. She had to, financially speaking. In fact, I can now reveal a secret; Del has always done my hair. She has played a huge part in the 'barnet' I have sported now for 50-odd years, as I began to recede at 22 and had gone bald on top by the time I was 28. I still maintain that the reason I lost all my hair wasn't because of the stress of being a football manager, but because Del kept putting me under the hairdryer to practise on me and it accelerated my balding by blowing it all off! These days the likes of Wayne Rooney have been able to fund full hair transplants. It was different in my day. I tried a few 'miracle cures', none of which worked. Then I remember one occasion when someone asked me if I had tried restoring it by putting paraffin on it. Paraffin? I'd have gone down in flames.

* * *

Carlisle was where my playing career really took off, especially in that first season after I arrived. I was fit, for once, and full of gusto. The manager, Alan Ashman, espoused good, fast, flowing football and he had a great man working under him, Dick Young, another Carlisle legend who was first-team coach from 1956 to 1975. Dick ran fantastic training sessions with the ball, based on passing and moving into space. He kept the game simple, forging a team pattern, while Alan scoured the country for players who could fit into that method and wanted to live in the northern outpost of Carlisle, developing a fearsome reputation for bargain-hunting as he did so. The club grew on paying peanuts for decent players who were on the fringe of the first team at bigger clubs and Alan pieced together an exciting side, playing one- and two-touch football. I'm going to claim I was one such player, ahem …

At the time, I didn't appreciate how good a coach Dick was. He trained us to pass and move, pass and move, just the kind of football that Manchester City have mastered under Pep Guardiola in recent seasons. At the time, the reference point was the great Liverpool team, as that era had begun under Bill Shankly. Dick Young's philosophy was on much the same lines. As players we would constantly moan about the repetitive nature of the training; pass and move, pass and move. We were so well-drilled, one- or two-touch all the time. 'They don't teach this at Lilleshall, Dick,' used to be our shout as we underwent the same drill for the hundredth time that day.

'Get on with it,' would be his gruff retort.

How wrong we were, as I would find out in the not-too-distant future. Honestly, players think they know it all, but often they are just big-headed lads who don't know any better and need keeping in line by an old, wise bird like Dick Young.

I really did not understand how good his training sessions were until I was older and wiser and I eventually incorporated most of his philosophy on how the game should be played into my own style and way of thinking. I ended up doing a lot of the things he used to do in training. Not only that, but I saw first-hand how this transfer strategy worked so brilliantly for the club and stored it away in the back of my mind for later use.

Carlisle United was a club that was very much on the up, having earned promotion to the second tier of English football for the first time in their history in 1965, boasting an average gate of around 10,000; well above historic levels. Ashman had promised me regular first-team football when he persuaded me to join. I was barely getting any at Huddersfield under Tom Johnston, so I felt this was too good an opportunity to turn down, especially as Carlisle were in the Second Division, actually slightly above Huddersfield, and had a chance of promotion to the top flight. I had also called my former Terriers team-mate Chris Balderstone, who had moved to Cumbria a year earlier for £7,000 and was loving life in the foothills of the Lakes. Chris really sold everything about Carlisle to me. He and his family loved it there. Once we arrived, Del and I used to go out with Chris and his wife on a regular basis, while Chris and I used to play a spot of golf, although, not surprisingly, he was also an exceptionally good golfer and regularly beat me. I told you he was annoying. Mixing together off the pitch really helped to create a bond on it and he and I struck up a good understanding. Many was the defence-splitting pass from Baldy that put me in on goal.

It was incredibly exciting and I played a lot more, suffering far fewer injuries, but the main memory I recall is scoring the best goal of my career for Carlisle against Bolton Wanderers when I hit a screamer past former England goalkeeper Eddie Hopkinson from 35 yards. Apparently, as I crossed the halfway line, carrying the ball forwards in a dribble, beating a couple of men in the inside-right position, and wound up my right peg to rifle the ball goalwards, coach Dick Young, who was sitting on the bench, shouted, 'He's not thinking of bleedin' shooting from there, is he? What the hell is he doing?' Once the ball had rocketed into the top corner of the net, Young roared, 'Great goal, Rudgie! I told you to have a dig!' The other lads on the bench rolled out of the dugout, creasing up laughing.

That was one goal in my only senior hat-trick, as we thrashed Bolton 6-1 at Brunton Park on the final day of the 1966/67 campaign. We were on a roll at that point and I had made an immediate impact, scoring seven goals in 14 appearances as we won five out of our last eight games to finish in third position, albeit six points adrift of Wolves, who ended the season in the second promotion place, behind champions Coventry. Sadly, only two clubs went up in those days. It wasn't increased to three until 1973/74, when ironically, Carlisle won promotion to the First Division for the first, and so far only, time in their history – in third position.

Still, finishing third and just missing promotion was, at that point, Carlisle's greatest ever season, even though we were disappointed not to have made it into the top division.

One thing that surprised me was that, when we were down in London staying overnight before a game at Charlton, my first away match in the capital, the squad headed off for a drink in Soho. I discovered this when some of the more senior players asked me if I wanted a bevvy just after we had arrived at our hotel.

'No, you're alright,' I replied, thinking I was being professional. I wasn't a big drinker anyway and, being a youngster, I didn't want to let the manager down as it may have jeopardised my place in the team.

'But we're in London,' they cajoled. 'It will only be a couple of pints.'

I caved.

In moments, I found myself amidst the bright lights of the West End, out for an evening on the sauce the night before we played a match. I couldn't believe it.

Even more memorably, my choice of drink got me a few funny looks and jibes from my team-mates.

'What you 'aving, Rudgie?' asked the skipper Peter McConnell, generously.

'I'll have a sweet sherry please.' I was never one for drinking pints.

Guffaws all round.

'Bloody hell, lads,' my new colleagues chorused to a man. 'What have we signed here? Rudgie's having a sweet sherry?!'

Those were very different times in terms of players' drinking; it used to be the norm, not like the modern era. Legendary are the antics of some of the footballers of the 1960s to 1980s. Southampton were dubbed 'alehouse brawlers' once by Liverpool's manager Bill Shankly, Jimmy Greaves and George Best were renowned for their drinking exploits, while the likes of Alan Hudson at Chelsea and then Stoke and Bryan Robson at Manchester United led drinking cultures of legend.

By the way, we lost at Charlton 0-1. Just in case you were wondering.

* * *

Unhindered by alcoholic intake in the main, over the course of the following 1967/68 campaign, I continued my decent form, scoring nine goals in 29 league and cup games as we posted a slightly disappointing tenth-place finish. By that time the manager had been headhunted by West Brom, with whom he won the FA Cup at Wembley in 1968, defeating Everton 1-0. Ashman was replaced by Tim Ward, the former Derby County manager, who was very experienced at Second Division level.

We only really had one high point under Tim, which was a fantastic FA Cup third round victory away at First Division Newcastle United. On Saturday, 27 January 1968, St James' Park was packed with over 56,000 fans, the biggest crowd I ever played in front of, for what was the first meeting between the two clubs. This was a very good Geordie team with the likes of strikers Wyn Davies and Bryan 'Pop' Robson, left-back Frank Clark and skipper Bobby Moncur, although their terror of a centre-half John McGrath didn't play as he was in the process of being sold to Southampton, so our paths would not cross for another 12 years yet. At that point, the Magpies were unbeaten at home that season and stood in fifth position in the First Division table. They would go on to lift the Inter-Cities Fairs Cup the following season, so that victory, courtesy of a goal from my strike partner Tommy Murray in the 12th minute, was a fantastic result; a giant-killing which gave me a taste for being the underdog and defeating teams with far greater resources. To set the seal on a fantastic afternoon, Alan Ross, our keeper, saved a penalty from Newcastle's Ollie Burton. Sometimes everything just goes for you and in those circumstances, smaller clubs can achieve incredible things.

That was as good as it got, really, as we went out to star-studded Everton in the next round, losing 0-2 at Brunton Park in front of 25,000 fans. Part-way through the subsequent 1968/69 season, we were struggling, in and out of the relegation zone and failed to win any of our first 12 league games. The manager was under pressure, we were bottom of the league – one fan was so angry that he painted the words 'Ward must go' in creosote on the turf in front of the directors' box.

We used to call Ward 'Gentleman Tim'. I'll never forget one match at Crystal Palace in September 1968. We lost 0-5. At half-time we were three or four down and Dick Young was quite rightly going through us like a dose of salts. Tim was just walking round the dressing room, seemingly in a daze. Eventually he went over to Chris Balderstone. We all held our breath for the manager's words of wisdom and even Dick Young paused his invective … but all Ward said was something like, 'Baldy, Clive Lloyd is 320 not out for the West Indies.'

After that game, it felt such a long way back to Carlisle on the coach, and, just to compound our misery, it went and broke down on the 'Shap', the steep road into the Lake District from Lancashire near the village of that name, between Kendal and Penrith. After waiting for ages, the driver finally got it going again and we arrived back in the small hours, only to awake the next morning to find out the gaffer had been fired. What a calamitous weekend that was.

The directors appointed Bob Stokoe as manager, poaching him from Rochdale. There was no in-between with Bob. He was ruthless, but I wouldn't say anything bad about him. He simply told you fair and square how it was. Unlike Ward, Bob was immersed in football, much more like myself. He took the game home with him; a bad result would ruin his weekend. And you'd know about it.

Of course, Bob would attain legendary status by leading Second Division Sunderland to victory over giants Leeds in the 1973 FA Cup Final and now has his own statue outside the Stadium of Light, frozen forever in his Wembley celebratory jig, famous trilby atop his head. There must be something about hats ...

The Saturday before Stokoe's first official game in charge, as the club was managerless, the directors actually picked the team and left me on the bench. The team went 16 games unbeaten, mostly unchanged, as Bob stuck with the winning formula the directors had found the week before, so I rarely made an appearance from the bench. I couldn't get a look in as the team recovered to finish 12th. It also makes me think that the cliché about directors knowing nothing about football isn't always true! Although this was to my detriment.

I really wasn't having much luck in that sense and neither was I with injuries, as my curse returned again. I cannot remember stringing together a run of more than about 15 games from this point in my career before some injury or other took its toll. The only blessing was that we had our first child, Lisa, in December 1968, which served to spur me on to ensure I could provide for my family.

This was where that work ethic my parents had instilled in me as a youngster held me in great stead, as I decided to gain my full FA coaching badges, despite only being in my mid-twenties. I coached boys' and amateur teams throughout my playing career, including, while I was at Carlisle, at a little local independent school. That extra money I earnt off the books, I spent very wisely indeed, getting myself through the FA badges until I was fully qualified not long after my 25th birthday. Not for me, blowing it on wine, women and girls; George Best I was not.

As part of that, I regularly travelled down to Lilleshall in Shropshire, then the national soccer centre, along with many other sports, to attend week-long coaching masterclasses with the crème de la crème of 1970s British football; the likes of Terry Venables, who was very much the up-and-coming *en vogue* manager at Crystal Palace, the Arsenal coach, and later manager, Don Howe, who would also become England coach under Ron Greenwood, and Bobby Robson, then of Ipswich and later England manager. I was only 23–26 years old at the time and learnt so much from them. Even after hours, when we had retired to the bar, the coaching discussions would go on using the classic beer mats and salt and pepper cellars to show different formations. There would be 40 or so of us in there, debating how the back four should react to certain situations or how to defend corners, with more experienced managers challenging us youngsters as to how we would set up, until we were thrown out at closing time.

During on-pitch sessions, us youngsters would be asked to play out those formations and situations, allowing us to understand how these leading coaches were thinking. I was in awe of them, sitting listening to them theorising and debating. This was a huge element that helped me formulate my own ideas, which I first put into practice at that private school with young kids. It also helped me realise what a superb coach Dick Young was as it opened my eyes to how practice and repetition makes such a big difference to players, making certain skills, ploys and tactical awareness second nature. It really was drilled into us and I took a lot of that with me when I became a coach and then manager. Talent has to be nurtured, not left to find its own way. Unless guided it often withers.

Not only were the tactics to prove useful, but, the connections I made would be critical as networking was to prove one of the most crucial aspects of making my managerial career a success. In the 1980s I continued to attend these sessions at Lilleshall, as I wasn't far away in the Potteries by then. There I met and socialised with Alex Ferguson, the then Aberdeen and later Manchester United manager, who I also saw when attending various reserve team games around the country. This was extremely important for me. I would use connections such as Alex regularly to plunder them for loan players or cheap signings from those youngsters who might not make it in the top flight, but would be brilliant in the third or fourth tier at Port Vale, nicking a play directly from Carlisle's repertoire. I remember on several occasions ringing Alex up and saying, 'Now then Alex, have you got anyone you can lend me who can play right wing? I've got injuries and no money.'

Alex would reply in that Glaswegian drawl of his, 'Bloody hell, Rudgie, you're a pain in the arse, you are.' I was, but he would often find a way of helping me.

* * *

My parental responsibilities weighed on me as I wasn't featuring often in the team and consequently not earning much in the way of bonuses to top up my wages. I began thinking about needing to move to get first-team football. I had clubs like Notts County, Chester and Crewe Alexandra showing some interest in me; Ernie Tagg was the manager at Gresty Road and was keen to sign me, but Crewe were glued to the foot of the Football League, with the reputation of being something of a 'Cinderella' club, so there was no way I wanted to go there.

In January 1969, manager Stokoe formally put me up for sale, finding a buyer right at the other end of the country, in ex-Scottish international Allan Brown, manager of Division Three Torquay United. The fee was £8,000, a big sum for the Gulls.

As it happened, Del had some relations down in Torquay and, when we discussed it, we felt that living on the south coast would be wonderful for our family. So, we decided to move ourselves lock, stock and barrel down to Devon. We put all the furniture in storage and Del lived with my parents for around three months until the house the club was renting to us became available. I stayed in digs for that period and travelled up to Wolverhampton to see Del, Lisa and my parents after each game.

When we moved into that club house, we quickly found it had a lot less ice on the windows. In fact, we were now in a subtropical climate, warmed by the Gulf Stream, which meant we actually had palm trees on our street. Although it was probably only five degrees warmer on average than Cumbria, it felt 25 degrees higher in Devon.

We fell in love with the place and decided to negotiate with the club to see if we could buy the house. Chairman Tony Boyce agreed so we purchased that property, our first, for £4,000. It was a lovely, semi-detached property just half a mile from the sea. The sun always seemed to be shining in Torquay; we had a beach a stone's throw away and we also bought a beach hut at Goodrington Sands, slightly further south down the coast, between Paignton and Brixham. We spent a great deal of time there. Lisa loved splashing around in the rockpools, making sandcastles and licking ice creams. A year or so after we moved, she was joined by a new arrival, our

Debbie, who was born in November 1971, just after I turned 27. We had a wonderful, almost idyllic life in the sunshine, which seemed to beam through an azure sky every day. How things had changed from living in Carlisle.

* * *

Torquay may have been a lovely place to live, but there were also plenty of distractions for the less dedicated and disciplined professional footballer, like the famous Shiphay Manor nightclub. In those days, as I mentioned, players had quite a liking for going out drinking and there was a big drinking culture. The Shiphay attracted many a less-disciplined player through its doors, but that wasn't for me as I was keen to establish myself and score goals on a regular basis. Untroubled by injuries for once, I notched 18 league goals in 1970/71, my best return. That season we also dumped fallen giants Aston Villa out of the FA Cup in the first round, winning 3-1 at Plainmoor. One pleasing thing that sticks in my mind from that game was that the match report in one newspaper said, 'The Villa defence was as slow and ponderous as a Russian moon buggy.' I took that as me making them look like that.

We had a decent side at Torquay. John Bond and Ken Brown, two former West Ham players, had moved to end their careers in the south-west. Both would go on to be successful managers. Also there was Allan Young, a former Chelsea centre-half. We finished sixth in Division Three in my first season and 13th the following campaign, 1969/70, then tenth in 1970/71; high-water marks for Torquay.

But my regular brush with injuries became a battle over that period. I felt that I would pull a muscle simply by jogging and, in an effort to save my own embarrassment, I would even go for treatment at my doctor's surgery and sometimes to hospital, without the club knowing, in a bid to get fit. I was that concerned that my career might be threatened. With a wife and two young children to support, it was a very worrying time.

* * *

After a poor start to the 1971/72 season, Allan Brown was sacked in October 1971 and Jack Edwards took over. But he couldn't stop the slide and Torquay would be relegated that season. However, I managed to avoid that ignominy as, in February 1972, I was to be on the move again after scoring 35 goals in 93 games for the Gulls over three years, although by the time of my departure in February 1972 I had only scored three that season. Edwards' big idea to avoid relegation was to bring back 'golden boy' Robin Stubbs, a striker who had been sold to Bristol Rovers after scoring 120 goals in 217 games, earning him the nickname 'The Prince of Plainmoor'. Despite him having finished as the top scorer at Eastville for the past two seasons, there was this huge clamour for him to become the relegation saviour and Rovers' directors seemed to bow to Stubbs' request to move. Stubbs also had a well-publicised marriage to TV star Anthea Redfearn (later to be Mrs Bruce Forsyth, following her many appearances on the *Generation Game,* one of the biggest entertainment shows of the 1970s and 80s), so really was the glamour boy. I couldn't compete with that!

The manager had this idea that, as I had effectively replaced Stubbs when he was initially sold to the Pirates, he could swap me for Robin to get him back. There was just one problem; I was crocked. Again. Rovers were, understandably, concerned about my injury record, so they arranged a friendly at Exeter to test my fitness. I actually played well, but as the game wore on, I could feel my groin was giving me problems and felt I would struggle to get through the full 90 minutes. To cover up, on around 65 minutes, I shouted up to the stands to the onlooking Rovers management team of Bill Dodgin and Don Megson, 'Haven't you seen enough yet?'

Fortunately, they had and the deal was done. Heaven knows what would have happened if they'd asked me to play the full 90 minutes before making a decision.

Because Rovers knew of my injury-prone nature, the deal they offered me was on a slightly lower wage than I was on at Torquay, so I went back to Gulls chairman Tony Boyce to ask him to compensate me for what I was losing out on. I knew he was so desperate to get Robin Stubbs back that I could have almost asked for anything. What made me even more confident when he turned up at my house to negotiate was that he parked his Rolls-Royce outside; he could afford to spare a bob or two to make this transfer happen. He did, and agreed to make up the difference, so we shook hands. I was on my way to Bristol.

The swap deal was as unusual then as it would be now and made quite a few headlines. I ended up being drawn into making a bet with Stubbs, mostly for the media's sake, as to who would score the most goals in the remainder of the season. It made for a great splash in both local papers. I won the bet as returning hero Stubbs did not score, failing to rescue Torquay from plunging into Division Four, while I netted three times as Rovers won 11 of the remaining 17 games that campaign.

When I signed, Rovers manager Don Megson announced me as a 'second Andy Lochhead' in the local paper. Lochhead had scored over 100 goals for Burnley in his spell there and then spearheaded Aston Villa to the League Cup Final in 1971. He was also the Third Division's top scorer in the 1971/72 season, so I was very happy to be compared to him.

* * *

This time, moving clubs meant we had to actually sell and buy a property, which turned into something of a saga. We did very well out of the Torquay club house we'd bought for £4,000 and we got £7,500 for it just three years later, but I found securing a property in Bristol a little trickier.

This was a time when gazumping was rife, making delving into the property market even more anxiety-inducing than usual. We had found a brand-new housing development we liked and, fortunately for us, discovered a Pirates fan working in the sales office. She told me that there was one house left which they had just put up in price from £9,250 to £10,000 and the person who had agreed to buy it was really unhappy about it. So, I immediately said, 'I'll pay £10,000, no quibbles. Ring me if he doesn't sign.'

The lady phoned a couple of days later to tell me the buyer had pulled out and we did the deal immediately. I bought her a dress to say thank you, as she had helped me out massively. Looking after people like that goes a very long way in life, I believe; even though £10,000 was a fortune to us. Far more important to me was that my family, having been uprooted again, were happy in their new surroundings.

I was now a senior professional. As apprentices at Eastville, we had two men who would become household names and future colleagues of mine when I became Stoke City's director of football; Gary Megson and Tony Pulis, who would both become managers of the Potters, and so technically my boss. For now, I was the senior pro and they were the young whippersnappers. They are about 14 or 15 years younger than me (as they keep reminding me).

I remember, actually, Tony played against me once in a practice match when we played senior attack against apprentice defence. Tony remembers this far more clearly than I do – he claims he never gave me a kick! That's not quite how I remember it, but Tony swears that's because I'm ageing. In fact, I swear he did give me a kick, but that was to the groin area.

My scouting report on Tony Pulis the player reads:

> A bread-and-butter player. A booter. Takes no prisoners. A ball winner, though never sees much of the ball. More of a cruncher than delicate skills. Motto: they don't limp fast.

As a manager, however, Tony turned out to be far more talented.

As it happens, also at Rovers was a left-back called Lindsay Parsons, who was so consistent he made over 200 consecutive appearances, out of a total of 421, reaching that milestone just after I signed. He was loved by Pirates fans, and by me, as he would join me at Torquay towards the end of his playing career. Then, some 30 years later, Lindsay and I ended up working together again when Tony Pulis, then manager at Stoke, brought him to the Britannia Stadium as his assistant manager in the 2000s.

Another Rovers star who would feature in my professional life was new player-coach Colin Dobson, who I had actually played with briefly at Huddersfield when he signed from Sheffield Wednesday in the summer of 1966. Colin would become something of a mentor for me in my managerial career.

I had a great start at Rovers as finishing the 1971/72 season so strongly meant we qualified for the Watney Cup, which was a pre-season tournament, sponsored by the brewery, that lasted four seasons from 1970, and contested between the eight teams, two from each of the four divisions, which had scored the most goals the previous season but were not promoted or qualified to play in Europe. The ties were one-off games and if they finished as draws went to a penalty shoot-out for the first time in professional football in England.

Under new manager Don Megson, who had taken over from the retired Bill Dodgin, who became chief scout, we took the 1972 competition by storm, defeating Burnley and Wolves without conceding a goal to face First Division Sheffield United in the final, which was played at Eastville. To give you an idea of how big those scalps were, Wolves ended up fifth in the top flight and qualified for the UEFA Cup, while Burnley won the Second Division title. Not bad for little Rovers!

I didn't play in the final as I was injured again, but I was there to watch as two attacking teams failed to score in 90 minutes, meaning the final went to penalties. I'd have loved to be out there to take one, but instead had to watch from the sidelines as, agonisingly, one by one players scored theirs after the long walk from the centre circle. The good news for us was that the manager had made the lads practise penalties, including that long walk from the middle of the field, over and over again during the days leading up to the final, which he regarded as a psychological part of the preparation. That paid off handsomely as Rovers players slotted spot kicks home without showing too many outward nerves. With us leading 7-6, goalkeeper Dick Sheppard saved Ted Hemsley's effort low to his left-hand side to secure the cup, which was presented by legendary four-minute mile athlete Roger Bannister. I remember huge numbers of fans from the 19,380 crowd invading the pitch to lift the players shoulder high and celebrate what was then – and still is – the only trophy either Bristol club has ever won.

* * *

I was mainly a striker, but by this time in my career I also liked playing in midfield and had a couple of memorable games there against Manchester United in the League Cup, playing against Bobby Charlton and George Best. We drew 1-1 at Eastville and I scored our goal past Alex Stepney, but in the replay at Old Trafford on 11 October 1972 we secured a famous 2-1 victory, in which again I scored our first goal. That goal is one of the few from my career that I recall perfectly; the ball came over and I leapt, using my full 5ft 10in height, to loop a header over Stepney and into the Old Trafford net. Told you I was taller than you thought.

Bruce Bannister bagged the winner. What a night that was, especially as our keeper Dick Sheppard became the man of the moment yet again as he pulled off a great penalty save from George Best. Scene stealer …

Winning at Old Trafford was the stuff of dreams, but it was a very different place back then to what it is now. It was cavernous, but often nowhere near full. For example, the crowd for our League Cup win was only 29,349, not the 75,000 or so Manchester United get at every home game these days, nor even near the 33,597 who had packed Eastville to watch the original tie. Mind you, Eastville was itself actually a greyhound stadium in between our football matches, with the track on which the dogs raced on Tuesdays and

Thursdays surrounding the pitch, with flowerbeds between the track and the stands.

Unfortunately, we got knocked out, losing 0-4 at my boyhood club Wolves in the next round, but those were great memories and we were building a fantastic team. That run netted the club over £22,000 and gave me a great insight into what a difference cup success can make. Cup ties are electric, especially night games under the lights. There is something about the British psyche which adores the story of giant-killing and Bristol Rovers winning at Old Trafford certainly fitted into that category. It galvanised the club and soon we were challenging for promotion from Division Three, with much of the impetus, and new arrivals, galvanised and funded by that cup success. I would never forget it.

Striker Alan Warboys signed from Sheffield United. I should have been worried about his arrival as he was a direct rival for my place up front alongside Bruce Bannister, but more and more I was dropping into midfield and saw what a wonderful understanding the pair quickly developed and how they forged a devastatingly lethal partnership which swiftly elevated us into promotion contenders. They became known as 'Smash and Grab' in reference to the strapping Warboys' physical playing style and the smaller, nippier Bannister's ability to get on to Warboys' knock-downs. Their partnership yielded 40 of the 65 goals our entire squad scored in 1973/74, an impressive proportion for a strike partnership.

By the way, yours truly was the next-highest scorer with four.

In my first full season, 1972/73, at the start of which we won the Watney Cup, we had finished fifth in the Third Division. That was very much a building season as the 1973/74 campaign proved to be a fabulous one which saw us win promotion, finishing in second place, just one point behind champions Oldham Athletic.

I remember we clinched promotion thanks to a 0-0 draw at Southend on Good Friday, only for our bus to break down on the way home after a celebratory dinner which the club treated us to before we set off. We arrived back in Bristol at 5am, tired, but still very happy.

We actually went unbeaten for the first 28 games of that 1973/74 season and had a rivalry with Leeds United, who were running away with the First Division and went unbeaten for the first 29 matches of their campaign. Leeds just pipped us after we were defeated 0-1 at Wrexham on 1 February 1974, but fell one shy of the then record of 30 unbeaten games from the start of a season in the First Division.

Amidst that great run, we went top on 22 September and, despite winning only two of our last eight games, we were still at the summit after drawing our final game at home to Brighton on 27 April. However, our closest rivals Oldham still had two games to play – at home to Charlton, which they lost 0-2 and then away at Plymouth, in which the Latics secured a 0-0 draw and that point was enough to take them clear of us, much to our annoyance. We had been top almost all season and ended up not being champions.

It was particularly frustrating that the draw against the Seagulls cost us the chance of going up as champions as, earlier that season, we won 8-2 at Brighton on 1 December 1973. The match was on TV, so we still have highlights to revel in all these years later. Warboys smashed four, after Bannister grabbed a first-half hat-trick. As the Brighton manager was Brian Clough, I can only imagine what the air was like in their dressing room after the game.

I was on the bench for that game and funnily enough, didn't get on, given how well the attack was doing. I was returning from yet another of my long-term injuries and only made my first appearance of the season in the following game in a 4-0 win over Southend, which featured yet another Warboys hat-trick. Three weeks later he got injured, so I started and scored in a 1-1 draw with Charlton and I continued filling in when one of Alan and Bruce was out, notching up 13 starts and six substitute appearances over the second half of the campaign, also scoring against Bournemouth in a 3-0 home win on 19 January and the winner in a 2-1 victory over Aldershot on 2

April. In between, I scored our consolation goal in a 1-3 defeat at Vale Park, of which more later.

* * *

For winning promotion, the directors rewarded the players with a trip to Australia, New Zealand and Bangkok which kept us away from home for six weeks. It was a fantastic opportunity for us all, although less so for our spouses. I remember going home to Del to tell her that she would be left with two young children to look after on her own. I put on a mopey face and said, 'I've got a bit of news for you, we're going on tour … really, darling, I don't want to go, but I have to …' She took one look at me and said, 'Don't tell so many bloody lies!' I was rumbled. Going abroad and being paid for it was the stuff of dreams.

It was a marvellous trip, but, as usual with most footballers, we did not appreciate it. 'I've arranged a visit of the area's cultural spots with the High Commissioner including the Sydney Opera House,' said the manager.

'No thanks, boss. Just drop us off at Bondi Beach!' we chorused. Our tans were well topped up by the time we returned. And that was in the Antipodean winter!

You can imagine the high jinks we got up to … well, actually you'll have to as my lips are sealed. All I'll say is that it was an unbelievable trip.

We were given spending money each day, but the club kept running out of cash, so we had to arrange another game to get a fee for it, then we used that money to fund the hotel rooms for another few nights before another match would be fixed up. We worked our way up the east coast from Adelaide like that.

One tale I can tell is that I remember Colin Dobson, our coach, who was a big mate of mine, getting on my nerves a bit, so I grabbed him while he was in his underpants and threatened to throw him over the fence and out of the hotel grounds. It was one of those impetuous things, half joking, half not. I can't remember what it was about now, but I can recall a snapshot of him half over the fence, with his pants hanging off him. That image is indelibly imprinted in my mind.

We stopped in Bangkok on the way back. Four nights. I remember as we got off the bus there were cars pulling up with fellers leaning out and shouting at us, 'You want live show, mister?!'

I went to bed. I can't tell tales on those that headed off out.

* * *

Throughout my time at Eastville, injuries had a major effect on my career to the extent that if I had been a racehorse I would have been shot. Robin Perry, Rovers reporter for the *Bristol Evening Post,* once wrote that I was the only player to pull a muscle while putting on my tracksuit. I wasn't best pleased with the comment, but he wasn't far from the truth.

Equally uncharitably, I myself once described my leg as being so wasted that there was more muscle on a chip. In 2009, in an interview for *Backpass* magazine, I was asked to give a scouting report on myself as a player and wrote:

> Bread-and-butter player. Quick, good in the air, decent scoring record. But not strong enough. Also injury-prone: hamstrings, calves, tendons. Gives everything he's got – for an hour. Then he's knackered.

Honest at least.

My hamstrings and calves were, at this stage, the problem, but they were already beginning to have knock-on effects on other parts of my body. As early as November 1972 I was out for a period with another 'muscle strain' and the local paper was reporting on how the club doctor had devised a special fitness programme, described as 'sweat and toil', in order to not only rehabilitate my injury, but build strength to prevent them from happening in the future. This programme entailed lots of sprinting and running up and down the stand. That worked and, once I got fully fit, I was in good scoring form, but every so often I kept breaking down.

I did manage to play at Old Trafford again, coming on as a substitute on 21 September 1974, although this time we lost a league game 0-2. It is remarkable to think now that little Bristol Rovers once played at the same league level as the mega-club which these days is Manchester United. Well, as it happens at the same time as we were getting promoted from the Third Division, United were being relegated from the First, ironically helped along their way by a deft back-heel from their former legend and my predecessor in my first bed at Huddersfield, Denis Law, who scored the winning goal in a late-season Manchester derby.

My 1974/75 season was something of a write-off due to injury. I only made three starts, plus ten more sub appearances for Rovers that season, but I did manage to notch a couple of goals, taking me to a total of 17 in 70 games for Rovers. Hardly impressive. So, although the team avoided relegation from Division Two by one place and a three-point margin, by the end of that campaign I would be on my travels again.

Chapter 3

There are No Beach Huts in Burslem

'One previous careful lady owner, low mileage and with a good heater.'

Don Ratcliffe, Port Vale director, January 1980

AFTER THREE happy years in Bristol, in March 1975, as transfer deadline day approached, my injury situation was such that Rovers manager Don Megson felt it was best I moved on. I couldn't argue with him. This time it was to another lovely coastal town, Bournemouth, signed by new player-manager John Benson, a former playing colleague from Torquay, who thought I would be a good addition. John signed me as an experienced head who had recently won promotion with Rovers from this very division. On this occasion, though, he was desperately trying to keep the Cherries in Division Three as the team were struggling in the drop zone.

We sold and bought houses again and settled into the social side of living on the south coast. One of my playing colleagues turned out to be Harry Redknapp, the former West Ham winger who had moved down to the south coast in 1972, but like me was nearing the end of his career and carried the battle scars of a career's worth of injuries. We became friends and I've had a good relationship with Harry ever since. When I was playing with him, we would go out quite a bit together or with the squad, and also with our families.

To say Harry was a character is putting it mildly. We had great fun, but, as I'm sure you won't be surprised to hear, Harry was a typical cockney, always on the make. He always had a deal going on the side, often cars. He was forever ringing me up trying to get me involved, but I consistently declined. I remember him once telling me he was going to make a killing on these cars he'd brought down from London, but then the deal went pear-shaped and Harry rang me, furious. 'Rudgie, I've been bloody done, here!' he howled down the phone. I was killing myself.

* * *

Harry had been injured for the first two-thirds of that 1974/75 season, but by the time I signed he was back playing and providing chances from the right wing again. I felt together we could produce the goals to earn us the points to get the club out of the drop zone and avoid relegation. However, it would not turn out that way as I detected a menacing lump on my Achilles tendon after playing only my third game and, after managing just four more matches before the end of that 1974/75 campaign, eventually needed surgery. My old injury jinx had struck again with a vengeance.

Despite winning our last two games of the season 4-2 against Watford and 2-1 against Peterborough, we couldn't save the club from relegation, finishing an agonising point below Aldershot. Arguably, those injuries both Harry and I suffered cost the club the points that ultimately led to us failing to overtake the Shots.

The biggest signing-on fee I ever received in my career was the £3,000 I banked when I joined Bournemouth. Sadly, the Cherries were the only club not to get value for money from me as, following the surgery, I missed most of the 1975/76 season with a ruptured Achilles tendon, and made only 11 league appearances in 1976/77, scoring twice.

Professionally speaking, my three years at Bournemouth were a nightmare, as I started fewer than 20 games overall. All too often I would break down while attempting to make a comeback. I was hardly proving a good buy, which made supporters grumble a bit, even though my price tag had been a bargain £7,000 to reflect my injury-prone status. It was not for the lack of trying. My body just wasn't up to it.

While I was desperately trying to get back fit through that difficult 15 months or so, I needed to earn a bit more money to make ends meet as I wasn't banking anything other than my basic wage. Unlike Harry Redknapp, I steered clear of dodgy motors and invested in a fruit and veg stall at Christchurch's market. This took me back to my youth when I had helped on my mother's stall. In fact, she was still running hers at this point, so I would regularly take tips from Mum on how to run the business.

Our stall was basically a collapsible, Meccano-style wooden shack, which I would put on the roof rack of my Vauxhall Marina and remove the front passenger seat to create space for the produce, which I would collect from local wholesalers each Sunday. It meant an early start for me to erect the stall for 6am on Monday morning and my 'staff' of Del and a neighbour would arrive later to do the selling. Although Lisa had started school at this point, our daughter Deb was about two years old and we would sit her in an orange box with crayons to keep her occupied. I would then go to the ground for treatment at about 9.30am and return to the market in the afternoon to be told in no uncertain terms by Del how much she hated it. I can hear her now, 'Up with the lark, humping boxes around, horse trading fruit and veg ...' This was really not her style.

Sometimes, while Del worked for me on the stall, I trained on the sands of Bournemouth beach as I tried to regain my fitness. I had been quite a while in hospital after my operation and was now trying everything I could think of to get back into contention to play again. It wasn't working; it was only a few sessions before I broke down once more. It became a never-ending loop. It wasn't a great time.

* * *

The end of any player's career is inevitable; just a matter of when it happens. You hope to be able to control that as much as possible, to make your own decision. Sadly, at that point, I realised that my dream was over at the age of 32. Overall, I scored a total of 78 goals in 267 appearances in all competitions over my much-interrupted career.

But, it was over. That was definitive and the question of 'what next?' reared its head far sooner than I had thought. Here I was with a mortgage, young family and just five 'O' levels, what the subjects were I couldn't remember by this time, let alone any useful information from them. My playing career had enriched my life far more than my bank balance. I needed to find work.

Thankfully, I never had any time to mope or think about my woeful lot as, in summer 1977, I was offered the opportunity to become player-coach back at Torquay United, under Mike Green, who had been appointed as the new player-manager a couple of months earlier. Mike and I had played together at both Carlisle and then again at Bristol Rovers, where Mike was a fixture at centre-half and club captain in the promotion-winning side, before he moved to Plymouth.

I jumped at the chance, turning down two other offers, to become player-manager at non-league clubs Weymouth and Atherstone in the process; not least because we still had the lovely beach hut at Goodrington Sands where we had spent many a happy summer's day. We had loved life in Torquay; the sea, beach, sun and outdoor life. It was for us.

Mike and I were new, young and fresh (Mike was actually only 30 years old when appointed, while I was just 32), but we had the experienced Frank O'Farrell, who had briefly been Manchester United manager in the early 1970s, as general manager and put together a fast, attacking team. We enjoyed the difficult challenge, working long hours. I recall a scouting trip to watch Jeff Hemmerman (later to play for Vale) for which we drove all the way to Hull and back, finally returning at 2.30am, then getting up to take training just a few hours later. It was a tough apprenticeship for coaching and management, but a wonderful one.

However, after a couple of successful years for Mike and I, finishing ninth and 11th in Division Four, it became impossible for me to play again at all, not that I'd featured much. Mike also took the decision to retire from playing and was wanting to take the first-team training sessions himself, which meant I was left to coach the School of Excellence, rather than the first team, so I was back to coaching youngsters which I felt I had progressed from by now. I also realised that being in Torquay meant I was out on a footballing limb and could soon be forgotten about if I wasn't careful. Once again, it was time to look for pastures new.

* * *

As I mentioned before, the contacts I had built through going to Lilleshall were vital for me throughout my career, but never more so than at this point as I cast around for a coaching opportunity to get me away from Torquay. It was the first time I saw the soccer grapevine truly in action. I had put it around that I was looking for something new. After an unsuccessful interview at Kettering Town, I was attracted by an interview at Crewe with Tony Waddington, the former Stoke City manager, who I knew could probably help me in my career further down the line with his experience. However, despite meeting Tony and looking around Madeley College where the club trained, and him telling me I would be first-team coach and he would be general manager, there was something holding me back. Crewe were at the bottom of the Fourth Division and my gut feeling about the potential there was not good. It did not help that, when I was touring Gresty Road, a pretty dilapidated stadium in those days, when we arrived at the directors' box, their inner sanctum, strategically positioned next to the tea bar, we found the door was padlocked. And no one had the key. Eventually the groundsman prised it open with a crowbar, but he needn't have bothered, as the room was not much to look at. I could not see what all the fuss had been about.

Clearly, I wasn't the right man for the job and Dario Gradi, who was appointed manager in June 1983, was. Dario propelled the club to unparalleled success and, by the time I became manager at Port Vale, he and I would prove to be the longest-serving managers in British football for the next 15 years, with Dario lasting until well into the 21st century.

Although Crewe didn't work out, it did give me a taste of the passion for football of the area around the Potteries. I had already had one brief sojourn in the area when Mike Green had sent me up to recruit Kenny Rapier on loan from First Division Stoke City, meeting him at the beautiful Trentham Gardens to discuss the move, so I had begun to know the area in which we now live. Although Kenny signed, that loan move didn't work out and he finished up leaving the game, joining the North Staffordshire Police and progressing to a very senior role. I was already storing away Potteries area experiences for when the right moment came.

1979: the winter of discontent in the UK. My personal version of this saw me on the soccer scrapheap, unable to play any longer and fed up with life in Torquay. This only added to the general national gloom of strikes, demonstrations and food shortages, plus a bitter period of weather which really rammed home how miserable everyone was. Unemployable as a player and with only a small amount of experience of coaching first-teamers at the lowest level of Division Four at footballing backwater Torquay, I spent that Christmas back in Wolverhampton with my family, but it was while we were sitting in the lounge of my sister Pat's house that I received the call that was to have a dramatic effect on my career.

The caller, John McGrath, had just taken over as manager of Port Vale and suggested while I was in the Midlands I should meet him at Vale Park. I had never spoken with John, although it transpired we had seen each other at Lilleshall on a course when I was doing my badges.

To this day I do not know exactly how he knew I was looking to leave Torquay, but undoubtedly it was that footballing network in operation in response to the jungle drums I had set beating. John had been the youth coach at Southampton and, after a playing career in the top divisions, knew nothing about the two lower tiers of English football, so he was looking for someone like me who had mostly operated in those lower reaches to become assistant manager and first-team coach. He had actually been given my name by Southampton manager Lawrie McMenemy, who I had met at Lilleshall and discussed tactics with once, but I have no idea how he had tracked me down to my sister's house! It showed me how tenacious a football manager had to be.

At least I knew where Port Vale was, unlike many! As I mentioned before, I had played and scored at Vale Park for Bristol Rovers, although we lost the game 1-3 in February 1974, with two of Vale's goals being scored by a forward called Ray Williams, of whom much more later. There was quite a story from that game which always stuck in my mind in that our goalkeeper Jim Eadie, who was so beloved by Rovers fans that he earned the nickname 'the flying pig', got injured in a collision with a Vale forward (it might have been Ray, but I can't remember), was carried off and taken to hospital. I scored our consolation goal in the 73rd minute, but then after the game was asked by Don Megson, if, as I was going to be stopping at my parents' house in Wolverhampton instead of travelling back with the team, I could pop back up to Stoke to check on how Jim was the following day, which was actually a Monday as the game had taken place on a Sunday, while the rest of the team and coaching staff went back to Bristol.

So come Monday morning, instead of spending my day off with my folks, I drove back up to Stoke to the hospital to find Jim was fine; conscious and lucid. Duty done, I headed back off to Bristol to training the following day. Even then, I was being seen as a senior player who would take responsibility and deliver on it. Another step along the road to management.

* * *

Back to Christmas 1979 and I turned up at Vale Park to discover I had walked into a 'land that time forgot' scenario. Far from being somewhere I would actually end up spending almost 20 years, this seemed more like a throwback to when I started my fledgling career in the late 1950s. Given that Vale Park had been (part-)built in the very late 1940s and opened in 1950, and had barely been touched since, this wasn't far off the truth.

John McGrath was a very big, imposing man who, I felt, dwarfed me as he enthusiastically laid out his plans during our long chat. He explained that he really needed someone who knew the Third and Fourth Divisions well and had some experience of coaching; he was basically describing me. This, I felt, was very shrewd and I could see immediately how I would dovetail with him, both in that way and in terms of personality.

Vale, like Crewe, were near the bottom of the Fourth Division, yet John was incredibly ambitious for the club, wanted it to live up to the ground's nickname of 'the Wembley of the North' which had been coined on its opening due to the extremely wide pitch, the second-widest in the Football League. This gave me ideas about coaching wingers, a position I had played quite a bit myself and had also benefitted from their service when playing as a striker.

The strange thing is John actually completely overawed me with his enthusiasm about what he was going to do at Port Vale. By the end of the meeting, I thought we'd be winning the European Cup within five years! He was so overwhelming, that after telling Del about it she said to me later, 'John, I can't understand why, but you don't seem enthusiastic enough about the job. Do you really want to take it?' Bear in mind she was also thinking about moving our family from our idyllic life on the south coast to the Midlands. But it wasn't that I was unsure at all, what had happened was that John had overpowered me with what he planned to do so much that it had knocked me for six. It felt like I was being apprehensive, when, in fact, I was struggling to process his vigorous determination that we would succeed when both history and everything I had seen on my visit to the club suggested the opposite.

However, there was one clinching factor that I kept coming back to; not inspiring the players to win trophies, not finishing off the shoddy ground, not the challenge of turning round one of the lowest-placed clubs in the Football League, not even John's inspirational, if challenging, enthusiasm … ultimately, I took the job because I was sold on the fact that the contract came with my first club car, an 1100cc Lada, which apparently had just the one previous careful lady owner, low mileage and was reputed to have a good heater (well, according to director Don Ratcliffe, club director, who owned the garage the car came from).

So, yes, a second-hand Lada changed my life. To have a club car as an assistant at that time was quite something. Don't knock Ladas, they're very good cars. OK, they weren't in 1980, but this was Port Vale – my club car clearly wasn't going to be in the Jaguar class, now, was it? Moving also meant we would have to part with our beloved beach hut. It wasn't the best swap deal I've done in my career …

You may not be surprised to hear that the car turned out to be rubbish. I mean really bloody awful. I remember driving that Lada to Southampton once to have a look at a player, as John McGrath made me travel down to watch this potential target he had been tipped the wink about at his former club. I can't even remember who it was now, as we didn't sign him. He clearly wasn't that memorable. Far more unforgettable was the diabolical journey I had in that car. In fact, I recall it as clear as day even now as some kind of dystopian nightmare. It was a heck of a long trip, especially on the way home after the game, with the Lada clanking and phutting all the way back to the Potteries. That car nearly was the death of me. I was constantly amazed that it got me anywhere.

* * *

Another reason I joined Port Vale was that, being located in the heart of the country, I felt the club was part of a 'hotbed' of soccer, in stark contrast to Torquay. However, that was the only thing hot about the Potteries. On my first day in the job, Del and I left Torquay in a balmy 18 degrees at 6am, but by the time we had reached north Staffordshire it felt like Ice Station Zebra. The temperature had dropped about 12 degrees, there was a wicked wind whipping in off the Staffordshire Moors and Burslem itself looked like a set from a mid-19th-century Arnold Bennett drama of the kind the BBC often put on in the 1970s and 80s. It was bloody freezing!

I remember stopping in Burslem town centre and dropping Del off, advising her to walk down Waterloo Road to Hanley, to do some shopping while I took training with John McGrath. I arranged to meet her back in the same place about 3.30pm. At the appointed time, I proudly drove up in my clanking Lada, heater on full blast, to find my wife at the side of the road looking simultaneously freezing and dazed.

'Are you alright, love?' I enquired breezily, flushed with the buzz of taking a first session as coach.

Del looked me in the eye and simply said, 'What the hell have you brought me to?'

I turned to her and said, 'There are no beach huts in Burslem, love.'

It was a long drive back down the M5 to Torquay.

Chapter 4

Rag Arse Rovers

'Welcome to Port Vale, we can hardly afford a pair of bootlaces.'

John McGrath, Port Vale manager, January 1980

JOHN MCGRATH was the man who had sparked Liverpool manager Bill Shankly into dubbing his Southampton side 'alehouse brawlers' after he infamously booted the Reds' record teenage signing, striker Alun Evans, into the West Stand terrace at the Dell after five minutes of a game. Evans had been hoisted on to a stretcher and Saints won 1-0, prompting Shankly's diatribe. Safe to say, John was to prove as 'combative' as a boss as he had been a centre-half. He was utterly formidable. Look up any description of him you care to online and it will be littered with phrases like 'no-nonsense', 'uncompromising disrupter' and 'aggressive in the tackle' ... He wasn't just controversial on the pitch, though; John's obituary in *The Independent* newspaper described how his 'lurid public persona was something between Desperate Dan and Attila the Hun'. Subtle, he was not.

As if I hadn't gathered this enough during my interview, I soon found out that John was a colourful, overpowering, but also inspirational character, who liked to be the centre of attention. It started on day one, when he greeted me with a handshake, a big smile and the words, 'Welcome to Port Vale, we can hardly afford a pair of bootlaces,' which set the scene for, though little did I know it then, the next 19 years of struggle, sweat, blood, tears and hard graft. I was pretty sure it wouldn't be dull.

The club we were taking over had no money and had been languishing in the lower reaches of the Fourth Division for years. It needed shaking up from top to bottom and John was determined to deliver. With no money to spend, it was very much a case of doing the best we could with the means at our disposal, which were none. Not a bean. The club had been poorly run and, to be frank, had poor players; far too many of them.

The one benefit of having a massive, oversized squad was that we could make savings by moving players on. Given that the previous management team of Alan Bloor and coach Gordon Banks had resigned with Banks telling the media as he departed, 'the players do not like hard work', the manager's focus was on weeding out squad members he didn't particularly think wanted to be there or who thought they were above fighting re-election, setting about this challenging task with alacrity.

John immediately identified about ten players from the vast squad of 30, making them train separately, with a few more following within weeks after failing to reach the manager's standards in training or in matches. The initial bunch included Bernie Wright, a beefy centre-forward, nicknamed 'Bernie the Bolt', who had played for Everton briefly earlier in his career, goalkeeper John Connaughton and Terry Owen (who would turn out to have a son called Michael you may have heard of, who I would sign for Stoke 30 years later). This band of reprobates quickly became known amongst the others as the 'lepers'. Some players made it easy for the gaffer to cast them into the 'leper colony', with others he just made choices. The lepers were booted out of the door fairly quickly, generating both wage savings and some small transfer fees, as well as stopping much of the infighting amongst those who didn't play much or were in a huff.

As if that wasn't enough, in order to make further impact, John actually announced to the local newspaper that he would be transfer-

listing the entire squad. This made an infamous front-page splash in the *Evening Sentinel* and caused something of a stir amongst the players, I can tell you. There were photos of them all on the front page, like an identity parade. This gave us all an early taste of how the manager could create a sensation fairly easily, giving us plenty to think about, whilst simultaneously administering a kick up the backside where he saw fit.

It caused a suitable jolt to the remaining players and made the point that John was in charge. For those remaining, it also partly boosted their egos because they felt wanted, deemed 'better' than the lepers. It also put the fear of God into them, as they now knew that they might be treated that way if they crossed the manager. They had better perform!

Once he had done that, just to ram his point home, John started the next training session with the reprieved players with a frighteningly dictatorial speech in which he declared, 'The holiday is over.' John demanded dedication and bloody hard work at all times; the players were in for a shock. A new fines system was also instituted, with various spurious reasons seemingly invented almost daily to allow the manager to make his point. Hitting the players where it hurt the most, in their pocket, also helped make them focus.

But it wasn't just sorting out the playing squad John turned his attention to. When we arrived, the club had a very shabby training kit. We looked like 'Rag Arse Rovers' according to the gaffer, so John rang Adidas straight away to replenish the kit. The players loved this and began to have some pride in the club they were playing for. It is often little things like that which can help turn corners.

Having generated a bit of cash and made some savings, John moved to bring in his first few signings in February 1980; goalkeeper Mark Harrison and defender Lee Harwood, from his former club Southampton, plus young forward Tony Sealy, on loan from Crystal Palace, who had also been at the Dell before moving to Selhurst

Park the previous year. Basically, they all joined the club because they knew John. The issue which was already becoming clear to me was persuading players to come to Port Vale. Not all footballers were impressed by second-hand Ladas as easily as me, even in the early 1980s.

You might think that all of this shock treatment was over the top or too much too quickly, but it worked; we went on a six-game unbeaten run to climb out of the re-election zone, with new signing Sealy netting three goals.

People began to notice that Port Vale were stirring.

* * *

During January and February 1980, until I could get the family moved up, I travelled at the start of each week from the English Riviera to Stoke-on-Trent. Regularly during that spring, I would leave Torquay at 5.30am on a Monday morning in short sleeves only to find myself taking training on Bycars fields in a blizzard – the drop in temperature in 200 miles was incredible. Perhaps my recent experiences in the south of England in places such as Bristol, Bournemouth and Torquay had softened me after my formative years in Wolverhampton, Huddersfield and Cumbria, but without doubt now I had hit the cold, stark reality of life at the foot of the Football League – in Burslem. It was brassic; in every sense.

After training was over, I'd spend my time looking for a house in Stoke, which I eventually found, settling in Trentham. During this initial period, I stayed at my mother's in Wolverhampton, only very occasionally being treated to an overnight stay at the George Hotel in Burslem, as the club's finances did not allow the luxury of a hotel room for long. In fact, I remember there were many times when John McGrath would sleep on the physio's table in the treatment room overnight in order to save some much-needed money. I would often arrive in the morning to find him grabbing a shave in the referee's room.

As befits a new manager, John spent a lot of time making sure the directors were on his side. He would have them in stitches with his ready wit and then baffle them with soccer science to ensure they were kept onside. It was incredible to behold. When we joined, Arthur McPherson was the chairman of what I would politely call an unstable board of directors. John quickly showed he was an expert at schmoozing the lot of them, especially as the chairmanship passed first to Don Ratcliffe and then to Jim Lloyd in October 1982. There seemed to be a lot of infighting, jealously and people moving from one position to the next. The club had gone through many managerial sackings before John and I arrived and needed some stability. We possibly benefitted from this in the sense that they had to give us time as they couldn't afford to sack us and start again.

I would take a lot of the training, but the other key element of my role as first-team coach was to listen to the players' gripes, which, as you can imagine given the scenario, were regular and I became a shoulder for them to cry on – an agony aunt if you like – and they would come to me as they quickly learned that John just wouldn't listen. This made some players, particularly those who weren't in the team, resent him.

I also had to cushion the blows that came in the players' direction from the manager. John was quite dictatorial with a cutting tongue, especially if he'd had a couple of whiskies, and there was always a danger of him going over the top. Some of the players were simply frightened of this huge man (in every sense) and woe betide anyone who would be so foolish as to challenge his authority, as he constantly gave it the 'big I am'.

Now, you'd think that there wouldn't be too many egos amongst a group of players so poor that they languished near the foot of the Fourth Division table when we arrived in early 1980, but you'd be wrong. That was part of the problem. I'd always known that talent was merely one facet of why players, teams and clubs are successful. Working under John allowed me to understand just how important character, motivation, hunger, desire and application needed to be drilled into players in order to allow them to let that talent shine.

He really had got into the players, shaken them up and bruised egos. I quickly became the cushioning buffer between the players on the one hand and John on the other, listening as they told me their fears or concerns. They would often come to me and ask, 'Has the gaffer gone mad?' or 'What is he thinking?'

I managed to turn this torrent of moaning into a positive, as an assistant or coach can often develop a better relationship with players than a manager because of the time spent with them, but also because of the effort spent mending fences. So, I became the person in some sort of authority that they could moan to when they weren't moaning amongst themselves. This wasn't constant, but it goes back to the old football truism for managers that the only 11 happy players in your squad are the ones you pick to start the next game. The rest are all sitting there thinking, 'Why are you picking him, I'm much better ...'

All players are essentially the same in that sense; if they are in the team then they are happy, if they are not then the manager is an idiot. That has slightly changed with the advent of huge squads and 18-man matchday teams, with up to five substitutes, in the last few seasons, but essentially it remains true to this day.

The players who aren't in the team are upset, but they know it is ultimately the manager's call as to who starts the games. I was the one who had to placate them and ensure everything was kept on an even keel, becoming the buffer, the psychologist and sometimes their mum and dad all rolled into one. Not exactly skills I'd learned when I was doing my coaching badges!

On top of standard selection issues, though, John would often belittle players, which I think sometimes is a problem for managers who have played at a high level in the game when they come down to the foot of the Fourth Division and players aren't as naturally talented. My approach was more of an arm around their shoulders, a softer touch. That obviously made me more popular than the manager, which is the same at every single club, although not all managers are as extreme as John was.

As coach, you are in a difficult position in many ways because you can end up a diplomat in a war of egos with entrenched lines, but in another way it is simple: you have to back the manager. Otherwise, you start a coup and that might not go so well and you could lose your job. Loyalty is nowhere near as prized a personality trait in football these days; the huge increase in salaries throughout the game over the last 40 years has seen to that. But back in the early 80s, it was one of the most important aspects of myself that I could bring to support John McGrath as he imposed his management style and ideas on the Port Vale squad. Being a new first-team coach, I simply had to back him when I was speaking with the players, but then try to address my concerns with him in private, by saying, 'John, calm down, you've gone well over the top here.'

He would mostly listen, but then make out it was his own idea to change tack from whatever volley of abuse he was launching forth with. I learned to intervene gently and guide him when he became too much. I believe he was emulating how Lawrie McMenemy had been at Southampton, as I understand he could be very difficult at times. To be fair, Lawrie did win the FA Cup in 1976 with Saints as a Second Division club, win promotion to the First Division and establish them as a top club, featuring stars such as Peter Shilton and Kevin Keegan, so his ego could be justified. John was just working on his.

So, I very much toed the line as the bridge between this inspirational, if slightly crazy, gaffer, and the players, although, looking back, I think I could have imposed more of my personality on what I did in those first months at the club.

John was very much his own man when it came to picking the team, but I had an impact on his selection at times, giving him news about niggling injuries and how well players were training during the sessions I took which he wasn't at because he was away scouting or trying to bring in new blood, or, often, speaking with the directors or the press. We may have been like chalk and cheese personality-wise, but we made a good managerial team and spent an awful lot of time together. When it came to watching games around the country in the evening, I would inevitably be the chauffeur. Well, I was the one with the plush club car with all mod cons.

As much as he had his brash, abrasive side, John could also inspire like no one I've ever seen before or since. When he was on top form, he could make you think anything was possible; playing in white shirts meant we were Leeds or Real Madrid, not Port Vale. I learned a lot about that aspect of man-management from John, but also other aspects of being a club manager such as being excellent at public relations, ensuring a never-ending stream of headlines. He instigated all sorts of publicity gimmicks, which I would sometimes get roped into. One famous occasion saw me being 'volunteered' to star in a photograph in which I wore a big Texan hat like the main character in the hit TV show *Dallas*, J.R. Ewing, wielding an enormous cigar. J.R. – see what he did? I felt quite awkward sitting on the pitch in this huge hat as I wasn't one for the limelight myself, but John was always pushing me outside my comfort zone which definitely helped me once I became manager. John was prepared to do absolutely anything that would capture a headline for Port Vale Football Club. In a way he had to; we had gates of under 2,000 and a crumbling ground.

A big issue was attracting better players to Burslem. The town itself wasn't anything to look at, while the club's facilities were, frankly, grim. The pitch was built on clay and flooded easily. It was often in terrible condition as there was no run-off or drainage back then. That's been improved a lot in the modern era. There was also one side of the ground which had never been finished and the stand only ran half the length of the pitch.

On top of that, the training facilities were non-existent. To start with we just used to cross the road and go into Burslem Park. Then we would try and borrow some of the big pottery manufacturers' facilities they had for their works teams, or go further afield to the universities at Keele and Staffordshire. It was beg, steal and borrow; a constant problem, with players having to clamber into their cars to drive wherever we were going that day, then, muddied up to the hilt, they would drive back to the ground to get showered. We were here, there and everywhere. There was a council field at the back of the stadium that would have been perfect, but we weren't really supposed to use it. When I became manager, I kept asking if we could buy it and build a training ground, but neighbours wanted to walk their dogs there, so we kept getting turned down. After I left, the council finally agreed and Vale now have a good facility right next to the ground.

Lol Hamlett was the physio. At least in name. He was a lovely man, but totally without any qualifications, so I don't know if he knew his own arse from his elbow, let alone the players'. He had been the club physio since 1958 and had played for both Potteries clubs in a career that also saw him appear in the First Division with Bolton Wanderers. Lol lived in Congleton and was a lay preacher in a Methodist church, as well as being a teetotaller, in complete contrast to John's liking for a tipple. To say Lol was strict was an understatement. Like John, he took no crap from anyone, although, as a religious man, he would never swear, something the players constantly tried to get him to do. Instead, he would say 'fizzing' a lot. And I mean a lot. Eventually, Lol had to retire due to illness in March 1983. He played a great part as one of the key members of the backroom team in that promotion season and it was such a shame he couldn't quite see it through until the end of the campaign.

The parlous state of the facilities had been matched by results and our initial task was to avoid finishing in the re-election zone. This was the scenario back in the 1980s, before automatic promotion was brought in between the National Conference and Division Four in 1987, whereby the bottom four clubs had to ask the other 88 clubs to vote for them to stay in the league, while one non-league club, or sometimes more, applied to get into the league and would replace your team if they got more votes. That was how clubs like Hereford and Wimbledon came into the Football League in 1972 and 1977 respectively, seeing Barrow and Workington drop out. Port Vale had never suffered the ignominy of having to seek re-election and we battled away in the second half of that 1979/80 season to ensure that did not happen, but that six-game unbeaten run was followed by a spell in which we lost six of the next nine games. Going into the last match, we were just one place above the re-election zone, but on the same points as Hereford United, although with a goal difference one worse than the Bulls. We won 3-0 against Doncaster, while Hereford only won their last game by two goals, not the three they needed to overtake us. They were actually leading by two goals at half-time but didn't score again and we were reprieved by the tiniest of margins, avoiding a plea for re-election by finishing fifth from bottom by virtue of goals scored.

The next season, 1980/81, we did slightly better, hitting the heady heights of sixth from bottom, although one game I remember that season which was particularly embarrassing was a humiliating 0-3 defeat at non-league Enfield in an FA Cup third round replay. John's tongue-whipping in the dressing room post-match turned the air blue.

* * *

While there was little on-pitch improvement, off the pitch, there was never a dull moment with John around. That made life interesting, but meant I, like the players, never really knew what was coming next. John's favourite saying was 'bullshit baffles brains' and there was regularly more of it flying around than at Leek cattle market.

Often people thought he had lost his marbles, but I knew that John was perfectly clear on what he was doing and why; even if it seemed utterly bonkers to most. He once managed to persuade the entire Vale first-team squad to go swimming in the freezing cold Irish Sea off Blackpool beach as part of a pre-season trip. I say persuade – it was mostly the fear of God he put into them.

John was strident and forceful in the dressing room and on the training pitch. In what is nowadays called the technical area, but back then we called the dugout, during games his voice would boom out across the turf and easily reach our winger on the far side. Given that we had relatively small crowds to perform in front of in those days, there could be none of that pretence, which has become more prevalent in recent years, that a player couldn't hear what John was screaming at him due to the noise and hubbub of the stadium.

Another thing John ensured was that the supporters loved him. He would commonly receive his own round of applause from certain sections of the crowd after a game – an art in itself which even the greatest manager doesn't always receive. John would commonly sit in the stand for the first part of a match to get a better view, but as soon as we scored he would appear on the touchline to take the plaudits from the crowd. He was a master at milking success and ensuring the limelight shone on him.

Ahead of the 1981/82 season, John signed midfielder Geoff Hunter from Crewe Alexandra, forwards Ernie Moss from Chesterfield for £12,000 and Stoke and Manchester United legend Jimmy Greenhoff, who was just returning to the area after a spell in North America with Toronto Blizzard, on a free transfer. Jimmy also became a coach, working alongside me. We lost just one of the opening eight games, but form suffered due to an injury crisis. In mid-season we then had another spell of 15 games unbeaten, before another spate of injuries caused a potential promotion campaign to wither into a seventh-place finish. It was definite progress, but John was never happy. He was constantly on at the players, beating one drum or another and laying down fresh challenges.

This was a huge driving force behind the improvement. Another was making sure the players gelled as a group. I remember one particular outing to Bernard Manning's nightclub in Manchester that went down very well. John was always looking to boost the image of the club in the press and to ensure we were being seen and reported on by the Manchester media, the players enjoyed the comedy and some drinks. This, he reasoned, would mean we could sign more players from the Manchester area clubs if they thought they would have fun by signing for Vale when they read about our night out in the *Manchester Evening News*. In fact, every Friday evening John would leave me with the players to finish preparations for the weekend's game to catch the train up to Manchester to schmooze the press to ensure Vale got a mention. He was a very social person and had a great rapport with a lot of the reporters, but, for me, imbibing with his press mates may have built useful relationships, but it also set a poor example.

John wasn't afraid to muck in on occasions, though, and he swapped his tracksuit for overalls to help paint the facilities at Vale Park, as we couldn't even afford to get decorators in during the first two years we were at Vale. John, Lol Hamlett and I painted the gym together, which was actually a good bonding experience early on in his reign, but I remember Lol and I painting the first-team dressing room, which was as shabby as Steptoe's Yard, including taking a lot of boards off, painting them and putting them back up, wondering where the gaffer was on this occasion. All of a sudden the phone rang – it was John telling us to watch out for a photographer from *The Sentinel.* As soon as this lad turned up to take the picture, John arrived, as if by magic, wearing overalls, with his paintbrush and even a strategically placed speck of white paint here and there on his face, to make sure he was in the photograph; never an opportunity missed. Lol and I were dumbstruck. I'm fairly sure Lol swore under his breath …

As abrasive as he was, John also had an amazing talent for getting people to do things for him. He could turn the charm on and somehow managed to persuade people like comedian Mick Miller to help raise funds for the club by putting on comedy evenings. But the best example I can give of this is when, in 1983, he convinced Stoke City manager Richie Barker that Mark Chamberlain's brother Neville was as good as his England international sibling. Neville had many qualities, but he wasn't in Mark's class, which I'm sure he himself would admit. Somehow John sold Richie this dream of two Chamberlains terrorising First Division defences and got £40,000 out of him for Neville. Remarkable.

* * *

The jewel in the club's crown at that time was undoubtedly local lad Mark Chamberlain, an England schoolboy winger, who was named in the PFA Fourth Division team of the year for 1981/82 after putting in some blistering performances on the right wing. This pleased me greatly as it had been something I had focussed on due to the size of the pitch. Mark was a tremendous talent who was a joy to coach, but we were desperate for money and, in the summer of 1982, Mark was sold to Stoke City, along with keeper Mark Harrison, for a joint fee of £240,000. The two clubs were poles apart in those days, but that sale of two young stars caused uproar amongst the black and white section of the Potteries. I still maintain that it was a good sale for the club at the time, as it gave us money to play with for the first time in two years.

Mark went on to play for England just a few months after that move, having caused a sensation in his first appearances in the top flight, devastating defences with that long, leggy running style and close control of his. He had a wonderful turn of speed and could beat a man with a sway of his hips. He scored on his international debut against Luxembourg at Wembley in December 1982, unusually for him heading home a cross, and in 1984 starred, alongside fellow winger John Barnes, as England won for the first (and still only) time ever in the Maracanã Stadium, Rio de Janeiro, beating Brazil 2-0.

I must say it was a privilege to coach him.

Meanwhile, John countered the unrest over the sale of Chamberlain by parading a new young signing on the pitch before a home game at the start of the campaign. The 17-year-old had just been released by Stoke after completing his apprenticeship and was spotted by our scout Ray Williams (remember him?). He found himself signing his first professional contract on a table in the centre circle at Vale Park, with the manager telling all and sundry that he was going to be the next big thing, revelling in the fact that he was signing a Potters reject that they had got completely wrong. That didn't go down too well amongst the home fans at first, until they realised that McGrath had unearthed a diamond in the shape of Robbie Earle, who would go on to become a Vale legend, play in the Premier League for Wimbledon and in the World Cup finals for Jamaica.

I say John unearthed him. It was Ray Williams, by now a coach and scout at Vale, who mentioned Robbie to John and I, suggesting we give him a trial. We liked what we saw. Robbie was raw, but had great energy and focus, so John signed him to great fanfare and he turned into an exceptionally good player. Whoever got rid of him at Stoke dropped a bollock, that's for sure.

Robbie's development didn't happen by accident, though. He and I spent hours in the gym together, along with two other young starlets, Andrew Shankland and Mark Bright. Robbie's first touch wasn't the greatest as he had wide feet, but his attitude was second to none and he would run all day long. He was competitive and could use his frame to get up in the air. It was obvious he had the energy to play in midfield and that was where I moved him when I took charge of the Vale first team, although he started up front for John McGrath.

I can still remember getting those three to work on heading in particular as I always felt that was a skill which can be improved through repetition, getting the power from the neck muscles, learning to deflect crosses which have pace on towards the corners of the net, etc. I'd often tell the players how I had worked so hard on my left foot but never managed to improve it, but my heading was the one skill which had come on for me greatly due to practice. I saw real improvement in particular in Mark and Robbie and both became renowned for scoring headed goals.

All three were desperately keen to improve, especially Mark, who had a Gambian father and English mother, but was fostered into

Stoke-on-Trent families as a kid after his parents split. Brighty was only part-time at first. He would go to work at Staffs Hydraulics in Kidsgrove at 6 or 7am and get to Vale Park for half past three. We would go round the back of the ground or into the gymnasium until it was dark, honing his skills alongside the other two youngsters, who were full-time. Mark earnt just an extra £10 a week from football until he turned pro, but I've never known such a determined and committed lad at his tender age of 18 and those sessions in the gym helped him secure his first full-time contract in 1982. I can still hear him now asking to keep going when I was ready to end the sessions at 5pm. Often, I would have to turn out the lights in the gym to get him to leave, he was that set on becoming a professional. I am so pleased Mark went on to do so well in the game, playing in the Premiership and both FA Cup and League Cup Finals. My reflected glory is that in his own book, Mark named me as the most influential person in his career, which I am incredibly proud about.

Both Robbie and Mark would break into the first team in the coming months and years and quickly establish themselves as top players who went on to have fabulous careers. Andrew Shankland was less fortunate, picking up a serious ankle injury which ended his career before it had really begun, a lesson in the fragility of being a professional footballer. Mark always maintained that Andy was the more talented of the trio and could have gone on to play for England were it not for the persistent injuries. Andy became a window cleaner, but a fall from a ladder in 2003 led to another broken ankle, which developed complications, eventually resulting in him having part of his leg amputated. He also suffered numerous other medical problems and we organised a benefit dinner for him at Vale Park, raising £20,000 towards paying for a new prosthetic leg. A sad, sad end to a promising career.

* * *

The sales of Chamberlain and Harrison also meant John could afford to make more ambitious recruitment efforts in the transfer market and in the summer of 1982, John tried to sign former England, Southampton and Manchester City striker Mick Channon, who had played at The Dell with John. But Channon (bravely) turned John down and instead joined Newcastle before ending up spending the twilight of his career at Norwich. I admired John for that, though, as it was an audacious attempt to bring a superstar to Vale Park and typical of him to try something like that.

But perhaps Channon's decision to head to the North East was a blessing in disguise as, instead of a landmark signing, we were able to afford the wages of defenders John Ridley, Wayne Cegielski and Les Lawrence (from my old club Torquay), midfielder Steve Waddington, winger Steve Fox, who arrived on a free from Wrexham like Cegielski, strikers Bob Newton, who arrived for £15,000 from Hartlepool, and Jim Steel, who we spent £10,000 on from Oldham, and goalkeeper Barry Siddall to replace Mark Harrison. These were all experienced players, well-versed in what it took to play in Division Four and we blended this team together, with the pieces falling into place very quickly as the 1982/83 season developed to be an excellent one, although, as we didn't score in any of our opening three league games, you wouldn't have predicted that in August 1982. Once we hit our stride we went on long runs; eight wins from ten games from mid-September, ten wins from 12 from mid-December and seven wins from 11 from mid-March.

Ernie Moss and Bob Newton quickly became one of the most feared strike partnerships in the division and were nicknamed 'the Kray twins' by John McGrath. They were a great double act, tailor-made for the lower divisions, and Ernie was one of the best professionals I came across – I was disappointed when McGrath sold him to Lincoln for £1,500 in March that season, believing him to be nearing the end of his fabulous lower-league career, aged 34, when in fact he played on for another six years. Ernie and Bob scored 30 goals between them that promotion season, with Bob getting 20 of them.

At the other end of the pitch, with just 34 goals conceded, we had the best defensive record in the Football League, alongside Hull, who were vying for promotion with us, Scunthorpe, Bury and Wimbledon. Five clubs into four promotion places did not fit.

We were defeated 0-1 at Hull on 26 March, but then lost just one of the next nine games (at champions Wimbledon, managed by Dave Bassett), also 0-1. Meanwhile others stuttered and promotion was clinched with a 2-0 win at Stockport County on 6 May, thanks to a brace of goals from Jim Steel.

Four Vale players were chosen for the PFA Fourth Division team of the season; Phil Sproson, Russell Bromage, Geoff Hunter and Steve Fox. Quite how neither Bob nor Ernie made it in beggars belief.

The directors were made extra happy by the club turning a profit for the first season since 1975/76 of over £100,000 as our average home attendance was the second-highest in the division. Urged on by showman John, they splashed out on some celebrations on the last day of that 1982/83 season before our final home game. McGrath asked supporters to turn up in fancy dress to create a carnival atmosphere and they responded with all sorts of outfits – we had a guy leaping around on the pitch dressed as a gorilla, cars flying through the air off ramps as part of the pre-match entertainment and John, dressed in a cream-coloured suit, ever the man to soak up the limelight and glory, signing a new contract on the pitch.

All that was wonderful, but only served to prove that distractions and having already won promotion often leads to losing games as struggling Northampton Town won the match 1-2.

No matter, we were on a huge high, having finished third in the table with a club record 88 points (under the new three points for a win system), seven points clear of Bury in fifth place. It had been a fabulous improvement over three years, led by this crazy, overbearing, yet inspirational gaffer and justified his unconventional methods and all the bruising the players had suffered as they could see the three years of hard work and a lot of home truths being told was bearing fruit.

It hadn't just been the players John had had a go at, though. He would also try to embarrass and undermine me at times, just to keep me in my place. An example which stays with me is that one of my roles was to go and look at forthcoming opposition and I would prepare a report on them for him. On one famous occasion, John had sent me on a round trip of over 200 miles to compile this report, which I duly submitted. To make an impression, in the dressing room before a game he got hold of that report and ripped it up in front of the players, with me there next to him, saying, 'That's what I think of this lot; it's not about them, it's about us!' as he did so. OK, so he was making a point that we didn't need to worry about them, only about ourselves and how we played, but he ridiculed my hard work whilst doing so. I swore I wouldn't do anything so showy myself if I ever became a manager. Mind you, I'm fairly sure John had read it in detail before putting on his performance for the team.

Even when we celebrated promotion that season, I was kept in the background and he would not even allow me on to the Edgeley Park pitch to congratulate the players I had worked so hard with because he wanted all the plaudits himself.

Having said that, I am eternally grateful for the opportunity John McGrath gave me in dragging me away from the footballing backwater of Torquay to be his assistant at Port Vale. It gave me an incredible grounding and allowed me to formulate ideas about how I might do the job were I ever to be given the chance. Little did I know that opportunity was just around the corner.

Chapter 5

Taking Over

'Even though someone made me a sign that had printed on it "J Rudge, Manager", I never had it put on my door. Football management is far too transient to risk that.'

John Rudge

DURING THAT promotion season, just after Christmas 1982, John McGrath had gone down with a virus and wasn't well enough to come into the club, so, as first-team coach, I was put in temporary charge of the team, with Jimmy Greenhoff to help me. We took 16 points from the six games I was in charge for (five wins and a draw), but, far from being great news for John, this seemed to have an unsettling effect on the indisposed manager. I would phone him straightaway with the good news after each game, but he didn't seem pleased that we were carrying on the good work without him, and it really was a continuation. I barely changed anything, just kept on picking the same team and demanding high standards from the players. I may have been quieter and less aggressive than John, but we kept the run going.

There was never any suggestion that I was after his job, even if ultimately, the mini run of success did me no harm. However, when John returned, I noticed a major change in his attitude towards me.

He clearly thought I had designs on his job and had been weaseling my way in with the directors. That wasn't true, even though I'd been given credit for what I'd done, although not by him. John's perception was I had taken the limelight away from him and he couldn't let that continue, so began a 'knocking-down process', which I believe led to his downfall. He stopped me going into the directors' room after games, I suspect, because he feared the directors might recognise the part I played in the promotion we eventually achieved. Our relationship somewhat soured and this was most likely behind the ripping up my scouting report incident.

As wonderful as winning promotion is, if you go up you need to invest to stay at that higher level, but Vale couldn't. There was just no money and, despite winning promotion, numerous players also were disgruntled over contract issues. Phil Sproson, our inspirational centre-half, had signed a lucrative long-term agreement which became known to the rest of the squad and it particularly agitated goalkeeper Barry Siddall and defender Russell Bromage, two experienced players, who fell into dispute with the club. John allowed this player unrest to fester as several others rejected new deals and four stayed at the club on weekly contracts only – this was despite the club paying the third-highest wage bill in the division of £9,000. That kind of thing can happen when players feel they aren't rewarded for achieving promotion.

It wasn't only myself and the players who had tired of John's manner by summer 1983. John was also in conflict with new chairman Jim Lloyd, who instructed him to speak to the press only on team matters. That did not sit well with the manager, who wanted as much media exposure about as many aspects of the club as possible.

In an effort to improve the running of the club, that summer the board appointed a new club secretary, Phil Shaw, who had been at Wolves. I think moving to Port Vale came as something of a culture shock to Phil, as did his relationship with the manager, which became an important factor in John's downfall. They had a combustible relationship, but Phil, as secretary, had the directors' ears, so that didn't help John at all, especially when trying to get some of his more eccentric ideas or more flamboyant transfer opportunities agreed, one of which, in true John McGrath statement style, was Gerry Daly, the former Manchester United and Republic of Ireland international midfielder. But money, as usual, and the board, no doubt prompted by Phil Shaw, turned the opportunity down on the grounds of cost, agreeing instead to sign loan defender Max Thompson, who had played for Liverpool and Swansea and was returning from a spell in America. That damaged John's ego significantly and the deterioration in his relationship with the board was only matched by that on the pitch.

He began to make some questionable decisions in my book. He offloaded the previous campaign's top scorer Bob Newton to Chesterfield early in the season in exchange for Martin Henderson, who was not a success. John did well to get Eamonn O'Keefe, a Republic of Ireland international who we signed from Wigan for £10,000. Eamonn was a combative, talented player who had very good body strength and could play in midfield or attack, which was where I preferred him. John, though, decided to play him in midfield, which for me wasn't his strength.

Another man we had also tempted to join the club in January 1983 was Alan Oakes, who had been a great player with Manchester City and won the Division One title, FA Cup, two League Cups and the European Cup Winners' Cup in a stellar career. In fact, Alan still holds their club record for appearances with 680. Alan had been player-manager at Chester for six seasons, bringing Ian Rush into the first team and then selling him to Liverpool. He was still super fit when he arrived at Vale Park after being sacked at Sealand Road in March 1982, with Chester heading for relegation and became player-coach, working under me. In fact, Alan was so fit he was able to turn out amidst an injury crisis in a home defeat to Plymouth Argyle when aged 41 years and 60 days old, his 776th and last Football League appearance.

* * *

I had become tired of John's ability to make enemies quickly and also my increasing sidelining since he had returned from his illness, and in the summer of 1983 I was tempted by an offer to go with Jimmy Greenhoff to work with him as he had just been appointed manager at Rochdale. On balance, though, having just won promotion, I felt I had a huge challenge in working in Division Three with Vale, so, after a lot of consideration, I turned the offer down. Jimmy lasted just nine months in the job at Spotland and never had another managerial job, while I would be the Port Vale manager by the turn of the year and remained so for a further 15 years. On such decisions are careers won and lost in football.

At the same time, Alan Oakes had an interview for the Manchester City managerial vacancy and asked me to go with him if he was given the job. But Alan was passed over in favour of Celtic manager Billy McNeill and I never got the chance to even turn that job down.

Both opportunities sorely tempted me, but my loyalty isn't quite as transparent as it may seem. Actually, what happened was that both of those opportunities landed in my lap at the same time. I really preferred the Manchester City option, so hung on for that, which meant missing out on Rochdale with Jimmy. When Alan didn't get offered the position at Maine Road, I was left with my existing job at Vale. I had bills to pay and a young family after all. I also had an inkling that John McGrath would self-combust in the not too distant future.

I had actually been under the impression that John was touting for the Manchester City job himself, hence his schmoozing of the Manchester press, but he wasn't even called for interview. He would have loved being a big-time club manager. Instead, he, like me, remained at Vale Park to take on the challenge of a new, higher division. It didn't go well.

We began 1983/84 with an appalling run of one win in the first 19 league games and were mired in deep relegation trouble. We were not a happy ship, but did manage to get through to the second round of the Milk Cup by defeating Wrexham, winning the second leg at the Racecourse Ground 5-1 to complete an 8-2 aggregate victory, and were rewarded with a tie against Ron Atkinson's Manchester United, the reigning FA Cup holders. That draw was tailor-made for John McGrath as it brought attention to little Port Vale – all we heard about for weeks was that tie and it overshadowed the importance of league games as points drained away. True, the two Manchester United games were great occasions for players and supporters alike, but we were fourth from bottom of the Third Division by the time we lost by the only goal at home in front of almost 20,000 supporters and then went down 0-2 at Old Trafford. Both were creditable performances, but they were soon forgotten when we became anchored at the foot of the league table amidst a run of one point from ten games. Dreadful form in anyone's book.

As the dismal results continued, so John sought to focus the blame away from himself, which meant on to me. I remember us getting thrashed 0-7 at Burnley in a game in which we were actually 0-6 down by half-time. When we conceded the seventh goal, John sent me on to the touchline to hand out instructions on his behalf, so I got the fans' pelters, while he stayed cosied up in the dugout. It was a major triumph how we managed to limit the damage to only one more goal in the second half – it was obvious things could not continue in this vein.

The next match, in the first weekend of December, saw Gillingham win 1-0 and we found ourselves propping up the rest of the table with just six points from 17 games. There was a certain irony about the following Monday because the TV cameras came to the ground to interview John about life at the bottom of the league. He was all smiles as usual, but, after the morning's training session, the board called him in and dismissed him. The TV interview went out that night with the announcer following it up by explaining that since it had been filmed John had been sacked. That must have been a brutal blow to John's ego.

I can picture him now, lying in the team bath while I sat alongside trying to console him. It was odd, actually, because I seemed more upset than him, confirming my suspicions that he had contrived his own downfall. I felt he had created a hole of his own making, which he didn't want to be seen to be getting out of, and so had instigated the confrontation with the board. He had ruffled too many feathers and there was only ever going to be one outcome. Given that he'd signed a new contract only that summer, John wasn't going to be out of pocket. In any case, he wasn't out of work for long, being appointed manager of Chester in January 1984 then moving on to Preston, with whom he won promotion from the Fourth Division in 1986/87.

Despite all the shenanigans, I have good reason to be very thankful to John. We may have been two completely different characters and he could be difficult to work with, but we blended well together, with me as the peacemaker to counteract his grenade-throwing style, and I learnt so much from him.

Sadly, John died of a heart attack on Christmas Day in 1998. Neil Midgley, the referee, rang to tell me the news. Ann, John's wife, asked me to speak at his funeral, which was a great honour. I recalled his time as a hard, rugged centre-half, who took no prisoners, and recalled the banter he would have with centre-forwards, asking, 'Do you like hospital food?' and 'Are you still in BUPA?'

I, of course, spoke about how I had a lot to be thankful to him for as John was the man who persuaded me to switch from Torquay to Burslem to further my career. He may have been a colourful character who liked to be the centre of attention, but he built the foundations for my 15-year tenure as manager at Vale Park.

John McGrath is sadly missed, but never forgotten by me. RIP big man and thank you.

* * *

Just before Christmas 1983, with Vale sitting at the foot of the Division Three table with just six points, I was given the job, initially on an interim basis, after my previous spell in temporary charge. When chairman Jim Lloyd called me, he told me the board didn't intend to advertise the vacancy if I did well. Obviously, the spell the previous season when I'd won five of my six games in charge while John convalesced had swung things in my favour, as had the fact that I was already on the books so they were effectively saving the manager's wage. I actually hadn't contemplated going into management so early in my career as I was quite happy being a coach and learning from John, so in that sense the situation was forced upon me, but you have to take opportunities when they present themselves in life and I seized this with both hands.

My first call was to Alan Durban, the then Sunderland manager, but who I had got to know during his spell as manager of Stoke City, to seek his advice. I had always got on well with Alan and I knew he had once been interested in signing me as a player while he was in charge at Shrewsbury. Alan's advice was to get hold of the more experienced players who would take responsibility, such as Barry Siddall and Eamonn O'Keefe; get them on my side and get them involved in what I was doing. This was very good advice.

I also moved to get some experience around me on the coaching side. Colin Dobson, who had been a coach at Bristol Rovers while I was there and with whom I had got on famously, despite the fence-chucking incident in the Antipodes, came to assist short-term, free of charge as we were not in a financial position to offer him an actual paying job, especially as the board had also sacked Alan Oakes along with McGrath. Meanwhile, Jimmy Greenhoff later came back to coach for the rest of the season after being sacked by Rochdale.

I moved O'Keefe up front and he responded by scoring nine goals in the second half of the season to finish as the leading scorer, with a total of 11 in 43 games, also being voted as the supporters' Player of the Year, with Mark Bright the only other player to make double figures in the scoring charts.

I soon realised that I had to have a different relationship with the players now I was no longer the coach who would put an arm around their shoulder, console and listen to them when John McGrath blew up at them. I was the boss. The players had to respect me or this simply wouldn't work. The players had called me 'Rudgey' when I was the number two, but now had to get used to calling me 'Gaffer'. It was a small win, but the first step on the road to putting my own mark on the club.

I carried on doing a lot of the coaching, despite being in charge now, as I enjoyed it so much and I wanted to stamp my seal on the team. Nowadays, managers don't coach that much, certainly Alex Ferguson didn't and he would change his number two regularly, but he had the resources to have a vast staff. I was the manager, coach, chief cook and bottle washer; literally. I always remember that, behind the scenes, Vale had the barest of skeleton staffing arrangements. There was just Estelle in the office, along with the club secretary, and I used to have to write any letters I wanted sending myself then give them to her to type it up. Nowadays there must be 15 staff in the Port Vale club office. The owners the Shanahans are incredible now; like chalk and cheese with the board situations I had to navigate during my time in charge.

Often, the coaches I had working with me would do a session, then I would follow on, but when it came to tactics I would step in and say what I wanted, making it clear to players what they were required to do. I would then decide what team I was going to play and we'd do shape, set pieces and marking in readiness for the opposition for the forthcoming game.

Fortunately for me, the response from the players was good. I think they were relieved that John had gone and that I, being more reasonable in their eyes, would not give them the same levels of pain. Not that I shied away from putting my views across forthrightly when I needed to and the players soon realised I had a steely side, despite being more reserved than their previous boss. But players will understand and accept that if they know they deserve it, by and large. And they did. Particularly those players who John had upset, who were now back in a positive frame of mind, ready to play for me.

When you have been in the game for any length of time you can 'smell' whether things are going to go for you and lads like Barry Siddall and Eamonn O'Keefe gave me a good feeling. A change in management can often have an uplifting effect, but we lost my first game in charge 0-1 at home to Lincoln City. We played pretty well and should have won, but the next match came as a rude awakening. On Boxing Day we got murdered 0-4 by lowly Preston North End and to make matters worse Phil Sproson got carried off with a hamstring injury, while Colin Tartt was sent off.

The following game was home to Sheffield United, who were second in the table, and I remember sitting in the office wondering what I was going to do. I brought in Wayne Cegielski to the defence as a fresh pair of legs, despite Sproson claiming he was fit, and O'Keefe played the major attacking role as we ran out 2-0 winners. Eamonn scored the opening goal, with my first ever signing as a manager, loanee Kevin Young from Burnley, who I had managed to persuade my former Torquay team-mate John Bond to part with for the remainder of the season, scoring the clincher.

We then went on a run of beating Bournemouth, Wimbledon and Southend and drawing at Bristol Rovers, to pick up ten points from the next 12.

That was the kind of run I needed to ensure I landed the job and, by the time I was offered it on a permanent basis in March 1984, we had gained 21 points from 15 games and climbed to fourth from bottom (with the bottom four all being relegated), but had momentum with us. From looking dead and buried, we had given ourselves a sporting chance of survival. I really thought we were going to get out of trouble.

I had changed the tactics slightly from John's approach as I liked to play 4-4-2 with wide players who hugged the touchlines. I always felt Vale Park, being a big pitch, offered great opportunities for our wingers to create chances. John had been less keen on wingers. Perhaps that is a difference between his playing career as a defender and mine as an attacker.

Although we temporarily climbed out of the bottom four, early in April 1984 we slipped up at home to Rotherham United, who were two places below us. We took a 2-0 lead, but then Alan Birch scored a hat-trick for them and we lost 2-3. I feel that game was the turning point, a significant nail in our relegation coffin. We only lost three out of the final ten games, but it was not enough to keep us up and we finished in 23rd position, six points off Brentford, who survived one place above the relegation zone.

If there was any satisfaction to be gained at all it was that people had forecast we were as good as down when I took over in the December and we had put up something of a fight in what had been a tough but educational apprenticeship for me as manager.

When the time came to negotiate my contract once I was offered the job full-time that March, I felt I was in a strong position. I'd been on £7,000 a year as first-team coach, but learned that John McGrath had been on £15,000. When I went to the board, they split the difference and told me I would be on £11,000. I responded by asking, 'So how is it that John McGrath was on £15,000 as manager, but you are only going to pay me £11,000?'

Chairman Jim Lloyd stared at me and said, 'You still have to prove yourself'. That was that. I had no alternative but to accept the offer as I was desperate to do the job.

To mark the occasion, taking a leaf out of John McGrath's book, I posed for a photo alongside the chairman by the sign on the door to the manager's office, although I was a little apprehensive when I saw it was written in chalk, while the dripping wet sponge on the floor nearby ready to wipe it off made it even more surreal. Hint taken.

Even though someone eventually made me a proper sign that had printed on it 'J. Rudge, Manager', I never had it put on my door. Instead, I kept it in a cupboard all the time I was at the club. Football management is far too transient to risk that.

Chapter 6

No Pots to Piss In

'Bloody hell, Rudgie used to be on to me all the time wanting something. When I got off the phone with him, I used to be in tears because of all the tales of woe about how little money he had.'

Sir Alex Ferguson

I FULLY believe that any manager is only as good as his players. Tactics, man-management, etc., are all key too, but recruitment is the most vital part of the job and, over the years, I was able to sign a lot of very good players, who rarely let me down. They were the most single important factor for me being successful. I'd like to thank each and every one of them.

But behind each signing there is always a story and in many cases at Port Vale often they were, let's say, unconventional, not least for financial reasons.

The saying goes that if you want to make a small fortune in football, start with a large one. We couldn't at Port Vale; we didn't have a pot to piss in, which was ironic given that the club is based in the Potteries.

Before John McGrath and I arrived, the board had allowed previous managers to splurge around £140,000 on the likes of Ken Todd, Peter Farrell (a club record £40,000 from Bury), Gerry Keenan and the original 'leper' Bernie Wright over the course of

1978, while in October 1979, just before we joined, Paul Bowles was signed from Crewe for £30,000. In the summer of 1980, the club allowed John McGrath to spend precisely £0, with all incoming players arriving on free transfers, while all of the aforementioned players left the club, with only Todd bringing in any money; sold to Portsmouth for £20,000 in October 1979.

Things didn't get a whole lot better, despite winning promotion in 1982/83, hence the sales of the two Chamberlains and Mark Harrison, and the club was still in a parlous financial state when I assumed the reins, so I had to call on all that experience I'd gained on the markets, learnt at night school and when networking in the school of hard knocks that is the football industry to cajole, persuade, beg, borrow, outwit, misdirect and, occasionally, plain deceive others to secure the signings I wanted at the price that Port Vale FC could afford. I often wonder if I could have done it so successfully without all these other strings to my bow, but I guess we'll never know.

Philosophically speaking, I wanted to play 4-4-2 with wingers who could get to the byline and cross the ball for the forwards, and then have midfielders who could control, pass, move, control, pass, move; based on what Dick Young had taught me all those years before and had proved successful at Carlisle. However, I knew that my players at Port Vale were not yet good enough and I needed to coach them more and, ultimately, bring in better players. Given the budget restrictions, that was a challenge on almost every front.

Here is an insight into what it took to make some of those successful (and some less so) signings and sales at Vale.

* * *

Like John McGrath when he took over the managerial reins, I had to shift a few players, partly because they weren't for me, but also because I needed to generate money for signings and wages or, in some cases, out of pure financial necessity. However, I didn't initially do this by calling the unwanted players 'lepers' and making them train on their own, blurting it all out to the press. I took almost the opposite approach, weeding them out one by one and selling them on, generating a small pot of cash which I could use to get my own men in, often telling the club they were destined for how brilliant they were in order to get them to part with just a little more cash.

Because I wanted a more mobile attacker, despite him doing well at the tail end of the 1982/83 promotion campaign, tall, strong striker Jim Steel was actually my first sale. I sold him to Wrexham in January 1984 for the same £10,000 fee John McGrath had spent on him ten months earlier in purchasing him from Oldham.

Another player I moved on was firebrand winger Steve Fox. Steve was a skilful wide right man who would always create a lot of chances. He could be argumentative, though, and fell out with me, and left for Wrexham on a free transfer, though he later admitted his regret at leaving.

I also found myself forced into selling Eamonn O'Keefe, who was a real character to say the least. Stocky, quick and fiery, Eamonn was a Republic of Ireland international, our top scorer and winner of the Player of the Season for 1983/84, but the day after picking up his award he put in a transfer request partly because we had been relegated, and partly because of his lengthy daily commute. I refused to sell him, though, as he was such a good player, which didn't endear me to him at all. There was never a dull moment with Eamonn. When a perimeter fence collapsed during our 2-1 FA Cup first round win at Macclesfield Town in November 1984, he carried two children to safety, which was heroic to see. Then, a few months later, in March 1985, he refused to play against Wrexham in a league game because he was due to play for his country the following night. That was the final straw for me. Three days later, I sold him to Sam Ellis at Fourth Division Blackpool for £17,500, after initially trying to persuade him to join John McGrath at Preston, but I think he'd had his fill of his former manager.

Although I had lost a potent goalscorer, I now had more money in the bank.

When defender John Ridley joined Stafford Rangers as player-coach in summer 1985, we felt we should be compensated as we didn't want John to go and he had played almost the entire season for us, despite being now 33. As he was continuing to play, not retire and just coach, we insisted, but Rangers refused to stump up, so the board took them to a tribunal, becoming the first Football League club to take a non-league club to a tribunal; we received £700, we were that desperate for cash.

Throughout my time at Vale Park my budget could best be described as modest or small. At the start it was infinitesimally miniscule. So tiny, in fact, that the board actually sacked first-team coach Alan Oakes in December 1983, at the same time John McGrath left, in order to save on wages. I insisted Alan return as my first-team coach the following August as I really needed him. There are only 24 hours in the day, after all.

Having the budget that would depress a pauper meant it was a case of me finding the players, negotiating the deals, doing the contracts and then getting it signed off by the chairman, so nothing could come back on me, before the deal was formalised. I really was a one-stop shop, where these days even smaller clubs probably have a team of people doing any one of those stages. Agents were non-existent at that time, so we never got approached by anyone. I had to go out looking for unpolished diamonds. I did have some much-needed help on that front. My scouting team included my old coach from Bristol Rovers, Colin Dobson, and former Vale striker Ray Williams, who helped out of friendship and his love for the club. I also occasionally used Eddie Tatton and Eric Foster. I knew all had a great eye for a player and so it proved, but these men were never paid for helping apart from petrol expenses and modest fees when players signed on. That was typical of life at Port Vale – begging favours and asking people to do things for nothing.

Even when they spotted a potential talent, I would still go and watch them for myself. That has always been key for me. These days, having cameras at every game at most levels, there is a lot of footage available, but you just never get the same feel for a player as you do when you can watch them live. For example, when the camera follows the ball down the other end of the pitch, what is the striker you are interested in doing to be ready for it to come back their way? Are they alert? Do they switch off? Even though I eventually signed players from Scotland, Ireland, Holland, Belgium, Sweden and France, I always went to see them, meaning long trips. I could never sign someone 'blind'.

For many years, we played our midweek home games on a Monday. That meant I could go and scout players by watching games every other evening. Once fans got wind of how much scouting I did, they used to joke that even though there weren't any professional games to attend on a Thursday night, somehow I'd find a non-league or even a parks game to watch.

My work ethic was constant and it meant that Del really brought the kids up, as I was here, there and everywhere; Swansea one night, Doncaster the next, then Bury, Lincoln, Wigan, around many non-league grounds. If I wasn't at games, I would be talking with managers about up-and-coming players we may want to sign. Sometimes, those would be from reserve teams from professional clubs, other times they would be young non-league stars on the rise. It was very much a boots on the ground operation.

I would study all the teams listed in the Sunday papers to see if I could spot any new names to check on. In that way I built up an encyclopaedic knowledge of players, their positions and backgrounds, strengths, weaknesses and form. I would pride myself in knowing almost every player in the Football League down to the colour of his eyes. That has never left me.

Signing players for a club like Vale requires hard graft, making contacts and phone calls, watching hundreds of games and using a hell of a lot of persuasion. This is how you unearth a rough diamond. The dream for any manager when at a non-league ground on a bleak winter's night, hoping to remain anonymous under a flat cap, is to identify a raw talent, sign him for peanuts and then turn him into a megastar and sell him on for millions. That became my hallmark.

Over a period of time, my criteria was always to ensure that at least 70 per cent of my signings proved to be hits. Those that weren't had to be moved on. I'd like to think I hit that throughout my 15 years as manager. We certainly had far more hits than misses.

To give you an idea of how player recruitment can also sometimes be totally random, I can now reveal the tale of how I signed midfielder Derek Monaghan in the summer of 1984. Derek had just been released from First Division West Brom and I had contacted him to see if he might be interested in joining us as I had seen him play for Albion's reserves on one of my regular scouting trips. So intent was I to sign Derek, that I then pursued him all the way to Spain, although this was more by accident than intent, or so I told my wife. The Rudge family set off to San Antonio, Ibiza for our annual two-week holiday and, while we were seeking entertainment for the children one night, we went to a hotel where there was a fancy dress evening going on. It turned out to be the kind of evening in which men were dressing up as women, and vice versa, and there was a lot of dancing going on. It was vibrant and fun, but to my amazement, who should I see pirouetting across the room in full drag but Derek Monaghan; my transfer target.

And yes, I did recognise him, despite his dress and make-up.

I approached Derek and had a laugh and a chat. I impressed upon him how interested I was in signing him and, the following morning, trialled him on the beach to see if his knee, which had stood up to the previous night's shenanigans, would stand the test of another season. Derek put pen to paper after returning to the UK, so I suppose it could be said I had signed something of a drag artist.

Sadly, Derek only played nine games before injury struck again and he had to move down to non-league level with Redditch United.

* * *

My first permanent signing on whom I spent money was Oshor Williams, a winger from Stockport County, who signed for £7,000 in November 1984. That was my entire budget gone in one fell swoop; all my other signings that season, such as Derek, Ally Brown, Alan Webb, Peter Griffiths and Billy Kellock, were free transfers.

Oshor was quick and sharp, with an eye for goal, at his most dangerous with the ball at his feet attacking the opposition full-back, just my kind of player. He cracked his left kneecap in a training incident in February 1985, but recovered his first-team place two months later to become an integral part of our 1985/86 promotion side, but then refused the terms the club offered him and I had to sell him at a bargain £2,000 fee in August 1986 to none other than my old boss John McGrath at Preston North End, who had actually been the one keen in signing Oshor in the first place, before getting sacked.

Negotiating with my old boss was less frightening than I had expected. John was fine with me, in one of his better moods. I think he thought he was getting one over me, and in a sense he did as Preston won promotion that 1986/87 season to join us in Division Three.

Two of those free transfers proved to be excellent signings; full-back Alan Webb and midfielder-cum-striker Ally Brown. Ally was a fine player, who had spent the vast majority of his career in the top flight, but was now nearing the end of his playing days. He became the brains for Robbie Earle's legs in the hub of our midfield. Alan won Player of the Season in 1984/85, as a marauding right-back who had a fine shot on him.

I was off to a good start, building a team around my existing stars such as Phil Sproson, Robbie Earle, Russell Bromage and Geoff Hunter, which could challenge for promotion from the Fourth Division. Geoff Hunter had been a mainstay of the club since my arrival as coach and was ever-present during the 1982/83 promotion-winning season and played 57 games in our next promotion season of 1985/86, scoring six goals as he helped us to escape the division for a second time.

With football being such a small world, contacts were a huge factor for me in my quest to sign talent, especially those connections via networking that I picked up at Lilleshall. Often that would mean picking up the phone to a fellow manager to ask about this player or that, or even request to take someone on loan as we often couldn't afford to sign players outright. But it could also work the other way when I needed to move someone on.

An example of this was with experienced centre-half John Williams. I bought him for £12,000 from Tranmere Rovers in the summer of 1985. John was one of the unsung heroes of our promotion side the following season, playing alongside Sproson, but at the level above I didn't feel they dovetailed well together, so I had to move one of them on. By December 1985 I was convinced the right one to retain was Sproson (which definitely proved to be the case), so gave my old mucker Harry Redknapp a call. Harry was by now manager of our former club Bournemouth and was persuaded to part with £30,000 for Williams. An £18,000 (150 per cent) profit is not bad for 18 months and a promotion out of a player. Harry still tells me John was his best ever signing and, to be fair, John did help Bournemouth win the division that season. You can't get every deal right!

In the summer of 1985 I also brought in experienced keeper Jim Arnold from Everton on a free transfer and signed defender Jon Bowden from Oldham Athletic for £5,000, both of whom would play the vast majority of games in that season's promotion-winning team. Jon was another who struggled at the higher level, so I sold him to Wrexham for £12,500 in April 1987; another 150 per cent profit in a player who contributed hugely to helping us win promotion.

* * *

Of course, the other side of making signings at a club like Port Vale is keeping hold of your best players because bigger clubs in higher divisions will always want them. It's a financial reality that the players will eventually, mostly, want to go and try their luck in the best leagues in the land. My job in those circumstances was to get the best deal possible for the club.

I first got a feel for this at the end of that 1983/84 season in which I took over. Every cloud is supposed to have a silver lining and, in that relegation campaign, emerging striker Mark Bright provided it with ten goals in 20 games, but this led to interest from several clubs and, despite me agreeing a new contract with Mark, First Division Leicester contacted him and he never signed it. In desperation, knowing I was almost certainly going to lose my protégé, I hit upon a plan and phoned Sheffield Wednesday to speak with their manager Howard Wilkinson and tell him how good Mark was, hoping to get evidence of other clubs being interested so I could bump Leicester's offer up. Mark even went over to train with the Owls for a few days and coach Peter Eustace really liked him, but Howard rang me back to say he wasn't going to take him. Ironically, Brighty would eventually end up at Hillsborough, albeit via a hugely successful spell at Crystal Palace, with Wednesday having to pay a fee of £1,375,000 in 1992!

So, stymied by failing to get another club to make an offer, I went to the tribunal, only to be disappointed with the result. Leicester were ordered to make a down payment of just £33,333 in June 1984, with two further instalments after so many appearances to total £100,000. I felt this was about half of what I would have valued him at. I was particularly disappointed after all that work I had put into Mark as a lad.

Incidentally, we never got the final payment from Leicester as Mark didn't play that many games for the Foxes, moving on to Selhurst Park in summer 1986, so he only cost Leicester £66,000 and they sold him to Crystal Palace for just £75,000, which was a steal. Not that I'm bitter about it at all.

One player we were able to keep hold of was Phil Sproson, who was a wonderful centre-half. Phil is a Port Vale legend and part of a dynasty, being the son of former Vale player Jess and nephew of Vale legend Roy. Utterly consistent, Phil played 500 games, placing him second in the all-time appearance chart for the club behind his uncle. I could also count on him to weigh in with four or five goals a season too, some of which proved vital. Tall and dominant in the air, Phil was a manager's dream and holding on to him was crucial to our progress until he suffered a bad knee injury in 1989. This I achieved when Stoke City came calling by making Phil's asking price ridiculously high so that even our city slicker, First Division neighbours couldn't afford it. One-nil to John Rudge's Vale in the Potteries derby before a ball was kicked. Incidentally, Stoke manager Richie Barker instead signed Coventry's Paul Dyson, which I don't think worked out too well.

* * *

My first major transfer success story was striker Andy Jones. And thereby hangs quite a tale.

I had been following Andy for a while, thanks to a tip-off about him from Ken Roberts, the former Chester manager, who I'd got to know at Lilleshall. I went with Alan Oakes to see Andy in a night game for Rhyl amidst the wind and rain, which ruined the match, making control really difficult, and so, although I thought Andy was a rough diamond that I could polish, I felt I needed another look. This led to me persuading Del that we should combine a family day out to the seaside, with watching him play against Matlock on a Sunday. Much to my dismay, Andy was on the bench with a heavily strapped-up knee. By half-time in a game of little interest, I felt incredibly guilty about dragging the family to such a dull match and was all for going off to the seafront to alleviate the boredom of the two kids, who we'd dragged along with the promise of sand and ice cream. It was Del who said that we might as well stay for the second half, which proved to be sound advice, as Andy came on with 20 minutes to go and produced a couple of great shots, one of which was a belting effort that hit the woodwork. He was quick and strong, had two good feet and was sure to score goals; my kind of striker. To this day Del reminds me that she is really responsible for me signing Andy Jones!

On my return to the Potteries, I heard that Arsenal coach, Don Howe, had invited Andy to Highbury for training, so, within hours, myself and Alan Oakes were at Andy's house in Ruthin, north Wales with the forms and we did not leave until he had signed for just £3,000, with a further £2,000 based on appearances.

Alan and I double-teamed Andy, who, when he tells this story, claims that he didn't even invite us in, we just barged open the door. I don't remember it quite like that, but we certainly didn't give him any opportunity to say 'no'.

Incidentally, Ken Roberts never received any bonus for signing Andy or when he was sold. The board rejected my request, with director Arthur McPherson saying, 'Let's wait until Ken asks us,' but Ken, on hearing this, said, 'If that's their attitude they can shove it where the sun don't shine.'

Andy was an instant hit, scoring against Stoke with a thunderbolt of a shot in a pre-season friendly to instantly earn cult status. His arrival really sparked the revolution at the Vale and he made a huge impact, scoring 18 goals in his first season, 1985/86, in which we won promotion, and then 37 in the next, 1986/87, to become the second-highest scorer in the country in any division behind Clive Allen. His total included five in the final home game against Newport and a hat-trick at Fulham. Andy liked the ball early and over the top to run on to. He had great pace and a good shot in either foot. His record proves he was a fantastic finisher and it was inevitable bigger clubs in higher divisions would show interest.

In February 1987, Alan Oakes, who still had great connections at Maine Road, had been tipped the wink that Manchester City, who were struggling near the foot of the First Division at the time, were considering signing Andy for around £250,000. This was huge money for us. Their scouts were due to visit for a home game against Blackpool on Saturday, 28 February 1987. Andy was on a run of scoring five goals in five games and this was the first time we thought we were going to get a significant offer. He had been told of the interest and was champing at the bit.

Come game day, things didn't go so well. Blackpool ripped us to pieces, winning 1-6 with striker Paul Stewart scoring five goals, to record our biggest home defeat since March 1957. After the match, an offer went in from Manchester City, but for Stewart, not Jones. Blackpool received a fee of £200,000, we got nothing, although I wasn't too sad as it meant keeping Andy for a few more months. Stewart went on to have a good career, playing for Spurs and Liverpool; on such events can football careers turn.

Mind you, a month later it was us scoring six goals away from home when we won 6-0 at Craven Cottage. Andy bagged that hat-trick to celebrate being called up for Wales, making his international bow four days later, scoring on his debut in a 4-0 victory over Finland. He then opened the next campaign with four goals on the opening day against Aldershot, leading to huge interest from top-flight clubs and it was inescapable that we would have to sell him. I had an enquiry from Alex Ferguson at Manchester United, but it was Charlton Athletic's manager Lennie Lawrence who signed Andy for a then club record outgoing transfer fee of £350,000. That's a profit of £345,000 and you can work out the percentage yourself.

We were top of the early season table at the time and selling Andy felt like I'd cut my right arm off. Inevitably, our form tailed off without his goals that 1987/88 season and we finished in mid-table. In my after-dinner speeches, I always claim we had to sell Jones as Vale needed match balls to get to the end of the season. Our financial situation wasn't actually quite so brassic by 1987, but it wasn't far off.

* * *

Quite often when you think you are at a game to watch one particular player, another can take your eye. That was certainly the case on one occasion in 1984, when I went to watch Dean Glover, who I would eventually sign many years later, playing for Aston Villa reserves. That night I spotted Ray Walker, whose passing ability was excellent and was clearly a different calibre to the midfielders I had at that time. Way above, in fact.

I first took Ray on loan in 1984 for two months before he went back to Villa to try and make it in the First Division as we just couldn't afford to sign him at that stage. Then, in the summer of 1986, after he hadn't managed to make the grade in the top flight and we had just won promotion to the Third Division, I found I had enough cash to have a hope of signing him and so got back in touch. The Villa manager Graham Turner was on holiday, so I rang Ray directly and arranged to meet him at the Hilton Park services on the M6, where we agreed our deal. But I still had to go to a tribunal to sort out the fee. The Aston Villa chairman Doug Ellis, known throughout the game as 'Deadly Doug' due to his financial nous, was confident he would manage to influence the tribunal to get at least £25,000 for a midfielder who I was pointing out had only actually played 23 first-team games for Villa in five years. For my part, Vale had precisely £12,000 in the bank, all of which I was prepared to part with for Ray, such was my faith in him. I needed a plan as this was clearly under half of what Villa were asking.

I rang the PFA, who I was well in with, and found out who was going to be sitting on the panel. I then spoke with each of them, pointing out that unless the fee was no more than £12,000, the deal would be off as, at that time, if you didn't agree with the figure the tribunal said you could still pull out. Lo and behold, when the day came, the tribunal set the figure at £12,000, but with a 50 per cent sell-on clause, which I was delighted about. Doug Ellis was seething. Not only that, but Ray went on to make a total of 424 appearances for us over 11 seasons, scoring 42 goals, and we never sold him. He left to become player-coach at Leek in the Conference after I gave him a free transfer in 1997, briefly taking over as caretaker manager later that season.

Amongst all these wonderful players, in my opinion, Ray has to go down as possibly the best in terms of value for money and he was one of the first to start the trend of better quality players that I needed to improve my squad. Ray was in a different class and it was no surprise to me that he was twice voted as Player of the Season. Known as the 'Hoddle of the lower leagues', Ray boasted all the qualities of a top-flight midfielder, except pace. His passing was immaculate and he had a fabulous shot on him.

To me, Robbie Earle and Ray formed the best midfield partnership in the Third and then the Second Division. They complemented each other perfectly. I will always maintain that Ray could have played alongside Robbie in the Premier League, but he was content at Vale and we managed to hold on to him. I had always envisaged grooming Ray to be my successor at Vale Park, or possibly Robbie, but it didn't work out that way.

I was amazed that the only club to try and prise Ray away at any point was Stoke City under Mick Mills in June 1988, causing Ray to submit a transfer request, but as far as I was concerned there was no way they were having him, despite the £300,000 on offer. I made sure the board flatly rejected it, bumped Ray's wages up with a new, long-term contract and he responded by having a fantastic season as we clinched promotion in 1988/89. He would now be playing in the same league as Stoke. More of which later.

* * *

Due to selling Andy Jones, I had some working capital for the first time in my career, which needed shrewdly investing. All too often you see managers wasting transfer profit and it's very common for clubs to inflate prices when they know a buying club has cash in their bank account.

First, I signed midfielder Darren Hughes from Brighton, a snip at £5,000. I used to joke he was quick enough to get booked for speeding, a trait he used to get round and cover Dean Glover's deficiency in that department after I converted him to playing at left-back, a position in which he had begun his career at Everton.

Then, in December 1987, I splashed out £35,000 on midfielder Simon Mills from York City. Skilful but adaptable, with quality on the ball and tremendous passing ability, I converted Millsy to become an excellent right-back, partnered with Hughes, and both became mainstays of the promotion team of 1989.

At the same time, I spent the same amount on intelligent right-winger Gary Ford from Leicester City, although the Foxes had only just bought him from York where he had played alongside Mills, under manager Denis Smith, so I was reuniting the pair, this time with Gary playing in front of Simon on the right-hand side.

On the left wing I signed the superbly tricky and dangerous John Jeffers; a real pearl. Kept out of Kenny Dalglish's all-conquering Reds team by no less a winger than John Barnes, John joined us in December 1988, on loan initially, but then permanently for £30,000. I kept the board happy by funding the transfer fee by selling Steve Harper to Preston North End for £35,000, so we were up £5,000 and had swapped one fantastic winger for another who wasn't playing often. That's how trading up works.

Jeffers' recruitment was a classic case of getting in first. I had heard about John on the grapevine and went to watch him at a reserve team game and there were about four or five managers or coaches there watching him as it was known he was too good to sit in the reserves waiting for Barnes to get injured. By half-time I had seen enough to know I wanted to sign him. John had such a good touch that his feet were like flypaper. The ball stuck to that left peg the moment it came into contact with it. I was looking for just his kind of wide left player who would take defenders on and commit them, then get balls into the box. I spent the whole of the second half hoping that he wouldn't have so much of the ball, which thankfully he didn't. I did my usual thing of sloping off early and not saying anything to any of the others who were there watching him, hoping to steal a march on them. They weren't quick enough as I contacted Dalglish before the game had even ended to do the initial loan deal.

John thrived on the wide pitch at Vale Park, where his jinking skills and pinpoint crossing gave us another dimension. His tendency to sometimes overdo things did infuriate some fans, let alone me. The classic Jeffers trick was to shimmy past his man with a drop of his shoulder, but then he would stop and do it all over again for good measure! However, when he was on form, 'JJ', often known as 'Jinking Johnny', was pretty unstoppable and he had pace to burn and a stunning left foot too.

He had an instant impact and, supported by the dynamism of Robbie Earle and hard graft of fellow central midfielder Andy Porter, was another to play a major role in the 1989 promotion campaign. The tenacious Porter cost us nothing as a youth recruit and eventually left for nothing, but in the intervening 13 years he gave the club valiant service throughout each of his 435 games. A lot of people queried what he had to offer, but 'Goober', as Andy was known, went on to prove that the team was often less effective without his presence in midfield. In short, Andy was one of those players who made others better. He gave 100 per cent all the time and, despite being small, he really was a hard little bugger. Quite frankly, he'd kick his granny, but also had a great attitude and determination and worked exceptionally hard to improve his game. Andy regularly asked Mike Pejic, who was by now my first-team coach, for extra training. Andy was also brilliant at taking instructions. I just gave him the shirt, told him what to do and let him get on with it. He did some great man-marking jobs when I asked him to, including on one occasion, on Boxing Day 1996, when he marked Manchester City's Georgian midfielder Georgi Kinkladze, who was the best playmaker in the First Division that season, out of the game. Everybody expected us to get thumped at Maine Road, but Porter snuffed Kinkladze out completely and we won 1-0 thanks to a goal from Martin Foyle. So tight did Andy keep to Kinky, that at half-time he actually turned towards the Man

City dressing room after coming down the tunnel off the pitch, rather than to ours!

Management would be easy if every player was like Andy Porter. I admit to having a soft spot for him and the players would refer to him as my son. Certainly, he was the only professional footballer I would have allowed a daughter of mine to marry! Mind you, he was the first to be knocking on my door if he was not on the team sheet and he did not relish being substituted either. Regularly, in the days before the modern, digital substitute boards, when the numbers 1–11 would be held up on printed boards to show who was coming off, during the pre-match warm up, Andy removed his number from amongst them, so it could not be held up for him to be subbed. I made Andy my captain towards the end of his time at Vale Park, he led the team out at Wembley against Genoa in the Anglo-Italian Cup Final in 1996 and we gave him a well-deserved testimonial against Derby County that same year.

Andy Porter was like a tiger, especially in the tackle, so much so that even Bob Hazell used to moan to me about him; 'Bloody hell, Gaffer, can you stop bloody Andy Porter annoying me.' Andy might have been small, but he wasn't frightened of anybody.

Talking of Bob, he was a huge man and a huge help to me when he signed in December 1986 from Reading on a free transfer. Bob was experienced at higher levels and had played in the FA Cup Final for Queens Park Rangers against Tottenham Hotspur in 1982. He did a sterling job for us. Like me, Bob was tempted by the offer of a car, courtesy of chairman Bill Bell on this occasion. The problem was it broke down regularly, so Bob wasn't best pleased and it was never a good idea to be around when Bob wasn't pleased. Damage would be done.

Bob dovetailed brilliantly with Phil Sproson in the centre of defence. His physicality frightened opponents at times and he took no prisoners, doing anything to prevent a goal. On the ball, he had much more skill and ability than he was often given credit for. In contrast, off the pitch, Bob was just the nicest feller, being quite softly spoken, but, even so, no one ever took the mickey out of him.

After his arrival, we kept three consecutive clean sheets and conceded only four goals in winning four and drawing two of the next six games. That run saw us move clear of the relegation zone into mid-table where we stayed, comfortably, for the rest of the season, avoiding becoming a yo-yo club between the lower two divisions.

Bob was such a dominant personality I made him my captain fairly quickly, becoming Vale's first black skipper in the process. I never had any concerns regarding racism at all during my time at the club and, as far as I am concerned, I only look at the player, their capabilities and work ethic. He was a mainstay of my side until January 1989, when a back injury meant he had to retire, becoming a sports prevention manager, working to help rehabilitate young offenders through sport. He did contribute a lot to the first half of that promotion campaign, though, and is one of those players that quickly springs to mind when I think of my Vale team of that vintage.

In the summer of 1986 I had signed West Bromwich Albion's reserve goalkeeper Mark Grew, who was looking for first-team football and took over from Alex Williams, who I had signed on the same basis from Manchester City the year before, but had now suffered a career-ending injury. That completed the framework of one of my favourite, and arguably my best, Port Vale teams; much of it thanks to selling on Andy Jones. You'd think losing all those goals that Andy scored us would make us a worse team, but I improved us all over the park with the money his sale brought in. That's how it works, sell on one star, buy cheaper replacements to turn into the next big thing. That was my hallmark. Having said that, I was still shopping in the bargain basement, unearthing diamonds where we could. That meant that not every new signing would make the grade; many 'diamonds' proved to be fool's gold. I signed one lad, Paul West, for £3,800 from Alcester Town in Warwickshire. Paul was a right-back who never actually made a first-team appearance for me, but that was because in a reserve team match against Everton he outplayed winger Peter Beagrie, marking him out of the game entirely, causing watching Bradford manager Frank Stapleton, who was out doing the same hunting for talent that I would habitually do, to table an £80,000 offer. I knew Paul had had the game of his life that day, while Beagrie, who was used to playing in the First Division by this time, may not have been completely motivated. So, I snapped Bradford's hand off and took the £76,200 profit on a player who would otherwise have been released and continued my search of random grounds for as-yet-undiscovered talent.

* * *

Trying to replace Andy Jones's goals proved, of course, very difficult. In late 1986 I tried to sign a young striker I had seen playing for West Brom's reserves. I liked his power, pace and eye for goal and I thought he could be the Jones replacement I was looking for, given that my star striker was almost certainly going to be snapped up at some point in the very near future. I couldn't persuade him to leave the Black Country, however, and he joined Wolves instead.

That young striker's name? Steve Bull. I wonder whatever happened to him?

I also enquired about another forward I liked, Don Goodman at Bradford City, but was quoted £100,000; a non-starter. Instead, in October 1987, I spent £20,000 on young striker David Riley, who could also play on both wings, from Nottingham Forest. He scored on his debut in a 2-1 win over Bristol Rovers and finished as joint top scorer that season with ten goals. He was sprightly and quick. Sadly, David would break his leg just before the end of the 1988/89 season, so missed out on playing in the promotion-winning play-off ties and eventually I moved him on to Peterborough for £40,000, another tidy profit.

Also scoring ten goals in the 1987/88 season was another diamond I unearthed in the form of Darren Beckford, a young

Manchester City teenager who I watched a few times in reserve team games and, after a successful loan spell, wanted to sign. This was the summer of 1987 and, with the player out of contract, but with the Bosman ruling still a few years off and Andy Jones not yet sold, we had to pay a fee to his former club. The only problem being they wanted £60,000 for Darren, while we could afford £5,000 at best, unless we sold off all the family silver. The case went to a tribunal panel and I knew I had to pull off another trick to land my target. On this occasion it was two-fold: first I pleaded at the panel for Manchester City to accept a much lower fee on condition they got a 20 per cent sell-on clause and, second, I convinced the board to agree to pay that lower fee of £15,000 if it was part-funded by supporters. In fact, it ended up with the board only paying half of the fee as the fans raised £7,500 in bucket collections outside the ground for our 'Buy a Player' appeal. It was a remarkable show of faith from the supporters in both my judgement of a player and in Darren as a young star himself. I really appreciated that; a truly magnificent effort.

In fact, I actually had my doubts about Darren as he had that big city arrogance about him. Although his ability and eye for goal were not in question, as a youngster he did have plenty of work to do to develop himself and in training his attitude could sometimes be difficult. But I knew the raw talent was there and in our position, I could only be grateful to have engineered his signing given the financial constraints, so, despite being advised not to take him because of his attitude, we signed him. Sometimes you take calculated gambles on players with attitudes. In Darren's case I could see how he would fit our system and, frankly, if I had sought out faults in every player I signed as Vale manager, I would have never signed anyone. Part of melding a team is bringing together players whose strengths complement each other and, in part, cover up others' deficiencies. The pressure on me to replace Jones was immense and Darren actually proved to be a tremendous asset to the side, particularly as it meant I could also make Robbie Earle a permanent fixture in midfield – for me his best position – where he once played 143 consecutive games for me; astonishing consistency.

Darren was strong and dynamic, a great runner, with a terrific turn of pace. He proved testing at times, as I had been warned. It was not unknown for him to stop a training session halfway through to ask me or the coach why we were doing such-and-such drills. The rest of the squad would be urging him to just get on with it, or we'd never get finished. Then, if someone upset him off the pitch, it could have an effect on his performance. He could be a nightmare at times and I once described managing him as 'like throwing blancmange at a wall, you just hope that a bit of it sticks'. He actually used to get very nervous and in the early part of his career would often vomit before games, not that you would know that once he got down the tunnel.

Darren had unbelievable spring in his legs and could finish. He was a terrific goalscorer and, as a striker, he ticked all the boxes. If we came up against a top team, we knew he was easily good enough to hold his own. He had scored four goals in 11 games in that loan spell, but after signing permanently, in partnership with the experienced Ron Futcher from 1988 onwards, Darren top-scored in 1987/88 with ten goals, 1988/89 with 23, 1989/90 with 21 in our first season up in the Second Division and 1990/91 with 23. Those are outstanding numbers by any measure. Darren also regularly scored hat-tricks, most famously in the play-off semi-final second leg in May 1989 to put us through to the final.

We eventually (and inevitably) lost Darren to Norwich for a tribunal-set £925,000 (I valued him at £1.5 million, but you can't win them all) in the summer of 1991, after he had scored 81 goals in 214 appearances. Just under £200,000 of that went to his old club via that sell-on clause, but his arrival had proven to be a crucial part of our progression into the league above and, in any case, meant I still had over £700,000 profit to play with to invest in the team.

Ron Futcher, Darren's partner in our promotion-winning campaign of 1988/89, was another player who joined us in unusual circumstances. After shaking hands with Ian Greaves, the Mansfield boss, Futch had actually been all set to join the Stags from Bradford for £35,000 when I swooped to sign him from under their noses. Like myself and Bob Hazell, it was the lure of the club car that did it and I sealed the deal at Bill Bell's garage by making Ron a counter-offer which included a car. Mainly because, at almost 32 years old, his brain was quicker than his legs, Futch dovetailed brilliantly with the dynamism and running of Beckford and he scored 17 league goals that season and 23 goals in 69 games overall.

Like Darren, Ron also proved to be an 'interesting' character, who had to be handled diplomatically. There was no point rollicking him in front of others because he would just blow up and cause unrest. Futch had to feel important, special and not just be treated as one of the lads. Coach Mike Pejic and Futch did not see eye to eye and fell out with each other many a time. I remember one training session when Pej shouted for Futch to spin and make a run down the right, so Futch would intentionally run down the left. This continued, upsetting Pej no end. Eventually they had a stand-up row, with Pej then telling me I had to get rid of Futch as he didn't take instructions. I couldn't do that as I needed him, so, instead, I took to taking Ron to one side and telling him how important he was to us.

Once he turned 33, Ron could only be effective for short periods in games, so I then moved him on, but he still made us a profit by signing for Fourth Division Burnley for £60,000, which was fantastic considering he didn't have many miles left on the clock.

* * *

When he first arrived in Manchester, I used to meet Alex Ferguson on occasions at games around the country. He and his assistant Archie Knox were fishing in a very different pond, of course, but they were such incredible football people that they wanted to see if they could spot any diamonds at the same matches I would frequent. We became acquaintances and, as Alex brought the huge success that he did to Old Trafford, I was able to approach him for help, usually for loan players. Later, whilst at Stoke, I would also sell him budding goalkeeping talent Ben Foster and take various youngsters on loan, so we got to know each other well.

Many years later, Alex was kind enough to invite Del and I to a dinner to celebrate his 25th year at Manchester United. I'll always remember, we were sitting at our table while he was giving his speech and he picked me out, saying, 'Rudgie's there, bloody hell he used to be on the phone to me all the time wanting something. What a bloody nuisance! When I got off the phone with him, I used to be in tears because of all the tales of woe about how little money he had.'

I had mastered that art, I'm proud to say and for five straight years my transfer philosophy, hard work and wheelings and dealings had worked, improving us from the Fourth Division to become an established Second Division side, but in the summer of 1991, as well as having to sell Beckford, we were forced to sell Robbie Earle, who wanted to test himself in the top flight, to Wimbledon for a tribunal-set £775,000, although we were also given a sell-on clause worth 30 per cent of any future sale (unfortunately Robbie was forced to retire due to a stomach injury in 2000, so that never came into play). I believe Wimbledon chairman Sam Hammam took a page right out of my transfer playbook in order to secure Robbie's signature by locking him in a small room at their training ground until he put pen to paper. Chapeau.

Robbie, who Vale fans christened the 'Black Pearl', had been a fabulous player for me. He had tremendous energy, would run all day and gave everything every single time he stepped on to a pitch. I had known and worked with him for over a decade by the time he moved on and he had scored both goals in the play-off final against Bristol Rovers in 1989 to bring his total for that season to 19; totalling 90 goals from 357 games. Incredible, especially as so many came from midfield. After that victory, overcome with emotion, Robbie sat in the tunnel and wept, a moment captured for posterity by *The Sentinel*'s photographer. It's one of my favourite photographs from my time at Port Vale and I'm delighted to be able to include it in the photo section of this book as it shows the total commitment this fabulous professional gave me, as well as Robbie being totally overcome with joy at winning promotion for his club.

So, I spent the summer of 1991 trying to replace the 34 goals the departures of Earle and Beckford meant. Feeling flush, I signed Martin Foyle from Oxford for what was then a club record fee of £375,000. Martin had been playing alongside Dean Saunders when I bought him and went on to become a Vale legend, scoring 108 goals in 296 games, which is a tremendous strike rate over almost a decade and actually made him Vale's leading post-war goalscorer until Tom Pope broke that record in 2020. It was a super investment and Martin turned out to be an exceptional professional, a mainstay of the team and a stalwart of my Vale teams of the 1990s. Not only that, but after persistent knee injuries forced Martin to retire from football at the age of 36 in 2000, he stayed at the club as manager of the youth team and then took over first-team responsibilities at the club in February 2004 after Brian Horton left. Under Martin's guidance, Vale narrowly missed out on a play-off place on goal difference at the end of that season. He really did prove to be a tremendous club man.

That nearly wasn't the case, though, as, in March 1992, Notts County came in with an offer for him of £400,000 on the afternoon of transfer deadline day. We decided to accept the fee as it looked like we were going to go down. The problem was we couldn't find him and the 5pm deadline passed with Martin still missing, none the wiser about how his future had just turned. In retrospect it was a good miss. I never did find out where he went, but I am very glad I couldn't track him down.

That same summer I also spent £100,000 on experienced striker Keith Houchen, who had been playing at Hibernian in Scotland, but was famous for the diving header he scored in the 1987 FA Cup Final as his Coventry side defeated Spurs, then, as short-term cover when Houchen got injured, Jason Beckford, Darren's younger brother, though he could not replicate his elder sibling's success and scored just once in five games.

As a quirk of the fixture list, Martin's debut was against his former club and he scored both goals as we started the 1991/92 campaign with a 2-1 victory over Oxford, although that proved to be one of only two wins in our first 11 games. Houchen got both goals in the other victory, 2-0 at Wolves, but we were clearly in relegation trouble after that poor start. Foyle finished as the leading scorer with 16 goals that first season and topped the scoring charts on three further occasions, but in 1991/92 it was in the context of Vale finishing bottom of the Second Division. We were relegated, as replacing all those goals that Beckford and Earle provided had proved too much.

Chapter 7

Giant-killers

'Not the day for you today, Ossie. It's a swamp.'

Spurs manager Terry Venables to star midfielder Osvaldo Ardiles before Port Vale 2-1 Tottenham Hotspur, FA Cup fourth round, January 1988

I BELIEVE that if you think of my Port Vale teams of the 1980s then you think of us as cup giant-killers, famously defeating the mighty Spurs. That result put us on the footballing map and marked us out as a club on the up. After that we regularly knocked out teams from higher divisions and no one who drew us out of the hat in either the FA Cup or League Cup could take us lightly, especially if we were drawn at home, where Vale Park and its boggy, sand-covered pitch became a graveyard of big clubs.

All that started in January 1988, although, as a Fourth Division club, we did draw 2-2 away at First Division West Brom in the League Cup second round in 1985, battling back from a two-goal deficit to do so thanks to goals from Andy Jones and Paul Maguire to bow out to a narrow 2-3 aggregate defeat. Now we were securely mid-table in the Third Division, I felt that we could generate some much-needed cash through the cups, as well as earn some much-needed publicity, and the mantle of giant-killers would suit us for a decade or more as we buckled some swash against some of the country's premier teams.

It does not necessarily take a good side to win a cup match or even, arguably, an entire cup competition. The luck of the draw and a few breaks can take you through, whereas promotion is the reward for a season's slog of up to 46 games. But, my goodness, doing well in cups was the making of Port Vale in my opinion, creating a fearsome reputation for us as cup fighters. These were the days when you would huddle around a radio at 12.30pm on a Monday to listen to the FA Cup draw broadcast from Lancaster Gate. You did not know your number and waited with bated breath as each ball was drawn out of the famous velvet bag. It was a part of the magic of the competition.

It all started when we were drawn out of the hat for the FA Cup fourth round with a home tie against the glamour boys of Tottenham Hotspur. Reacting to the draw on his ITV show *Saint and Greavsie*, pundit Jimmy Greaves reckoned that, 'The only trouble Spurs will have at Port Vale, is finding the place.' As a former Tottenham player, Greaves should have known that would only serve as a red rag to a lower league club like us and I used it as motivation running up to the tie.

The mighty Spurs, managed by Terry Venables, boasted an array of stars and were one of the most attractive sides in the land. The tie captured the imagination of the country and beyond. Port Vale seldom attracted national attention, but suddenly everyone wanted to know us. Swedish television took the game live, with the match also broadcast on radio in Australia, which enabled us to sell a lot of advertising space round the perimeter of the pitch. That was a tremendous financial boost for us and lifted our profile.

I persuaded the board to spend some money on taking the players to get new suits at Review, a gentlemen's outfitters in Newcastle. The chairman Bill Bell was delighted to get some great publicity and so shelled out for the suits so the local media could run stories about the forthcoming FA Cup tie. That also boosted the players' egos and they were relishing being underdogs against Tottenham, who had reached the final only to lose to Coventry the previous season.

When Spurs did find Vale Park they were in for a shock. Our pitch was always heavy when it rained and it had been an extremely wet week; the good Lord answering our prayers. Tottenham's star striker Clive Allen had been scoring goals for fun, netting 49 the season before whilst winning the PFA Player of the Year award, so I had to find a way of stopping him. The best plan I could come up with was getting the fire brigade to hose some more water on to the already sodden pitch to turn it into an absolute quagmire. We sanded large areas of the pitch as a result, so the surface was very difficult, which led to Terry Venables taking one look at it after their team arrived, turning to Osvaldo Ardiles, their Argentinian World Cup-winning midfield maestro and saying, 'Not the day for you today, Ossie. It's a swamp.'

We had detailed Robbie Earle to shadow Ardiles as part of our game plan and I think his absence gave us an added spur, allowing Robbie much more freedom than he would otherwise have had. He and Ray Walker had the better of the midfield battle with Spurs' Terry Fenwick and Paul Allen and we took the game to them in a packed, raucous atmosphere amongst the crowd of 20,045.

In those days centre-halves could have a free whack at a player and so, early on, Phil Sproson went through the back of Clive Allen, getting up and saying to the referee David Scott, 'That's my first tackle, ref ...'

Bob Hazell could hold a grudge and was determined to gain some measure of revenge after he had lost the 1982 final against Spurs when playing for QPR. Ironically, Clive Allen had been a team-mate of Bob's in that 1982 final, but that counted for nothing as Bob also flattened him in the opening minutes, leaning over and telling him, 'You're going to get that for the next 85 minutes.' Allen went and played on the wing for much of the rest of the game after that second assault; superstar striker dealt with. It wasn't all pretty football when I was in charge at Vale. We could do dark arts too.

We survived an early scare when Chris Waddle's toe poke from eight yards out skimmed the post, but then, as we applied pressure, Neil Ruddock's back pass beat his own keeper and only just rolled wide. On 12 minutes, a long ball forward by Sproson caught Mitchell Thomas out of position and he had to go to ground to nick the ball off David Riley, which meant he couldn't recover in time and Gary Ford nipped in to nudge it to Ray Walker, who was unmarked 25 yards out. Ray took it on a couple of touches before lashing a right-foot shot which sailed over the static Tony Parks and into the top left corner of the net. It was a magnificent, dipping shot, hit with his instep, with a little bit of curl on it; classic Ray.

Vale Park exploded.

On 24 minutes, astonishingly, we doubled our lead when Walker's floated free kick tempted Parks out of his goal to collect it, but he didn't get there and ended up in a crumpled heap on the floor along with his central defender Chris Fairclough. The ball ricocheted around a bit, notably off Darren Beckford's chest, before falling to Phil Sproson, who lashed it home from five yards with his left foot.

The place went ballistic once again. This was dreamland. The stuff of fairy tales. Port Vale 2 Tottenham Hotspur 0.

A moment later Parks pulled off a brilliant reaction save from a close-range Beckford header to keep them in the game as we poured forwards. It really was a superb performance from the lads in that first half.

I remember we came into the dressing room at the break and I was totally lost for words. I had rehearsed so many scenarios in my mind about what I would have to say, but I can reveal that none of them were that we would be 2-0 up against Spurs! I really didn't know what to say except, 'Well done, boys, go out there and do that again.' It was slightly bizarre. I do remember cracking one joke along the lines of, 'Can you get some boards for the goals and nail them inside the goalposts …'

We had never been in this position before and we all knew we would be under the cosh in the second half. Sure enough, on 64 minutes Ruddock headed in a right-wing free kick from six yards and the game was very much back on. That triggered a frantic final half hour or so, but our fans urged us on with a wall of sound as we hung on for grim death with the pitch playing a large part as it churned up, meaning the likes of Waddle couldn't run with the ball and Spurs' passing game was badly affected. The closest Tottenham came to an equaliser was four minutes from the end when Gary Mabbutt shot and Mark Grew pulled off a fingertip save. Sproson also made a fantastic tackle, lunging in front of Allen to block a Thomas cross from reaching him.

We managed to hang on and the final whistle sparked off wonderful scenes. One banner in the Bycars stand proclaimed 'White Hart Slain' as Vale's glory-starved fans invaded the pitch in their thousands, while Venables strode off down the tunnel with his hands thrust deep into his coat pockets. To think that he had only returned from Barcelona the summer before and now here he was losing at Vale Park was quite delicious.

* * *

The entire world seemed to want to know the story. There were cameras, reporters, lights, cables and newspapermen all over the place. We were the lead game on *Match of the Day* that night and highlights were also broadcast around the world. The club received £80,000 for the game from the BBC. As well as making us renowned giant-killers, that game was the start of being able to generate some more money which allowed us to move forward.

I also remember local broadcasting legend Nigel Johnson of Radio Stoke asking Ray Walker hardly the most appropriate question in our hour of glory, along the lines of, 'How would you feel about joining Stoke City?' as Mick Mills was interested in signing him. Nigel must have felt suitably awkward because he called a few days later to apologise, a mark of the man.

It was so appropriate that Walker and Sproson, two of my key players, should score our goals and share the limelight because they were so crucial to our success throughout that period. That glorious moment almost never happened, though, such is the fickle nature of football. We were goalless with non-league Macclesfield and not playing well at Vale Park with just five minutes to go in the third round and, unbeknownst to me, before the game, chairman Bill Bell had approached Phil Sproson to fill in as caretaker manager while they found my replacement if we lost, as we were only just above the relegation zone in 18th place, having lost six of the last seven league games and won none of the last 12. Then up popped Kevin Finney, a YTS graduate in his first season as a professional, with a headed winner to put us through and pull Tottenham out of the hat. Our reward was another home draw, this time against Steve Harrison's Watford, featuring Malcolm Allen, Luther Blissett and Kenny Jackett. We were chosen for TV coverage, meaning we got extra income and 22,483 turned up, an even bigger crowd than we had for the visit of Spurs and the largest crowd at Vale Park since the visit of Liverpool in 1964, so the board were ecstatic. We couldn't quite nick the goal we needed to win that tie, drawing 0-0, although we scraped the post with one shot. We lost the replay 0-2, but we were now on the football map and also £175,000 better off in prize money thanks to reaching the fifth round in our cup run. That led to a huge profit of over £410,000 that season, which stood us in fantastic stead moving forwards. Port Vale FC was very much on an upward curve.

* * *

The year after that, which was our 1988/89 promotion season, we drew Norwich City at home in the third round of the FA Cup and were chosen as a live television game on the Sunday of third round weekend, which meant we generated further revenue. Norwich were managed by Dave Stringer and were top of the First Division at the time, with players like Bryan Gunn, Mike Phelan, Andy Townsend and Robert Fleck in the team. We lost 1-3 after being a goal up through Alan Webb's rasping drive at half-time, but it was another marker of our progress. Norwich reached the semi-final that season and ended up finishing fourth in the top flight. Earlier that season, we beat Second Division Ipswich Town in the League Cup second round first leg 1-0, thanks to a goal by Phil Sproson, but lost the second leg 0-3.

In January 1990, in the FA Cup third round we drew 1-1 at home with Derby County, who had Peter Shilton, Mark Wright and Dean Saunders in their line-up, thanks to a Darren Beckford goal, before travelling to the Baseball Ground for the replay on the following Wednesday in which we beat them 3-2 with a superb smash and grab performance; an absolutely brilliant display, although, as we were only one division below the Rams by then, perhaps less heralded amongst our giant-killing feats.

We forced an own goal when Rob Hindmarch hooked a back-pass over Peter Shilton and into the net as Darren Beckford put pressure on him. Then, after Craig Ramage had equalised following a scramble at a corner, Ray Walker slammed home another beautifully struck cup goal. The winner came after Darren Hughes ran two-thirds of the length of the pitch before slamming a cross-shot towards the far post where Nicky Cross slid in to convert. I can still see that cross being fired across goal in my mind's eye. It was superb from Darren and typical of the experienced Cross to be in the right place at the right time.

The last ten minutes, after the giant Kevin Francis had pulled one back, were nail-biting, with some great saves by Mark Grew and a few last-ditch tackles preventing opportunities, but we held on by the skin of our teeth, showing a lot of quality, spirit and determination. I remember running on to the dreadful Baseball Ground pitch to celebrate with our 5,000 travelling fans after the final whistle. They were as magnificent as our players had been and I remember the procession of Vale supporters' cars all the way back to Burslem with scarves hanging out of car windows. I am sure there were a few sore heads in the morning.

Our reward was a trip to Villa Park in the fourth round, where we came down to earth with a wallop. Graham Taylor's team were riding high in the First Division and they thrashed us 0-6. Too many of our players froze in the driving rain. It didn't stop Neil Aspin playing in his customary fashion and he clattered into David Platt with a tackle that attracted a lot of bad publicity. Post-match Taylor ranted and raved that his player could be out for three months, when in fact Platt played the following Saturday. It was a lot of fuss over nothing really.

* * *

One unexpected side effect of being such famous cup fighters came in early 1990 when Geoff Wakefield, secretary of the Port Vale supporters' club, came to see me and explained a bizarre situation which had occurred in Northern Ireland, which had led him to receiving a phone call from a police sergeant. This sounded alarming at first, but it turned out to be a quite brilliant story.

Apparently, a group of friends over there had got together to form a team and entered a local competition. On completing the entry form, the club secretary had been asked the question, 'What is your team name?'

The only problem was, they hadn't actually discussed a name, so this chap blurted out 'Port Vale', as he had seen us on telly beating Spurs and taken quite a liking to us. Having registered the name, he sheepishly explained to his fellow committee members what he had done, whereupon the chair proposed that they should cross the Irish sea to visit Vale and take in a game if they were going to be named in honour of the club.

The problem? They had no idea where Port Vale was located!

So, naturally, this being pre-internet, the chairman and secretary of this brand new club took the decision to visit their local police station to ask how they could find out where Port Vale came from. The police officer on the desk had then phoned the Vale supporters' club to explain the situation, which is how Geoff ended up sitting with me telling me this incredible story.

Without a second's thought I agreed to meet these Irish lads if they could find their way to Burslem. They did so, visiting for a home game against Newcastle United and we made them feel like football royalty. My training under John McGrath in spreading the good word of Port Vale as far and wide as I could had come very much into play.

* * *

Our next cup exploit came in September 1991 when we drew 2-2 at Anfield in the first leg of a second round League Cup tie thanks to an early header from a Simon Mills corner by Robin van der Laan, which saw us take the lead to huge scenes of jubilation in the Anfield Road End, and a late equaliser by Martin Foyle, who benefitted from a mazy run and cross by former Liverpool winger John Jeffers, who revelled in returning to his old stomping ground. We lost the home game 1-4, but getting a result at Anfield was a landmark performance for us.

In January 1994 we claimed another notable FA Cup scalp in Southampton, after a creditable 1-1 draw at The Dell with Andy Porter netting our goal. The third round replay was another of those nights when conditions had their say and the Vale Park pitch was similar to when we beat Spurs. In truth, I had serious doubts as to whether it was playable, but I was desperate to get the game on because Saints had just sacked their manager Ian Branfoot, which meant Lawrie McMenemy, who had been John McGrath's mentor back in the day, took over as caretaker manager. Bernie Slaven, a master finisher, struck an early blow and it was enough to see us through.

That was in the middle of our 1993/94 promotion campaign and we were just embarking upon a run of one defeat in 11 league games, so that victory over a club two divisions above us gave us huge confidence. We lost at home 0-2 to Second Division Wolves in the fourth round, though, allowing us to concentrate on the league!

Two years later we were again drawn away in the third round at high-flying opposition, this time Crystal Palace, and drew again, 0-0 on this occasion. Palace had an excellent team, including Nigel Martyn, Ray Houghton and Dougie Freedman. Their supporters were very boisterous, so to get a draw at Selhurst Park was superb. The replay, on 16 January 1996, was an all-time cup classic. Ray Walker scored twice, Martin Foyle got one then Andy Porter scored the winning goal in a 4-3 victory after extra time.

In the fourth round, we were again drawn away at a top-flight club, this time Everton, the FA Cup holders. We drew 2-2 at Goodison Park in a magnificent performance. Foyle bagged a second half equaliser after Everton opened the scoring, but, with only minutes remaining, our goalie Paul Musselwhite dropped a harmless-looking cross to present Duncan Ferguson with a goal. Everton's blushes seemed to be spared, but with one minute left Ian Bogie saved the day for us with a shot from long range that took a deflection and looped over Neville Southall to allow us to take them back to the Potteries for a replay. Everton, managed by my good friend Joe Royle, joined the ranks of the fallen in the replay on Valentine's night in which our wing wonders, Steve Guppy and Jon McCarthy, played starring roles. It was another great occasion at Vale Park, but one which Guppy and Andy Hill might have missed out on. Such were the crowds thronging the approach roads to the ground that Steve had to abandon his car and run the last mile or so to make the team sheet, while Andy needed a police escort to Vale Park after getting stuck behind the Everton fans' coaches. It was one hell of a warm-up and Guppy proved to be the outstanding player on the night, crowning his performance with the run and cross that led to McCarthy claiming a famous winner in a 2-1 victory in which Bogie had again scored our opening goal. Vale had not put out the cup holders since beating Stan Matthews' Blackpool in the quarter-final in 1954.

We were unfortunate not to win the next round at Leeds, again taking the Premier League club to a replay, and Howard Wilkinson's team, who were playing in the UEFA Cup that season and also reached the League Cup Final, ran out 2-1 victors back at Vale Park, with Gary McAllister netting both goals and Tony Naylor replying for us.

* * *

Two years later, in 1998, we again found ourselves drawn against a Premier League team away from home. This time it was Arsenal, so we visited Highbury, with its marble entrance halls and underfloor heating in the dressing rooms, to face Arsène Wenger's team. I particularly enjoyed our trip to north London; the Gunners had been one of only four teams we had not played in my time as Port Vale manager (the others being Chelsea, Wycombe Wanderers and Coventry City), so the draw was something special for me and I relished pitting my wits against Monsieur Wenger, who I believed shared a similar footballing philosophy to myself. We had been struggling in the league near the foot of the First Division table, but the players responded magnificently and worked their socks off to contain the likes of Ian Wright, Dennis Bergkamp, Patrick Vieira and the pacy Marc Overmars, who I was worried about on the counter-attack, to come away with a 0-0 draw. I remember the Arsenal defender Martin Keown saying, 'Why the hell don't you play like that every week?'

There was an air of keen anticipation for the replay and again we were shown live on Sky TV and we set about Arsenal with the same formation of one man up front with two wide and three in midfield to give them the tight game I wanted.

The game again ended goalless after 90 minutes, although Tony Naylor spurned a fabulous chance when he had a clear shot on goal with only David Seaman to beat from ten yards, but somehow spooned the ball a whisker past the post. Mind you, on one of his trademark breakaways Overmars hit the inside of the far post with Paul Musselwhite beaten all ends up, but the ball cannoned across the goal line and somehow curled out for a goal kick. Gareth Ainsworth missed two very presentable opportunities and Ian Wright had a shot on the turn from five yards flicked on to the post by Musselwhite as somehow a very entertaining match ended 0-0, but Arsenal finally broke 190 minutes of deadlock ten minutes into extra time, although I found that goal intensely annoying.

Before the game I had pulled Neil Aspin aside and said to him, 'Neil, that Bergkamp, you watch him and he will always turn to his right-hand side. That's the way he wants to go, so don't let him do it when he's anywhere near our penalty area. Make sure you put him on to his left side.' Lo and behold it was Bergkamp who shifted the ball on to his right-hand side and curled a shot in the top corner to give them the lead in extra time.

'Bloody hellfire, Neil,' I shouted. 'What did I tell ya?'

'He's a bit bloody good, boss,' came the reply.

We showed our fighting spirit, though, and Wayne Corden scored his first senior goal for the club, half-volleying home from six yards after a driving run down the right side of the box by Ainsworth led to a far-post cross, to take the tie to a penalty shoot-out after a 1-1 draw.

Penalty shoot-outs are nerve-racking to say the least, but even more so for managers as all you can do is stand and watch, once you have established who the first five to take are. This one started brilliantly for us when Lee Dixon, struck his spot kick low to Musselwhite's left and our keeper got down to save. We were in pole position, but then Mark Snijders had his penalty saved by David Seaman and eventually it all boiled down to the last kick. Allen Tankard needed to score to send us into 'sudden death', but blazed his penalty over the bar and we were out 3-4 on penalties. Nevertheless, we had put on another super show and, tactically, it was one of my most pleasing performances. I felt we matched Arsenal in all departments and I am sure they heaved a heavy sigh of relief to get through as we were just a whisker away from claiming another notable victory. That the Gunners went on to win the double that year shows the level we were playing at.

I'm sure our supporters remember that as one of those fantastic matches which could have seen us add another famous scalp to our long list of giant-killings. I do too, but I also have a very different memory from the day before the game which always springs to mind when I think about that replay.

I was with Mark Grew at the tactics board in my office talking about how to approach the game, when a knock came on the door. It was Jill, the lady who did all our kit washing. She said, 'Sorry to interrupt, John, but you'll need to ring Creda straightaway as the washing machine has broken down. It's an emergency because if you don't we won't have any kit for tomorrow.'

'OK Jill, leave it with me,' I said.

Once she had gone, I looked at Mark and said with a straight face, 'Blimey, I wonder whether Arsène Wenger's got the same problem?' Grewy creased up laughing! But that was Port Vale. There was never any chance of us living above our station. Mark loves telling that story to this day.

And yes, I did have to ring Creda to get them to come out and fix the machine. They don't teach that at Lilleshall!

* * *

We weren't always the giant-killer, though. I never liked being the bigger club in a cup tie and that reminds me of an incident in a game which lives long in my memory because of its bizarre nature. Back in November 1986 we had been drawn at home in the first round of the FA Cup to non-league near-neighbours Stafford Rangers, which stirred up a lot of interest in Staffordshire and actually brought in or second highest gate of the season at just under 6,000. I always started watching the games up in the directors' box to see the pattern of play and then moved down to the dugout after about five minutes, as you are just so removed from the action and cannot influence the game from there. After this match kicked off, I set off through the inside of the stand and down the stairs to the dressing rooms and tunnel, ready to emerge pitch side, only to be met by Andy Jones making his way off the pitch.

'Jonesy, where are you going?' I said, bewildered that I should meet him as he was supposed to be on the pitch scoring the goals to get us through to the next round and avoid utter embarrassment and local derision.

'I'm off to have a bath, Gaffer,' Andy replied.

I still didn't get it.

'What do you mean?'

'I've been sent off,' Andy said, trudging towards the home dressing room. 'Their centre-half kicked me all the way from the centre circle to the edge of their box and when I asked the referee if he was going to do anything about it he sent me off …'

Let's just say Andy may not have been quite as polite as that.

Andy's blushes were spared when Robbie Earle managed to nick a goal, so we squeezed through 1-0.

* * *

Of course, we never reached the latter stages of either major domestic cup competition, but that doesn't mean we didn't play under Wembley's twin towers. In fact, I led Port Vale out on to that hallowed turf three times, which for someone who had not been anywhere near the place as a player was magnificent; the stuff of dreams for me as manager, the staff, players and, of course, the supporters.

We first drove down Wembley Way in our Bostock's club coach on 22 May 1993 to face Danny Bergara's Stockport County in the Autoglass Trophy Final; they had lost the previous season's final against our city rivals Stoke, so were desperate to win the trophy. They could have not been more of a contrast to my team. They had 6ft 7in Kevin Francis up front, who was the focal point for their long-ball style and had joined them from Derby where we had played against him in that epic cup victory in 1990. Their team was generally full of players of six foot or over and the ball didn't spend much time on the lush Wembley turf.

The final was actually the third time our two clubs had met in seven days as we had edged out Stockport 2-1 on aggregate in the Second Division play-off semi-finals, drawing 1-1 at Edgeley Park, before Martin Foyle scored the only goal of the return leg to send us through to the play-off final, which would take place at Wembley against West Brom seven days after this final. We were heading to the Mecca of football twice in a week; incredible.

At the old Wembley, the tunnel used to be at one end and managers walked out with their team, leading them to line up in front of the Royal Box and the famous twin towers to meet the dignitaries. That was a wonderful thing to be able to do, a great privilege and honour for me, especially as it was the first time Port Vale Football Club had ever been to Wembley.

Ray Walker was ruled out due to injury which was a blow, but Ian Taylor and Robin van der Laan were superb in the centre of the park. We struck early when Bernie Slaven turned in the centre circle, drove forward and slid a pass through the Stockport defence for Paul Kerr to run on to and fire home past Neil Edwards with the outside of his right foot in just the fourth minute. The over 28,000 fans amongst the crowd of 35,885 wearing Port Vale's black and white went berserk.

Half an hour later, Dean Glover clipped a ball in from the left which Martin Foyle turned into the path of the onrushing Slaven, who controlled on the run and directed a low, left-footed shot into the far corner of the net. We really were all over them.

As a manager, your half-time team talk when you are 2-0 up at Wembley is a lot harder than you might think. I told the lads to keep doing what they were doing, but to not take their feet off the accelerator, expect Stockport to come back and watch out for the giant Francis up front. We started the second half well and Porter had a good chance cleared off the line by Mick Wallace, but after Andy Preece came on for Stockport the tide began to turn. Musselwhite made a brilliant double save before, on 65 minutes, a right-wing cross was headed in by Francis. We had 25 minutes to hold on, which passed slower than a snail going the wrong way up an escalator. It really was excruciating. I was on the edge of my seat because our legs seemed to go and we had to hang on grimly and I've never known such excruciating pain as when the board went up to show there would be six minutes of injury time at the end of that second half.

The final whistle brought huge relief, but also a wave of elation and we went and celebrated with our supporters before collecting the trophy. I had great pride in lifting a cup for Port Vale, which was presented by Sir Bobby Charlton. What a feeling winning at Wembley is.

On the bus home, the players gave a rousing rendition of *You've Lost That Loving Feeling* by the Righteous Brothers, which had become something of an anthem for us that season, I know not why. We then returned to the Potteries for an open-top bus tour, with thousands of supporters wearing black, white and yellow (our away colour) 10 or 20 deep all the way round our route. That was wonderful. I remember coming back to Burslem Town Hall to show off that trophy, the first in the club's history, to the celebrating hordes; one of my proudest moments as Vale manager.

To cap it all, Joan Walley, MP for Stoke-on-Trent North, tabled a motion in Parliament to congratulate Port Vale on our win. We really were on the map now.

* * *

Each time we went to Wembley we made a big deal of it, taking the team to stay away for a few nights before the game, often in Watford, so we were back there a few days later preparing for our second Wembley visit; the 1993 play-off final against West Bromwich Albion, ironically managed by the same Ossie Ardiles who had been left out of the Spurs team by Terry Venables five years earlier due to the Vale Park pitch. Wembley's green baize was somewhat different that late May day and I felt confident as we had finished four points ahead of West Brom in the league table, only just missing out on automatic promotion by a point, had won both of that season's league games against them, 1-0 at the Hawthorns thanks to a Taylor goal and 2-1 at home with Cross and Foyle the scorers, and had just won under the twin towers.

We kept the build-up very much the same and, as Walker hadn't recovered from injury, the team was exactly the same. Over

60,000 fans were there this time, although about 40,000 were from West Bromwich. The game was evenly contested but goalless until the hour mark when Albion striker Bob Taylor raced clear on to a through ball and, as he approached the D of our penalty area, Peter Swan lunged in to try and win the ball, but only succeeded in tripping and bundling Taylor to the ground, just outside the box. Swanny was shown a straight red card by referee Roger Milford, who had actually not sent off a player in the entire season until that point. After that, we capitulated and conceded three goals in 24 minutes to lose 0-3 as West Brom swept forward. Our ten men just couldn't keep Albion out.

That red card decided that match and our fate after a long, hard season. Not that it wasn't a sending off. It was. There's no denying that.

That was a huge disappointment and I honestly cannot remember feeling any lower during my entire career. We had finished with a higher points total than any other team who hadn't won promotion previously and indeed the following season we only got 88 points, but went up automatically, with champions Reading only getting 89, the same as we had done the previous campaign in not going up. To have gone through everything we did that season, come so close to winning automatic promotion and then lose out in the play-off final was devastating. You can't ask much more of a team than to get 89 points over a season, but football can be a very cruel game. If I had a choice, I probably would have preferred the victories to have been the other way around; won the promotion play-off game not the cup final, but at least we won one of the two. Poor old Stockport lost at Wembley four times between 1991 and 1994 and only went up to the First Division when they won automatic promotion under Dave Jones in 1997.

My final visit to Wembley to lead Port Vale out was on 17 March 1996 for the short-lived Anglo-Italian Cup Final. The competition in this incarnation only ran from 1992/93 to 1995/96 and in that last season we beat Ancona and Perugia (winning 5-3 in Italy in a fabulous performance) to reach the latter stages. We then defeated Ipswich 4-2 at Portman Road and West Brom 3-1 over two legs in the English semi-final and final respectively to earn our spot in the overall final at Wembley where we would play Genoa, who we'd actually drawn 0-0 with in the group stages.

Genoa were a fantastic side and we were 0-3 down by half-time, then 0-5 down as former Italian international Gennaro Ruotolo completed his hat-trick, while fellow striker Vincenzo Montella, who went on to play for Sampdoria and Roma, becoming a full Italian international, was sensational. Martin Foyle netted two consolation goals to make the final score 2-5. Genoa were an exceptionally good team and we were well off their pace in that game, but defeat at Wembley didn't carry the same pain on that occasion as it had in 1993.

I did go to Wembley on one other occasion as Vale manager, a couple of months after the Anglo-Italian final, in May 1996. That followed our victory over cup holders Everton in the fourth round and I was presented with the 'Giant-killers' trophy on the pitch before the FA Cup Final between Liverpool and eventual winners Manchester United. I feel that was a great recognition for what we did at Vale in the 15 years I was in charge, not just for that defeat of the reigning cup holders, but overall. I am so proud of what we managed to achieve in cup competitions. They really were magnificent days and nights that put Port Vale on the footballing map. There is now a video called *Port Vale: Giant-killers* celebrating our achievements on which you can relive those fantastic ties. It's a good watch, unless you're a Spurs/Everton/Crystal Palace/Southampton/Derby fan.

Chapter 8

Going Up

'MBE: Mills, Beckford, Earle – goal!'

Robbie Earle, describing his promotion-clinching goal against Bristol Rovers in May 1989

NICE THOUGH the glory of winning cup ties is, and everything that went with those fantastic victories that put Port Vale on the footballing map, doing well consistently over a season in the league is the holy grail for football managers. Each August you aim to lift the title, win promotion, to succeed. Clearly, only a handful achieve that. Going up was always my aim as making progress in the league meant an awful lot to me. There is nothing like winning promotion for real satisfaction.

In my 19 years at Port Vale I was involved in four promotion campaigns, two relegations, two sets of play-offs and those three Wembley finals. The first promotion season (1982/83) came when I was assistant to John McGrath, but it never feels the same when you are the number two as when you are the manager. Plus, John's negative reaction to my efforts when I was in charge for a short spell that season when he was ill left a bit of a sour taste in my mouth and I felt left out of the celebrations.

I had suffered relegation at the end of my first part-season as manager, but had done well enough to be given the job on a full-time basis, so clearly my aim had to be to regain that higher-league status. I had my own designs on how I wanted to play the game, but it took me a couple of years of all that wheeling and dealing to assemble a squad capable of doing it 'my way'.

In my first full season, 1984/85, shorn of Mark Bright's goals, we finished in mid-table, following a season of rebuilding the squad. Veteran striker Ally Brown top-scored with 21, whilst young midfield dynamo Robbie Earle notched 19.

The 1985/86 season saw the arrival of Andy Jones and, amidst a blizzard of goals over the next few seasons, we established ourselves in the Third Division. You are never going to win games of football, certainly not enough to gain promotion, without scoring, so a good eye for goal was one of the key things I looked for in signing players for attacking positions. Andy was a great example; as much as he had a fantastic shot in either foot, could head the ball and knew how to finish, he also had a tremendous hunger for goals, which is so crucial for strikers. He was desperate to score. I'll give you an example; Andy was 21 when we signed him. The elder statesman of the team, Paul Maguire, was on penalties at the time and was very good at them, having been a regular taker in the top flight when with Stoke City. Jonesy, having that insatiable thirst for goals, was eager to take over. As soon as Maguire missed one, Andy was on at him in training, saying, 'Mags, your confidence is shot. I'm having pens now.' He duly took over and scored bundles of them.

Even when Darren Beckford arrived on loan and was paired with Jonesy, Andy wouldn't let the new arrival take a penalty towards the end of the game, which would have seen Darren get off the mark on his debut. Beckford actually picked the ball up to go to put it on the spot, but Andy grabbed it off him, put it down and slammed it home. Darren complained in the dressing room, 'But I could have scored on my debut.'

'Could've,' came back Andy's north Wales drawl.

Many of Andy's goals came from crosses and he benefitted from having Maguire and Paul Smith consistently delivering the ball early for Jonesy to make his run and get on the end of it. Timing is everything when a cross is coming into the box. It's important the striker knows when it's being delivered and where it is being targeted, so he can get a run on the defender. I always remember when Andy came back on loan after picking up an injury playing for Charlton and needed some game time at our level before going back up to the top flight, he told me that he was fed up with Addicks team-mate Paul Mortimer failing to give him the same level of service he'd been used to at Vale. Mortimer was skilful, but spent his whole time trying to beat players, rather than delivering the ball. Andy was fed up with making run after run but not receiving the ball, or if he did, it would come in behind him, aimed at where he had run from, not where he was running to.

But it isn't only skills and goalscoring on the pitch that wins matches and promotions. Before the start of the 1985/86 season, I spoke with Alan Hodgkinson, former England goalkeeper, on a coaching course at Lilleshall. Alan reckoned that if you could keep 20 clean sheets you would get promotion, so I offered the lads the incentive of a tenner out of my back pocket for a round of drinks every time they kept the opposition out; bear in mind that a pint would have been around 70p at the time, so this is a lot more generous than it sounds! It worked. We kept 19 clean sheets in the league, conceding just 37 goals, the second lowest of the entire 92 league clubs that season, only being bettered by Manchester United. Early in the campaign, we went nine without defeat to leap into the promotion race, including three 4-0 wins in Burslem against Hartlepool, Wrexham and Southend. After suffering a bit during a spell when big John Williams was injured, which upset our defensive balance and shape, we enjoyed an unbeaten run of 18 games from early January to late April to achieve promotion. Aside from Robbie Earle and Phil Sproson, other stalwarts were Alan Webb, Jon Bowden, Geoff Hunter, Russell Bromage and Maguire. Andy Jones was helped in no small way by the wily Ally Brown, his ageing but experienced partner up front. And goalkeeper Jim Arnold was an inspirational, intelligent man, who was a great shot-stopper.

We clinched promotion with a 1-0 win at Torquay United on a Saturday night, with the majority of the 3,421 in attendance being Vale fans on an away weekend. As a result, we were featured on television, which was unusual for Port Vale in those days. Afterwards the lads went out on the town to celebrate and I recall a bit of a problem at that same Shiphay nightclub I'd frequented back in my day, which led to a police presence, but it was nothing serious. Thankfully.

I wasn't happy with how we finished the season after that, though, as we lost two and drew one of our final three games and I accused the players of lacking professionalism as that lost us the chance to head into the Third Division as runners-up. Instead, we finished in fourth position on 79 points, albeit seven points clear of Orient. Of greater concern, however, was that in order to achieve promotion the club had actually run up a sizeable loss for the season of almost £80,000. We would have to sell to survive. Could we manage that financial imperative and not fall foul of the relegation which had followed our last promotion? That was an immense challenge facing me throughout the summer of 1986 and the following season.

* * *

Success brings recognition for a manager, as does the ensuing exposure in the press. By this time my trademark flat cap, which was initially worn solely to cover my balding pate from the north Staffordshire winter weather, became much remarked upon and even copied by some Vale fans. Wearing a flat cap became synonymous with me, to the extent that it now forms part of the title of this autobiography, but it was never that much of a conscious style choice or anything like that. This wasn't David Beckham's latest fashion statement haircut, after all, although people still tell me I am a style icon.

I also felt that the flat cap was the headwear of the working man and here was I trying to play the working man's ballet on a working man's budget, so I was almost never without a flat cap on a matchday, whatever the weather. It also served as a disguise when I was out scouting until the media coverage blew my cover and I became so renowned for it I could hide no longer.

The flat cap reached its zenith with the 'flat cap march' which took place after I was sacked, of which more later, but it also became woven into things like interviews and matchday coverage. I remember once hearing that sports reporter George Andrews made a big thing of it during commentary in a game in which we scored a late winning goal. In his excitement, George shouted down the microphone, 'Oh, if my lip reading is up to standard, Bobby Downes has said "let's all have a disco" and Rudgie has thrown his cap in the air and I've nearly caught it!' When you think that George's commentary position was at the top of the Lorne Street stand in a kind of garden shed sticking out from just under the roof, you can tell he was playing fast and loose with the facts, but that wasn't the point; the flat cap had entered folklore and I wouldn't be seen without it.

My cap may have started out merely for keeping my head warm whilst on the touchline, but there's no doubt it quickly became a 'thing' and I soon got approached by a cap manufacturer, Kangol, who sent me a few for free on the condition I wore them and got pictured wearing them. That became a long-standing relationship and, when I retired, Kangol presented me with a cap which says 'JR 843' on it. You'll find an image of that cap in the photo section of this book.

* * *

After that tremendous success in winning promotion in 1985/86, which I felt righted the wrong of that relegation I couldn't stop, we had a couple of seasons of ebb and flow in the Third Division, finishing respectably enough in 12th and then 11th place, the first of those being the 1986/87 season in which Andy Jones plundered that record 37 goals. I had learnt from the failure to invest after the promotion we'd won under John McGrath and brought in better players where I could, starting with the goalkeeping position as Jim Arnold was nearing the end of his career, signing Mark Grew from West Brom. At 28, Mark was approaching his prime and would be a mainstay for Vale for years, eventually becoming one of my coaching staff. Mark was a shot-stopping goalkeeper, who mostly remained on his line and relied on his defenders to deal with crosses, which was why it was so vital to have Bob Hazell, who arrived a few months later after I moved John Williams on to Bournemouth, and Phil Sproson in tandem. Simon Mills and Darren Hughes arrived as my full-backs and that defence proved to be the cornerstone of our 1988/89 promotion challenge as we had the meanest back line in the division, conceding just 48 goals in 46 league games and Grew was voted as Player of the Season, which shows how much he contributed, because when a club goes up it is usually an attacking player who the supporters focus on. I had also signed Ron Futcher to partner Darren Beckford up front and, with Robbie Earle breaking forward to score from midfield and Ray Walker chipping in with John Jeffers and David Riley or Gary Ford on the wings, we were an impressive outfit. There was also a greater feeling of expectancy amongst fans because we had beaten Spurs in the FA Cup the previous season and the club were perceived to be 'on the up'.

Arguably, this was the best-balanced Port Vale side I ever conceived and we started the 1988/89 campaign well, being solidly in second place behind Graham Turner's Wolves, who were powered by Steve Bull's goals, for much of the season, with Sheffield United our main rivals for the second automatic promotion place. Then disaster struck. In January 1989 both Hazell (back) and Sproson (knee) picked up injuries which not only ended their seasons, but their careers. To lose one of my titanic centre-halves could have derailed our promotion push, but both caused me a huge problem. I had no choice but to jump into the transfer market, which you could in those days as there was no August transfer deadline back then. Replacing our twin pillars of strength was a mammoth task, but I managed to sign Dean Glover for a club record £200,000 from Middlesbrough. Dean became 'Mr Cool' at the back and stayed for ten years. Gary West filled in too, but that meant we were a bit less consistent throughout the remainder of the season, although from early February 1989 we lost only four games, and were overtaken by Sheffield United. We won the last three matches, including beating both Bristol Rovers and Fulham, two of the clubs in the play-off zone, but that wasn't enough and finished on the same points as the Blades; 84, with an inferior goal difference of +30, compared to their +39. Devastating, although I remember Dave Bassett, the manager of champions Sheffield United, sent me a 'good luck in the play-offs' card from their club holiday base in Spain.

The play-offs had been introduced in 1986/87 to add extra spice to the end of the season. Prior to that, the top three teams from the Third Division went up automatically. Now, we had to play sixth-placed Preston North End, who happened to be managed by my mentor John McGrath, over two legs, in order to reach a two-legged final, as Wembley did not stage play-off finals in those days.

Pitting my wits against my mentor and former boss was something I enjoyed as I knew how he would want his team to be set up and to play. The first leg at Deepdale was tight and ended 1-1, with Earle scoring our goal. The return match was on 25 May and we felt confident as we were on a great run of form and that proved true as our goalscoring quality produced some excellent strikes. Darren Beckford scored a fabulous hat-trick in a 3-1 victory, to secure a 4–2 aggregate win. The team we were to face in the final? My old club Bristol Rovers, who were a dangerous side under manager Gerry Francis, who I would work with at Stoke some 20 years later, and had thrashed Fulham 5-0 on aggregate in their semi-final.

The first leg was away and again we drew 1-1 with Earle heading the crucial equaliser 17 minutes from time, setting us up for a memorable decider at Vale Park where the entire season's work was at stake. That, to me, is what you call pressure.

We had nearly nicked the first leg after Beckford's header was cleared off the line in the last minute, so we all felt confident, but there are so many uncontrollables in a game of football, we couldn't take anything for granted. A crowd of over 17,000 packed into Vale Park. Nerves and tension play a big part in play-offs and with so much riding on the outcome you rarely see a flowing game. Play can often be hectic, but early on Rovers keeper Nigel Martyn, who would go on to find fame with Crystal Palace, then Leeds and England after becoming the first ever million-pound goalkeeper that summer, made a great save from Beckford from close range and held on to a volley from 25 yards from Glover. In the second half, Futcher was put clean through on goal by a long ball, but Steve Yates somehow got back to tackle him on the edge of the area just as he was about to shoot.

Enter our secret weapon; the MBE routine.

Not only was Simon Mills a stalwart in our defence, but he was also an excellent set-piece taker, assuming those duties from the retired Paul Maguire, who could drift the ball into the near post like a 9-iron into a hole at St Andrews. Simon had now become part of our 'MBE' corner-kick routine: Mills taking the corner, which was flicked on at the near post by Beckford for Earle to run in and head powerfully home. It was a finely tuned routine which we practised for hours and hours and we regularly scored goals from it. Millsy could put in a brilliant delivery and it almost bore fruit early in the second half when Beckford actually went for goal, instead of a flick-on, and hit the bar. But the crucial goal finally arrived in the 52nd minute when Mills, who had actually postponed his honeymoon to appear in the play-offs, clipped the ball from the right corner flag to the near post, where Beckford flicked it on for Earle to race in and bury his header. In fact, Robbie scored headers in all four games against Bristol Rovers that season.

It was the only goal of the game, although Rovers piled forward and Devon White shot tamely at Mark Grew when well-placed centrally and then some feller called Ian Holloway fired just over the bar from the edge of the penalty area. We clung on and referee Keith Hackett's final whistle sparked off wonderful scenes of celebration amongst the crowd of over 17,000 that began in the stands, spread on to the pitch and went on long into the night. It was, without question, one of my most memorable occasions with the Vale and I remember telling the players as they were starting their lap of honour not to run, but to walk; it was a moment to savour and not to get over quickly. I remember, too, the warm and sporting reception that the Rovers supporters gave us from a packed Hamil End, sickened though they must have been by the result. It was to be my former club's turn a year later. It was after this that the photograph of Robbie Earle sitting in the tunnel, quite overcome by the emotion of the occasion, appeared in *The Sentinel.* Robbie was a massive influence on the team through both promotion seasons and, of course, now actually has a well-deserved MBE of his own, awarded in 1999 for his services to football, while in 2009 he was inducted into the English Football Hall of Fame as 'Football Foundation Community Champion'.

For me, guiding Port Vale back into the Second Division goes down as one of my greatest achievements and I realised one of my greatest ambitions; achieving parity with local rivals Stoke City. Vale, understandably, had been labelled a Third or Fourth Division outfit after kicking around the lower divisions for so long, so it had become a burning ambition of mine to lead the Valiants back into the second tier for the first time since 1957, an absence of 32 years.

* * *

I knew as a group of players my team could play at a higher level, but we also had to bring better quality into the squad in key areas, so I signed Neil Aspin from Leeds for £150,000 to partner Glover in defence and the pair became the mainstays of our back four for years to come. Up front Nicky Cross arrived from Leicester for £125,000, while I also signed veteran winger Ian Miller from Blackburn Rovers. We had a good first season in the Second

Division, surprising a lot of people by finishing 11th when we had been the bookies' favourite to go straight back down. Often, though, the momentum of promotion can carry you forward and it is the season after that which becomes a bigger test when you are no longer an unknown quantity. We dropped to 15th in 1990/91, with only Kevin Kent as a major incoming transfer arrival, and that summer we faced the chilling prospect of losing two of our most talismanic players and goalscorers – Earle and Beckford – due to freedom of contract. Their sales brought a smile to the face of the chairman and the club's bank manager, making £1.7 million, but left me with the monumental task of finding suitable replacements to cover their 30–40 goals a season.

My signings, Martin Foyle, Keith Houchen, Paul Kerr and Peter Swan, fitted in well, but 1991/92 turned into a season of unrest, culminating in the departure of my first-team coach and right-hand man Mike Pejic. Around Christmas we were mid-table, but we then went 18 games without a win as we also had the influential Walker sidelined for five months with ligament damage. His absence was a significant factor in our struggles. Instead of Walker and Earle, we had two Dutch lads, Robin van der Laan and Nico Jalink, patrolling our midfield. Robin, who I once described as having the 'lungs of a horse', was my first import, with his success prompting me to sign Nico. Unfortunately, Nico, despite his exceptional talent, could not really cope with the rough and tumble of the English game and went back to Holland after dropping a clanger with a back-pass that cost us a goal in his last game at Derby. After losing our last two games away at Cambridge and at home to Grimsby, we ended up being relegated, five points from safety, with the club in turmoil, both on and off the pitch.

In the modern era you would expect a relegated club to sack their manager. In fact, there is a decent chance he would have been sacked part-way through the relegation season in an attempt to shake things up and stop the demotion happening in the first place.

There were plenty of rumours and rumblings about me losing my job, but the supporters were wonderful for me, making their protests more about the board and the sale of players, not about me. To be fair to them, I don't think the board had any choice but to sell.

For whatever reason, the board kept faith with me, as they had eight years earlier following that initial relegation, and, despite relegation normally being looked upon as a disaster, in this instance, it sparked off two of the most successful years in Port Vale's history.

* * *

Going straight back up was always our aim and 1992/93 turned into a titanic campaign, which led to us missing out in that Wembley play-off final in which Peter Swan was sent off. I had signed a new goalkeeper, as Grew was nearing the end of his career and I let him go to Cardiff on a free transfer. Paul Musselwhite, an experienced keeper from Scunthorpe, cost just £5,000, which rose to £17,500 due to appearance clauses. That proved an absolute steal as Paul made over 360 appearances for Vale over eight seasons.

The other legend to join that season was Ian Taylor, a gem of a dynamic midfielder who we found playing for Moor Green, of which more later. Ian was superb in the centre of the park for us, top-scoring with 19 goals as we finished third in the league, won the Autoglass Trophy and then lost at Wembley the following weekend. That season also contained five Potteries derbies, a club-record stretch of 22 games without failing to score and a run of five consecutive away wins, picking up clean sheets in all five between 20 March and 24 April 1993. It was epic and we finished on 89 points. Yet, at the end of it, I found myself sitting in that Wembley dressing room totally devastated. I can picture myself now; so forlorn I was actually short of words for once. The players didn't need telling anyway. They shared my desolation. We were all bereft for weeks afterwards at the stark reality that defeat meant we had to go and do it all over again the following campaign. I had never felt so low and never would again in my career.

On the bus home the mood got lifted slightly when Paul Kerr found the champagne which we had ready in case we won and the players grabbed me, telling me they'd win us promotion and I agreed we could do it if we stuck together. They then put Madness on the stereo at full blast, donned shades and did the 'One Step Beyond' dance up and down the bus aisle. You'd never have known it was us who lost!

However, the hangover continued well into the start of the following season on the pitch, and it was apparent the disappointment of missing out in the play-off final weighed heavily on the players' shoulders. I would need a forklift truck to try and lift them out of their depression.

My mood was not helped either when Ray Walker had to undergo a cruciate ligament operation that September, which caused him to miss most of 1993/94. We won just one of the first seven games to slump to fourth from bottom by mid-September, although that one victory was remarkable enough, coming after an early red card to our new signing, defender Peter Billing, which seemed to fire the players up. Our opponents Barnet were overwhelmed and both Foyle and Slaven scored hat-tricks in a 6-0 thrashing, Martin's being a 'perfect' hat-trick, netting left-footed, right-footed and headed goals. Heaven only knows how many we would have scored if we'd had all 11 men for the whole game.

Yet we managed to turn that poor start around and win promotion. That was not easy, but it all hinged on one managerial call, at least that's how I tell it. We had spent some of pre-season, as we regularly did, in the Isle of Man, playing the tournament there. We won the first two games and all we needed to do to get into the final was avoid a three-goal defeat in the last pool match against Wrexham. Wanting to knit some new signings into the squad including left-back Allen Tankard, who I had just paid £87,500 for from Wigan, I promised the lads a team night out if we made the final. We lost 0-3 and I was spitting feathers. This may have been a pre-season tournament, but the performance had the hairs standing on the back of the neck as the pressure of needing to win promotion really began to tell. When I got them back into the dressing room, I told them they could 'stick that flaming night out up your backsides'. The players were banished to their rooms after dinner under strict instructions not to even think about attempting to go out. The players knew my rules, they were grown men and knew they would be for the high jump if they stepped over the line.

Or so I thought.

At breakfast the following morning, one of the waiters said to me, 'Your boys were a bit noisy when they came in last night.'

I couldn't hide my surprise. 'What time was that?'

'About 1.45am.'

'How many did you see?' I replied.

'Five or six.' Fuming, I told my coach Bobby Downes that we would just do training that morning as normal and not to let on that we were wise to anything as I didn't yet know who the guilty players were. I asked him to, 'Run the bollocks off them today, Bob,' so they got a very tough workout. After the training session, with them all panting after a hard grind, I sat the players down in a circle and stood over them, because you are always better off looking down on lambs to the slaughter.

It was a nice day and I imagine that they thought they were just going to have a bit of a chat when I suddenly spun round, changed my demeanour entirely and pointed a finger straight at Bernie Slaven, the goalscoring striker I had signed on a free transfer in March 1993 after he fell out with Middlesbrough manager Lennie Lawrence.

'Did you let me down last night?' I snarled.

Bernie looked up at me, startled, and, much to my surprise, said, 'Yes boss.'

It was very handy for me that he owned up straightaway because he had set the ball rolling. So, I continued going round the circle pointing in the face of every one of them. Everybody who had been out owned up except for one, Ray Walker, but he soon confessed once we got back into the hotel as he felt so guilty. I was not in a position to send them all home as we had a final game to play for third place in the tournament and too many were guilty, so I told them I'd sleep on the punishment.

The next day, I informed the half a dozen players or so that had been out, that they would be fined a week's wages, but that I wasn't going to tell their wives, any of the directors or press that they had let me down. Instead, rather than giving the fines back to the club, I was going to use them to place a bet on us winning promotion. There was method to my madness. What it meant was that every week I could say to them that not only had they got their win bonus to play for, but also their 'promotion money' as I called it. I told the whole squad any winnings would be shared by all the players, not just the miscreants, and the winnings would provide them with spending money for their holiday at the end of the season. It was a 'carrot' every time we had a team talk.

These days, of course, this entire scenario would be highly illegal, as the Ivan Toney case shows, but in those days you could bet on yourselves to win, just not on anything else. I asked a friend of mine to place the bet, as I didn't want to be seen gambling myself, but, before the season started, we were amongst the favourites to go up at 2 to 1 as we had come so close just a few months before, so I deferred its laying. That poor start meant our odds lengthened to 6 to 1, so I felt that was the time to place the wager. Throughout the season I'd joke with the players about the bet looking good. It worked out to be quite a motivator as, once it had gone on, we won eight of the next ten games to rise to the top of the table.

We kept the bet strictly between us and nobody on the outside ever knew about it; not even the directors. The ploy paid off handsomely because, once I'd placed that bet, over the course of the rest of the season, we won 25 of the remaining 39 games, losing only seven, to finish in second place on 88 points. Martin Foyle top-scored with 20 goals, while the tireless Taylor really came to the fore in midfield, hitting 16, with Cross also scoring 13 and Slaven bagging nine, while Paul Kerr could make the difference in games when he was on form.

As well as scooting up the table, we knocked Premier League Southampton out of the FA Cup thanks to a Slaven goal, which proved to be his last for the club. That helped our momentum and, back in the league, even Neil Aspin scored in a 4-1 win in his native North East at Hartlepool, while young centre-half Gareth Griffiths netted a brace as we beat Rotherham at home. We went on a tremendous surge and a run of six wins out of eight earned me the Manager of the Month award for April, only losing what felt like a crucial game 1-2 at Stockport, who would finish the season three points and two places below us.

That left us with two away games to go. We knew if we won both, we would clinch promotion. A 3-1 victory in midweek at Cardiff City set us up nicely to travel on to Brighton for our last game of the season. Over 6,000 Vale supporters hit the road to the south coast that day to throng the open side of the Goldstone Ground. We were on such a good run that we were always confident of winning, although back home Del could not bear to listen to the local radio coverage and went shopping instead. We had the best start with Foyle and Glover giving us a two-goal cushion by half-time and, although Brighton pulled one back, Martin scored again. It was just as well because third-placed Plymouth, managed by Peter Shilton, beat Hartlepool 8-1. It was a fabulous day and another for the memory bank.

The promotion celebrations were fantastic. I remember the chairman descending from the stand with bottles of champagne and we joined the supporters who had surged on to the pitch. I emerged sometime later having lost my tie from around my neck. Five years later, I met up with the guy who admitted to having taken it. The players were stripped of almost everything they wore, but just about managed to preserve their dignity.

Winning promotion gives you a tremendous feeling of satisfaction and is what you live for professionally and it was made especially sweet after a relegation and such a close call in the previous two seasons. We'd got our second tier status back, albeit a year too late as far as I was concerned, but that was tempered by collecting our winnings and sharing them out. Ironically, Bernie Slaven, whose honesty triggered the whole thing off, never received his share, as he had left to play for Darlington in February 1994.

I like to think that getting Vale into the Second Division (as I think of it still, although by the time we achieved it that second time it was retitled as the First Division and now goes by the name of the Championship) on that second occasion is one of the greatest feats of my career, up there with winning all those fantastic ties against the big boys of British football. It also put us back in the same division as our local rivals Stoke City once again. The game was, therefore, very much afoot.

Chapter 9

El Ceramico

'No matter which side of the divide I was on,
I always wanted "us" to win!'

John Rudge

THE BIGGEST games in many ways during my time at Port Vale weren't promotion-clinching nail-biters or famous giant-killings at all, but the iconic Potteries derbies against our bitter local rivals Stoke City. Perhaps the most famous of these came in November 1992 in an FA Cup first round replay which was televised live on Sky TV, who enlivened pre-match with dancing cheerleaders and put on a giant sumo wrestling contest on the sodden pitch at half-time.

Coming out of the hat with your local rivals is always going to lead to huge anticipation. Given that this happened in a season when we were already promotion rivals, that was multiplied ten-fold. We had drawn the initial tie 0-0 in front of a sell-out 24,500 at the Victoria Ground and, eight days later, brought Lou Macari and his powerful team back to Vale Park for a titanic match in atrocious conditions. Few of the 19,810 fans who witnessed the replay will forget the weather, even if Stokies prefer to forget the result. The game didn't start well for us as an over-the-top tackle from Stoke's combative Steve Foley nearly broke Neil Aspin's leg. Neil was a very strong boy, but he had to come off after just 15 minutes, which he never did unless he had to. You couldn't get away with anything like that these days with how refereeing standards are, but that was very much an accepted part of the game back then and somehow Foley escaped a red card, while Neil had to go to hospital to get checked, but at least could watch the game on the screen in the waiting area. Before he had even reached A&E, though, events took over as the Potters scored through Lee Sandford's close-range tap-in on 24 minutes. That was the signal for the heavens to open. I have never seen rain like it!

The monsoon conditions quickly transformed the pitch into a paddy field, which we seemed to adapt better to and equalised when, two minutes later, Foyle took advantage of a long ball floating over Ian Cranson to control and hammer right-footed under Ronnie Sinclair in the Potters' goal. Then, right on the strike of half-time Porter lashed home a left-footed shot from the edge of the box to put us into the lead after Stoke's supposedly huge defence was outjumped for another long ball in the lashing rain.

Down and down it came and, on 66 minutes, the pitch, which was by now a total quagmire in places, played its part in the drama of the night. Musselwhite had raced out of his area to deal with a long ball which had evaded our defence, but only succeeded in miskicking it to Dave Regis, who was 25 yards out, centrally, just outside the D. His side-foot shot looked destined to find the net, but instead stopped dead in the growing pool of water on the six-yard line with the goal gaping, thus denying them an equaliser. I remember in a post-match TV interview that night describing the Vale Park pitch as 'a bit sticky', albeit with a large grin on my face.

A late breakaway goal by Foyle earned us a wonderful 3-1 victory, rounding Sinclair to slot home left-footed. It was a fantastic night and a great atmosphere. My satisfaction was that, not only were we in the second round, but the Vale fans had bragging rights the next day back at work.

* * *

That FA Cup victory was my favourite game in a long run of derbies which lit up the decade; an incredible era and I am delighted I was part of it. Of course, when I arrived the only derbies were pre-season friendlies, with Stoke City the First Division giants and us the Fourth Division paupers. There was a chasm between the two clubs in the city which seemed uncrossable at that point. But in 1985/86 we won promotion and were now only one division below our city rivals, who, following relegation from the top flight in 1984/85, had former Ipswich and England captain Mick Mills in charge as player-manager.

During the period just after I arrived at Vale Park, I had learned that supporters used to go to watch Stoke one week and Vale the next. That stopped altogether as we achieved parity alongside the Potters, even overtaking them at times. The city became that divided, and memories are that long, that even when, in December 2018 (a gap of almost 17 years since the previous league derby), Vale's first team pulled Stoke's Under 21 side out of the hat in the EFL Trophy, the rivalry flared up again. Big time.

I'd got a sense of how deep-lying the rivalry was when, earlier in the 1980s, I had signed both Paul Maguire and fellow winger Peter Griffiths, both of whom had played for Stoke. A sizeable portion of Vale's fans were decidedly unhappy and targeted Griffiths, in particular, because he was a former Stoke City star, although he played his part in improving us.

The links between the clubs were numerous. Robbie Earle had been released by Stoke as a youth player before joining us, as I've mentioned, while Mark and Neville Chamberlain plus Mark Harrison went the other way, being sold to Stoke by John McGrath, while, by the time of the first derby in decades, I had former Stoke star Mike Pejic on my staff as assistant coach. In fact, Mike would prove to be someone who crossed the divide to Vale and then went back to coach at Stoke under Lou Macari. I managed to keep hold of Ray Walker in the summer of 1988, despite Mick Mills' £300,000 offer. Partly that was loyalty, partly his new contract, but also, we had created a wonderful environment and enjoyed cup and league success at Vale and winning promotion in 1988/89 meant we would now be facing our deadly city rivals in a competitive fixture for the first time since April 1957. Our supporters fervently awaited the publication of the fixture list that summer and when it came out there was only one club's name they were hunting for as they looked down the list. As it turned out they didn't have far to go as the first competitive Potteries derby in 32 years was scheduled for 23 September 1989. To be even in the situation when Port Vale were going to be playing Stoke was absolutely immense for us.

I don't think anyone realised just how great the rivalry was to turn out to be until we played each other that first time, nor how patronised Vale would be in the media. In the build-up to the first derby game the local press referred to Stoke as our 'big brother'. It was almost as if we were just going to the Victoria Ground for a lovely day out. I also remember a Stoke fanzine described chairman Bill Bell as 'dedicated to making Vale the No 1 team in the Potteries', but continued, 'Bill also wants to find the lost city of Atlantis, be the first man to walk the Channel and skateboard up Mount Everest.'

So, it was a particularly sweet moment when we took the lead five minutes after the break through Earle, who latched on to a Jeffers pass to turn and net in front of our ecstatic fans. That was incredible for Robbie, a nice revenge for being let go those years before.

Stoke equalised through Leigh Palin's deflected shot 15 minutes later and the game ended 1-1. We nearly won it though, when Jeffers crossed for Futcher to head against the bar and Ronnie Jepson headed the rebound wide with the goal gaping. Mind you, Cranson's header also rattled the woodwork at the Boothen End towards the end of the game. Honours even was just about fair.

The attendance that day was 27,037, almost a sell-out, and one of the largest gates in the country, being higher than games at Leeds, West Brom and Newcastle. The Potteries derby touchpaper had been set alight.

I say alight – the return game that February was the dampest of squibs, with Stoke happy to defend in depth to nick a point as they were by then struggling at the foot of the table. Come season's end, they were relegated, Mills was dismissed, and we stayed up comfortably, eventually finishing in 11th place. That meant, for the first time since 1955/56, Port Vale finished above Stoke City in the league table. Ambition achieved.

* * *

Despite Stoke's relegation, we couldn't crow for too long as 1991/92 saw us suffer the drop too. So, 1992/93 saw both of us in the newly renamed Division Two, thanks to the advent of the Premier League. Having survived getting the sack following that relegation I had to prove to the board and supporters alike that I would be the right man to get the club back up again and take on our bitter rivals who were now also vying for promotion alongside us. It was always a special occasion when we met Stoke, but we were really spoiled that 1992/93 season because we clashed no less than five times – twice in the league and once in the Autoglass Trophy as well as those two FA Cup ties. Each was witnessed by massive crowds and preceded by huge fervour, with the build-up seeing local news pieces on the clubs on both BBC and ITV, often focussing on myself and Lou Macari. The games were momentous, starting in September 1992 when we visited the Victoria Ground for a league fixture that is still talked about today.

Paul Kerr curled in a lovely goal to put us ahead halfway through the second half, but a minute later we relaxed and let a Kevin Russell free kick reach the back post, where Cranson rose to power his header into the roof of the net.

It seemed that honours would be even as the game drifted slightly towards its end, but, four minutes from time, a long punt down the right-hand side found Mark Stein making one of his characteristic, lung-busting runs. Stein just beat Musselwhite to the ball inside the penalty area and went down. I thought there was no contact, that Stein had taken a dive. The referee disagreed and awarded a penalty. After a fair amount of chaos, Stein lashed the ball home from the spot, despite Peter Swan telling him we would find out what he was made of as a way of trying to unnerve him as he waited to take the spot kick. First blood went to Stoke in the remarkable 1992/93 season of derbies.

By the time the return league fixture arrived at the end of March, we had not only defeated the Potters in that epic FA Cup tie, but had knocked them out of another cup too; the Autoglass Trophy at the Southern Section semi-final stage. Make no mistake, neither Stoke, nor us, took this game lightly. That we knew we would be facing each other in a do-or-die league fixture later that month only added spice to an already tasty tie.

Stoke were the holders, having defeated Stockport County at Wembley the previous May, but we were on our way to completing a remarkable Potteries double over the Hatters, winning our first ever Wembley final 2-1. We got past Macari's men in front of a bumper crowd of 22,267 at the Victoria Ground on 3 March. This time Stein hit the post with a penalty for the Potters on 12 minutes after Taylor tripped Shaw in the box. Stein then had a goal disallowed for offside as we rode our luck, but in the second half we came back into it and van der Laan scored the only goal of the game, getting his head on a Chris Sully free kick to beat Ronnie Sinclair at his near post to secure Port Vale's first victory at Stoke in a competitive fixture since November 1927. We were making history match by match in these titanic derbies.

The ensuing league game proved extremely costly for us, however, as we lost 0-2 at Vale Park. Losing those six points in the league cost us dearly as Stoke finished as champions a mere four points ahead of us, with Bolton just one point above our incredible total of 89. That could have been so different even up to the very last week of the season, however. As luck would have it, in their penultimate game, Stoke, who had already clinched the title, visited Bolton, who needed to win to climb above us into the automatic

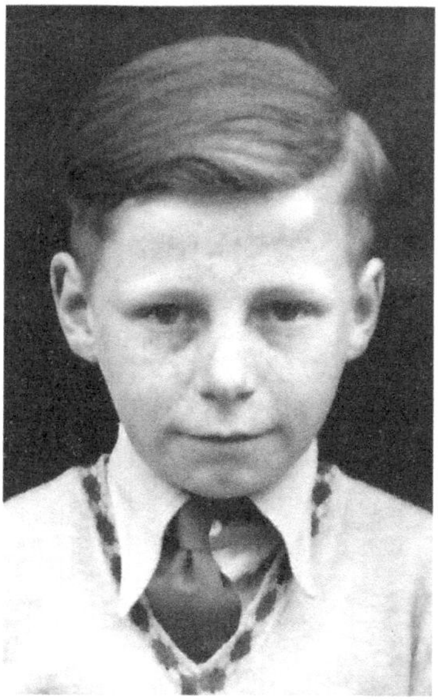

Far left: As a young lad I played for Wolverhampton schoolboys. I had hair to comb back then, but never quite got my tie straight.

Left: With my cousin Gordon Potts (left), whose family had a carpet stall on Wolverhampton market alongside my mother's fruit and veg stall.

My school team in 1955. I was captain and no one was getting the ball off me.

I was also a good enough cricketer to captain the school XI.

The wonderful Edith Longbottom (left), known to us as 'Auntie', who took Del in aged ten and leased the hairdresser's in which I then met my future wife.

Posing with Del, mom and dad.

The 1959/60 Wolverhampton Boys' team. I'm front row, second from the right, with a full head of hair. It wouldn't last. Graham French, who joined Huddersfield with me, is on my left.

Out with Del, Pat and my brother-in-law Peter Clark, who mentored and inspired me.

The happiest day of my life, marrying my incredible wife, Del.

Gordon Potts (right) reminding me how lucky I am to be marrying Del outside St Patrick's Church, Huddersfield.

Mam and dad.

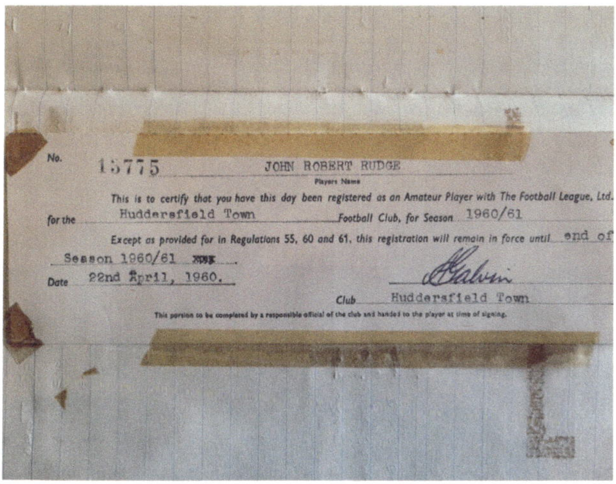

No. 15775 JOHN ROBERT RUDGE

Players Name

This is to certify that you have this day been registered as an Amateur Player with The Football League, Ltd.

for the Huddersfield Town Football Club, for Season 1960/61

Except as provided for in Regulations 55, 60 and 61, this registration will remain in force until end of Season 1960/61

Date 22nd April, 1960.

Club Huddersfield Town

This portion to be completed by a responsible official of the club and handed to the player at time of signing.

My first player registration, on signing as an apprentice for Huddersfield, aged 15.

I signed pro for Huddersfield at 17, after two years as an apprentice.

Huddersfield reserves. I am front row, second from the right. Allan Gilliver is on my right.

(Third from left) Scoring for the reserves against Rotherham in a 6-1 victory. It looks like a deft flick to beat the defender on the line. That's what I'm going with, anyway.

The second of the four

Inside-right Len White making the header which gave Town their second goal against Swansea Town at Leeds Road last evening. The Swansea player in the picture is Davies (P).

Teenagers play a big part in Town's 4—1 win

IT was "teenagers' night out" at Leeds Road last night, where there were sparkling displays by young hopefuls Gilliver and Rudge in Town's 4—1 win over Swansea Town before a 7,964 crowd.

The non-stop drive and enthusiasm of the two eighteen-year-olds who were making their debuts worked like a blood transfusion to the Town forward line.

Unquestionably, this will go down as their match. Gilliver, particularly, had a night to remember. Playing against Wales Under 23 centre-half Johnson, the

Making headlines in the Huddersfield newspaper, along with fellow debutant Allan Gilliver, in May 1963.

Signing for Carlisle under Alan Ashman.

Training at Brunton Park in the late 1960s. My control, heading ability and turn of speed were my biggest assets.

Carlisle's greatest moment; defeating mighty Newcastle United in the FA Cup third round in January 1968 before the biggest crowd I ever played in front of. On the left, we are celebrating in the dressing room afterwards. Goalscorer Tony Murray is holding a bottle (centre). I am on his left with my friend Chris Balderstone to his right.

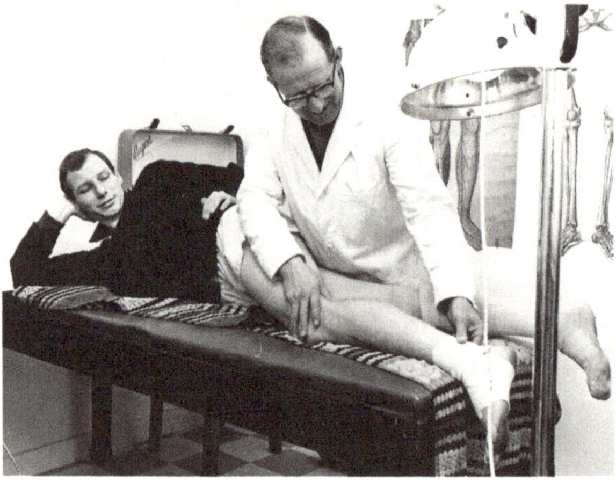

Receiving treatment on my dodgy ankle. To be honest they both were, and my Achilles ... I became a regular on the Carlisle physio's massage table.

Rising high against Middlesbrough in 1968.

Warming up against Chelsea in the FA Cup in January 1969.

Signing for Torquay United, with manager Allan Brown.

After moving to Torquay, Del and I bought a beach hut on Goodrington Sands.

Losing out to my future team-mates Frankie Prince (left) and Don Megson whilst playing for Torquay against my future employers Bristol Rovers.

Following in as all good strikers do as Torquay defeat local rivals Plymouth 2-1 on Boxing Day 1970.

Our two daughters, Lisa (right) and Deb, arrived while we lived in sunny Torquay.

With the family in our sparkling new £10,000 house in Bristol. Mom was worried I'd never be able to afford it. So was I!

At Bristol Rovers as a grizzled veteran of, ahem, 27 years of age.

Scoring at Old Trafford in the League Cup replay was the stuff of dreams. Very happy I am that far off the floor!

Celebrating promotion in 1983 with John McGrath, the big man in every way. The gurning chump behind me is Wayne Cegielski, with Phil Sproson next to him.

John taught me a lot about using media photo opportunities, like this one with me as J.R. Ewing from the 80s TV show *Dallas*. See what he did there?

Taking over as manager thanks to chairman Jim Lloyd's subterfuge. That sign doesn't exactly look permanent does it?

Football management soon took over my life. I was out on the road, scouting players and opposition every night when I wasn't on the bench.

This was what passed for our open-topped bus tour to celebrate winning promotion in 1986. Coach Alan Oakes, who was a great help to me, is to my right.

Signing Ray Walker from Aston Villa in 1986 after I shanghaied the tribunal to ensure the fee was only £12,000. 'Deadly' Doug Ellis, Villa's chairman, was livid.

Ray Walker's shot is on its way into the back of the Spurs net and the greatest giant-killing in Port Vale's history is on. Our 2-1 defeat of Terry Venables' glamour boys put us on the footballing map.

Full-back Darren Hughes in control as we hold on to beat Spurs in January 1988.

Our two goalscorers in the famous win, Ray Walker and Phil Sproson, listen in to the FA Cup fifth round draw in January 1988. We pulled out Watford.

Getting used to TV and media duties as manager once we'd gone global; the flat cap became my trademark brand.

Accepting Manager of the Month awards, on the right with Bobby Downes, a good coach.

And the Football Writers' Association (North) Manager of the Season award in 1986, or was it 1989, 1993 or 1994? I can't remember, but I won four of them!

Those coaching sessions at Lilleshall were crucial for me; they taught me almost everything I knew about football management... Until I started doing it, that was. Ray Graydon, who helped me in 1998, is second row, fourth from left.

The dilapidated state of Vale Park would soon become a major bone of contention between myself and chairman Bill Bell ...

... although occasionally we could stand to be in each other's presence for a photo or two.

Celebrating beating Spurs with coach Mike Pejic (right) and physio Richard Gray.

Robbie Earle reflects on his winning goal against Bristol Rovers, after all the fuss had died down. This is my favourite photograph from my time at Port Vale as it shows just what winning promotion meant to a local lad.

The 1988/89 promotion-winning squad.

Despite being a combustible character, Mike Pejic was an excellent coach for me. This is a rare photo of Pej smiling during training. Ron Futcher must have been behaving himself ...

With Lou Macari, the Stoke City manager through those classic Potteries derbies. We were both paid-up members of the 1990s tie club.

Celebrating with the Vale fans after winning the Autoglass southern section semi-final at Stoke's Victoria Ground in 1993 ...

… then, rather more professionally, commiserating with Lou and Chic Bates.

Thanking Robin van der Laan for his part in securing a famous Wembley victory in the 1993 Autoglass Trophy Final against Stockport, with Ian Miller in the foreground.

Open-topped bus tours had gone up in the world by the time we got to drive around the northern end of the Potteries to celebrate that Wembley win.

Del always says I looked more lustfully at that trophy than I did at her!

The 1993 Autoglass winners.

Listening to a cup draw after defeating Premier League opposition yet again with a youthful Andy Porter, a player who graduated though the ranks to play 432 games for me and did an incredible job in midfield and, latterly, as captain.

Bernie Slaven scores the goal which defeated Premier League Southampton in an FA Cup replay in 1994. It proved to be his last for the club before he headed back north.

Celebrating defeating FA Cup holders Everton in a replay in February 1996, having knocked out Crystal Palace in the previous round. Colin Dobson, a great friend and assistant, has his arms aloft (left).

After the Crystal Palace victory.

That win earned us the 1996 Littlewoods Giantkillers trophy, which I was presented with at Wembley before the cup final.

My testimonial match in 1993 against Aston Villa at Vale Park celebrated my decade in charge; with Martin Foyle, who brilliantly scored over 100 goals for Vale, in the foreground.

spots. Perhaps not surprisingly, at least not to me anyway, the Potters lost 0-1 at Burnden Park. By all accounts they put up a pretty tame effort and there was the bizarre spectacle of Stoke fans in the away end celebrating Bolton's goal and victory because it meant most likely Vale wouldn't go up. Did Stoke deliberately lose to ensure we didn't win automatic promotion? I don't believe the game was 'fixed' in any way at all, but I think we can all agree no one was surprised when the already-promoted Potters barely lifted a finger. There really was that little love lost.

Although we won 4-2 away at Blackpool, Bolton's 1-0 victory over Preston on the final day of the season, courtesy of a late penalty which we heard about via the radio we had on the bench, left us in the play-offs on course for that Wembley heartbreak. Fair play to Bolton, they had won eight of their last nine, while we only won six, drawing twice, the second of those stalemates being the penultimate game at Exeter which ended 1-1 and handed the momentum to the Trotters.

* * *

That 1992/93 season set the tone for the tribalism, drama and tetchiness of Potteries derbies which endured for a decade. It featured some of the biggest games during my time at the helm of Port Vale, with some of the biggest attendances. The two clubs had very different philosophies and playing styles at that time, which added to the intrigue of the matches. Lou's team was a long-ball, powerful side, but with some very skilful players such as Nigel Gleghorn and superstar striker Mark Stein. Up front, we had Slaven and Foyle, with Kerr and van der Laan in midfield. I wanted them to play one- and two-touch football, but you couldn't in those games really. They were frantic, with tackles flying in left, right and centre from the centre-halves on both sides; Aspin, Glover and Swan wearing the white of Vale and Cranson and Overson donning the red and white stripes of Stoke. The likes of Foley and Porter weren't backwards in coming forward in a challenge either. That made for extremely competitive, incident-packed matches. It was a fantastic rivalry, but, of course, things would often spill over amidst the intensity, atmosphere and vivid spectacle of a local derby.

You may not believe this, but, down on the benches during those titanic tussles, there was actually huge camaraderie and respect, with plenty of great, friendly banter between myself and Lou and our respective backroom teams. Despite the fierce rivalry, all that passion never spilled over between us on the sidelines, even amidst the white-hot atmosphere on the pitch and in the stands. It just didn't get tasty on the touchline, perhaps because we were winning all the time!

In the build-up to derby games, some of the papers liked to try and whip up some kind of hatred between us, but that just wasn't the case. Lou and I respected each other a lot. We would occasionally see each other outside football at some function or other and we always got on. In fact, I was invited to Stoke's celebration dinner of the 1992/93 season promotion team, at which I kept having to remind them all we did win promotion the following season ...

Lou and I have ended up living only a few hundred yards from each other nowadays and I fully respect the incredible work he does for the homeless across the city of Stoke-on-Trent. When we see each other, we talk about how we used to be travelling up and down the country by car or on trains watching reserve teams to see if we could cherry-pick players. In both our cases, we came up trumps with some superb signings; for Lou, Mark Stein and Mike Sheron spring to mind, while for me, Ray Walker, Ian Taylor and Dean Glover are great examples.

Back in 1994, our promotion meant Potteries derby hostilities resumed again, but this time it wasn't Lou Macari in the opposition dugout, but Joe Jordan, who managed Stoke for 18 months or so between Macari's two spells in charge. What you may not know is that it was very nearly not Joe who was given the job, as autumn 1994 was the first occasion that Stoke chairman Peter Coates approached me to become the manager. Despite the larger salary on offer, I turned him down as I had just got Vale promoted again and we were on the up, while Stoke had just sold star striker Mark Stein to Chelsea and you could see that their promotion team was needing to be rebuilt. In any case, I was more than happy at Vale Park and had no desire to join our bitter rivals. It would be another three years, after Lou had left the club for a second time, before I got as far as agreeing that contract.

As it happened, the fans had to wait months for the first Potteries derby of 1994/95 as the game at Vale Park didn't take place until the middle of March. It took just three minutes for Tony Naylor to open the scoring, lashing home after a lovely move; a goal to be proud of as a manager, when everything comes together. Lee Sandford netted the equaliser with a close-range header, so this game really exemplified the differences between our two approaches with the two goals being so different. We then won the return in late April when Foyle headed home Guppy's corner for the only goal, the 18th of his 20 that season. Stoke's Cranson earned a second yellow card late in the game to become the first player ever sent off in a Potteries derby and we were home and dry; our first league win at the Victoria Ground since November 1927, which helped us finish 17th, steering well clear of relegation in our first season back up.

In contrast, the first derby of the following campaign was scheduled for the third match of the season and was marked by Sir Stanley Matthews and Robbie Williams parading on the pitch before the game for Central TV's cameras; Robbie actually emerged from the paddock where he was in amongst the fans. The result was the same, though, another 1-0 victory for us, with new signing Ian Bogie, who was in sublime form, sliding the ball under Carl Muggleton at the near post to score the only goal of a tight game, while another new signing, Andy Hill, actually made his debut having never met or trained with the rest of the squad, but did brilliantly for me.

The return in March was in midweek under lights, which always brought a more magical touch to Potteries derbies, especially on this occasion as there had been snowfall and there were piles of the white stuff around the almost frozen pitch. The result was the same, with the same scorer, but this time the goal was all the more remarkable as Bogie scored after just 12 seconds, yes twelve seconds, following us taking the kick-off and Hill playing the ball forward for Foyle and then Lee Glover to both dummy it to leave Bogie racing in on goal. His stunning right-footed strike into the top left corner from 20 yards saw the ball lodge satisfyingly in the stanchion of the goal. I believe that is still the fastest ever goal scored by Port Vale, full-stop, let alone in a Potteries derby. In celebration, some of our players threw and kicked snow high into the air, making for fittingly magical fairy-tale pictures. Sheron hit the inside of our post, but otherwise we held on well for the remaining 90 minutes to record our third consecutive 1-0 victory in Potteries derbies. We were well on top in the local rivalry at this stage – literally their Bogie team – although it was Stoke who made the play-offs at the end of that season, while we finished a respectable 12th, knocked both Crystal Palace and holders Everton out of the FA Cup and reached the Anglo-Italian Cup Final.

The following season it was our turn to be in play-off contention. Honours were even in the first derby at Vale Park on a sunny Sunday afternoon in mid-October. Kevin Keen looped in a header to put Stoke in front, which I was very unhappy about as he was one of the smallest players on the pitch and it looked like the Potters would steal a 1-0 victory, but, in the third minute of injury time, Guppy crossed for Lee Mills to rise above Mark Prudhoe to head home. That one felt like a victory, even if it was only one point earned.

As the 1996/97 season came to a climax, we sat in fifth position as we travelled to Stoke, with just three games remaining, for what would be the last ever Potteries derby at the old Victoria Ground. We were riding high on the back of a run of four successive wins and the news that Lou Macari would be resigning at the end of the season to fight his court case against Celtic had just broken (little did I know that announcement would lead to the second of Peter Coates' approaches to me to take over at the Vic). So, you would think we were in prime position, but I suppose I should have expected Stoke's players to be as up for this game as much as any other derby.

Nothing went to plan that day, starting with two Potteries legends coming to blows; no, not Port Vale and Stoke, but local radio commentator George Andrews and legendary Stoke kitman Neil 'Nello' Baldwin, who, if for some reason you don't know, is the subject of the BAFTA-winning film, and the award-winning play, *Marvellous*. George had been winding up Nello all season about how Stoke were below Vale in the league. Neil being Neil, had revenge foremost in his mind. When Lou Macari jokingly told Nello not to let 'that bastard' into the ground, a plan formed and, before the game, Nello and an accomplice from the Stoke office staff kidnapped George, stowing him away in a kit hamper before running it into the laundry boot-room under the main stand. They then threw George in a chair and gaffer-taped his mouth up, securing his arms and putting a ring round his neck with a piece of cardboard on it saying, 'George is a Stokie', leaving him locked in there alone. George was supposed to split the commentary with Nigel Johnson, who was doing the first 22 minutes before handing over, but, come the midpoint of the first half, when George didn't appear, the producer went down to the dugout and at that point Lou realised Nello had gone over the top a bit and sent the physio to open the door to let the kidnapped commentator out. Ever the professional, George managed to cover the rest of the game alongside Kevin Kent. It was the only thing I could laugh about all day.

We just really didn't turn up. Andy Griffin, City's 17-year-old left-back, kept Jon McCarthy extremely quiet, when I had hoped for joy down that side, especially against an inexperienced player, and I had to substitute him. Sheron scored two goals from distance, one via a wicked deflection off Glover's chest in first half injury time to put them ahead and another after an easy clearance had been blocked. That was a painfully poor performance, arguably our worst in a Potteries derby with me in charge, and the 0-2 defeat cost us our place in the play-off zone. We couldn't recover, losing to Wolves and drawing with Crystal Palace to finish eighth, ending on 67 points, just four off the play-offs. Had we won two of those last three games we would have made the play-offs instead of Steve Coppell's Palace, who then went and won promotion, defeating Sheffield United with a last-minute David Hopkin goal in the Wembley final.

Despite that disappointment, I take great pleasure from having finished above Stoke on several occasions, including three points and four places higher that 1996/97 season; a huge achievement for me because of where we had started. The nonentities had risen up above our big city rivals. There were some great headlines about our rise, one I remember saying I had masterminded 'the greatest miracle since Lazarus'.

Disappointing though the end of that campaign was, it still represented the club's highest finish since 1933/34, only having been bettered once in the club's history, when Tom Morgan's team finished fifth in 1930/31. It was also the closest I would ever get to winning promotion to the Premier League as manager, having once come agonisingly closer as a player. Given that we had joined Vale with the club rooted almost to the foot of the entire 92-club Football League, this was some achievement, but it proved the zenith in terms of league position and it was only downhill from here. History has shown that kind of season is very difficult to emulate at a club like Port Vale.

Around that era, there was occasionally talk of the two clubs ground-sharing or even, unbelievably, merging. Both seemed to me to be ridiculous and the supporters on both sides agreed. There was uproar. Bill Bell always said, 'Our fans would rather see me shut the gates than merge with Stoke.' A lot of the chat about ground-sharing stemmed from Stoke's new Britannia Stadium, which had been constructed on the hill overlooking the old ground and opened in summer 1997. Could it be used by one club one week and the other the next, much like the San Siro in Milan is used by AC and Inter? It was a total non-starter as far as I was concerned, although

I understood the financial savings which could be made and both clubs were struggling for money at that time. It got a lot of people worked up, spawning phone-ins, column inches and online chat, a new phenomenon which was at the very beginning of being in my consciousness and would obviously grow with fanzine forums, Twitter and the rest over the next 25 years.

All that meant the first Potteries derby at the Brit was a charged affair. The atmosphere was very different compared to the Victoria Ground, though, as the new ground had three open corners for the wind to howl around and Stoke's fans were still finding their feet in it. That derby started badly for us when Richard Forsyth headed home from close range from a Keen cross after just four minutes. It nearly got worse when Forsyth rounded Musselwhite, but shot wide of a gaping net. We really weren't at it, but then equalised out of nowhere when Naylor somehow got his head to Rogier Koordes' cross from 15 yards. Stoke got a second, though, when Graham Kavanagh ran 60 yards with the ball, which annoyed me, and crossed for Keen to fire home the winner. Even though that goal was scored just before half-time, both keepers made superb saves in the second half, allowing Stoke to edge the game.

The return saw both clubs in relegation trouble. Consequently, it was a feisty affair on and off the pitch, which ended 0-0, with Stoke at that point being managed by the short-lived Chris Kamara, who had replaced Chic Bates as the Potters' season fell apart. That would prove to be my last Potteries derby as Port Vale manager, as Stoke got relegated that season, while we stayed up.

From 1993 to 1998, in particular, we had huge success, at least for a club with Port Vale's history and size, notably in Potteries derbies and my overall head-to-head record as manager of Vale against Stoke City reads:

Won 5
Drew 6
Lost 4

Considering we were three divisions apart when I joined Vale, I'm very happy with that.

* * *

The season after I joined Stoke, Vale got relegated and so we had a series of Potteries derbies again, but this time with my successor Brian Horton as Vale manager and me on the red and white side. You might think this would provide me with difficulties or divided loyalties, but, honestly, I didn't really find it difficult to adjust as I passionately want to win, irrespective of any history I may have. That's the mark of a professional. I am not really coloured by the same feelings fans have. It was an odd scenario for me, but once I crossed over the divide, that was it.

Perhaps surprisingly, neither set of fans had a problem with me. But I think that was because I was the director of football, not the manager in the Stoke dugout. It is one of the many significant differences between the two roles. As manager you are the figurehead and in the limelight all the time; fans of both teams either hate you or loathe you most of the time.

As director of football you are much more in the shadows, although I did find myself being sought out for comment every time a Potteries derby came around. There was always banter whenever I met Vale fans whilst I was working at Stoke, but there was such a respect between us that it was never an issue. I also would never walk away from them, but instead would walk towards them and smile, acknowledging them. I really believe that helped me overcome crossing that seemingly uncrossable divide without causing a riot.

Cross-city hostilities were resumed on 19 September 2000, with me up in the stands, not on the bench next to Stoke manager Gudjon Thordarson. It still felt very strange for me to be on the red side of events on game day and I was a little relieved when, in that first season, the two league games both ended up 1-1, although I would have far preferred a Stoke win or two.

I remember going back to Vale Park for the first time and sitting in the directors' box as a visiting official. That felt strange. My loyalties had changed and it was now my professional job to win for Stoke. I had to set aside the fact that I had been at Vale for 19 years. There were a few chants from Stoke fans taunting Vale supporters along the lines of 'He's red, he's white, he hates the Vale sh*te ... Johnny Rudge!' which obviously wasn't true, but did allow me to muse on how times had changed. Marc Bridge-Wilkinson opened the scoring with an early header, but then Kavanagh crossed for Nicky Mohan to head towards goal. Although Mark Goodlad saved, Kyle Lightbourne lashed the rebound home. We hit the bar twice after that, but couldn't score the decisive goal.

I was happy that my first Potteries derby as a visitor to Vale Park had ended without defeat, but would have preferred a victory. Despite what you might think, no way did I want Vale to win. I was desperate for us to win those games. In fact, everything I heard about Vale's financial situation was dire, with Bill Bell engendering fan protests on seemingly a weekly basis, so I was, quite frankly, glad to be out of it.

* * *

We also found ourselves drawn away at Port Vale in the Football League Trophy that season, but, after a couple of postponements due to the poor pitch at Vale Park, the tie got switched to the Britannia Stadium. It didn't help, though, as Vale won 2-1, with Bridge-Wilkinson scoring the deciding goal from a penalty on their way to lifting the trophy again at Wembley.

Overall, while I was at Stoke, we only played five Potteries derbies, but what was now my team never actually won any of them. There were three 1-1 draws, that defeat in the Football League Trophy and a 0-1 home defeat in the last first-team derby played to date in February 2002. The only goal of that game was a farce. A long throw from Matty Carragher was headed clear by Sergei Shtanyuk, except it hit the back of Micky Cummins' head from close range and looped up and span, just out of reach of goalkeeper Birkir Kristinsson, into the far corner of the net. Cummins didn't even know he had scored. We didn't really get going and Vale hit the bar before running out deserved winners, although Stoke won promotion under Gudjon Thordarson that season and the two clubs have not been in the same division since, so I haven't been put in the position of having to decide which 'side' I am on for over 20 years.

* * *

Despite the intense rivalry, there are several examples from my time at Port Vale which I can point to that show how the two clubs could actually work together, when the cause was right, for the common good. One that springs to mind came in January 1989, when Vale legend Phil Sproson suffered a severe knee injury during training and was forced to retire. Stoke agreed to play a testimonial match for Phil, which was held on 21 March 1988. The game was as fiercely contested as any Potteries derby and finished 1-1, with Sproson collecting £12,000 as a thank you for his wonderful service.

Another came in November 1998, when the Ipstones village Lights and Market Committee decided that the managers from both Stoke and Port Vale should turn on the Christmas lights and approached me to see if I would do it. I was delighted to agree and, at that point, my opposite number at the Britannia Stadium was Brian Little, so I rang him and suggested we show some unity and travel across together, which we did, with our wives, in his car. The 'stage' was the upper deck of an open-top double decker bus and there was a huge mix of red and white and black and white scarves amongst the sea of excited faces as we counted down to the big switch-on. Apparently, it was the largest turnout in the event's history, which I remember included a competition for the best-dressed house, and was another great example of how football clubs can make a difference in their community by bringing them together. A score draw in a different type of Potteries derby, I suppose.

But, of course, whenever it is played, the Potteries derby is always a massive game, partly because it doesn't happen that often. There hasn't been one for over 20 years now, which is sad, but there will come a time when it returns, I'm sure, and when it does it will still be one of the most intensely competitive rivalries in the country, if not the world.

For over 15 years, having reignited it by getting Vale into the same division as Stoke, then crossing that great divide to see what life was like from the other side, I was synonymous with the fixture. All of those derbies were electric and live long in the memory. Each and every time a Potteries derby was looming the talk in the city would be of nothing else. The build up could last weeks, on some occasions months, as the hangover from the previous game's events became huge talking and debating points: Stein's penalty, the ball stuck in the mud, Bogie's goal after 12 seconds, George Andrews being kidnapped, celebrations in the snow. As they say in the Potteries, you couldn't make it up, youth.

The derby game has now been dubbed *El Ceramico*, after the Barcelona–Real Madrid derby title of *El Clasico*, in honour of the city's pottery heritage. It has only happened once since 2002, when Vale drew Stoke's under-21s in the Checkatrade Trophy in December 2018. That night showed how the passion remains, although it spilled over into a load of nonsense inside the ground with Stoke fans ripping out seats and toilets. But it gave the modern supporters, who have become used to Vale being below Stoke again, a flavour of those halcyon seasons 25–30 years ago when the two clubs competed on the same, even footing. It will give me great pleasure to see that happen once again, although, given Vale are a division below Stoke as I write, that will have to be via a promotion, not a relegation. I have to stay neutral.

In fact, I often get asked whether I'm Vale or Stoke. I choose to be diplomatic, because of course it may depend on who is asking and what colours they are wearing at the time, but my answer is, 'No matter which side of the divide I was on, I always wanted "us" to win!'

Chapter 10

Slightly More Pots to Piss In

Neil Warnock: 'What's this about you being interested in signing Ian Taylor? I sent my chairman to look at him and he is signing for us.'
John Rudge: 'He won't be,' I said. 'He's already signed for us'

AS TIME went by, begging, borrowing and persuading players to join Port Vale became more difficult, especially as the club established itself in the second tier. If you want quality you have to pay for it, and rightly so, but that means risking far larger sums of money on each signing. You are staking your reputation on each and every arrival and, while our financial situation was a lot better than it once had been, we most certainly couldn't afford to lose vast amounts of money on a disastrously expensive signing. Thankfully, my wheeling and dealing now meant I could start to buy the better players from teams in the lower leagues, fringe players from Premier League teams or from foreign climes to attract them into the First Division to play for Vale. But that gave me new problems to have to face; signing good players can be rather more troublesome than you think, as it can often take a lot longer, months of coaxing and persuading, then all of a sudden it can happen in the blink of an eye. You're never sure you've secured the deal until the player has actually signed on the dotted line. My first signing which raised more than a few eyebrows was that of Dean Glover from First Division Middlesbrough for a club record £200,000 fee in February 1989; not because anyone questioned whether Dean was any good – he was clearly a very good central defender – but because people thought the fee had one nought too many! After all, the previous higest fee we had spent at the Vale had been £40,000, but first Bob Hazell's retirement and then Phil Sproson's injury shortly afterwards, which led to me offloading him to Birmingham for £60,000, forced my hand in terms of needing to recruit and Dean was someone I'd had my eye on for year. He was actually the player I had gone to scout when I spotted Ray Walker in Aston Villa's reserves five years earlier. Dean had moved on to Middlesbrough to play first-team football, but was now out of favour. He was an established player, though, so came with a price tag. Thankfully, I had been able to generate enough money to afford him.

Rather than being a like-for-like replacement for either Hazell or Sproson, Dean brought a new dimension to the team as we could now really play out from the back thanks to Dean's cultured left foot, which brought silky skills, rather than mere brawn, to the heart of our defence. He was not over-blessed with pace, but read the game exceptionally well, which meant he could also play in midfield. I must give credit to Bill Bell for sanctioning the deal. He was not frightened to part with money if it was available, nor was he shy of pushing me to sell if needs be.

Despite that enormous fee for Port Vale, Dean proved to be excellent value for money, starring for over ten years. I remember his debut was against Wolves and their legendary striker Steve Bull, who was a dynamo and, incredibly, earned an England cap at the end of that season whilst playing in the Third Division. Dean kept Bull quiet as we drew 0-0 with the runaway leaders. He helped us become known as a good footballing team, starting with that promotion campaign of 1988/89, which he arrived half-way through to spur us on when all seemed lost after Sproson and Hazell retired.

Over time, Dean picked up long-term ankle and back injuries which we had to manage him through, but he battled back to be ever-present in 1993/94 and was selected in the PFA's Second Division team of the year. His reputation may be as a quality player, but Dean had some grit and determination as well.

Alongside Dean, forming an incredible partnership which lives on in legend, synonymous with my great Vale side of the 1990s, was Neil Aspin. Neil arrived in July 1989, following our promotion to the Second Division for another sizeable fee for Vale; £140,000. I spoke with Howard Wilkinson, who was by now manager at Leeds and had just won promotion into the top flight, who told me that, although Neil would not be good enough for him in the First Division, if I took him, he would be my next captain.

Howard was right. Neil was voted Player of the Season in his first campaign, helping us establish ourselves in the second tier. During a ten-season stay at Vale Park, he made 410 appearances in all competitions, being named in the PFA's Second Division team of the year in 1993/94 alongside Dean, but pipping Glover to the Supporters' Player of the Year award. Neil was wonderful for me and I once told the press I would not sell him at any price and did well to beat off a challenge yet again from Stoke City, this time when Lou Macari was manager and a big admirer of Aspin.

Neil was very different to his centre-back partner. He didn't have silky touches or great passing ability, but he was as strong as an ox, a good marker and an adept tackler who earned respect throughout the game as an honest and genuine professional who gave everything. They dovetailed brilliantly, complementing each other perfectly, becoming the heartbeat of our team throughout that incredible 1992/93 season, the 1993/94 promotion campaign, reaching the Anglo-Italian Cup Final and the push for promotion to the Premier League in 1996/97.

£340,000 very well spent, then. When you consider that those two cost significantly more than the £212,000 I had thus far spent on all of my signings collectively since becoming manager five years earlier, then you can see how this was a sea-change in transfer policy at the club.

As his manager, I found Neil could be a bit strange at times; sometimes he could just go missing, being completely uncommunicative. Despite this, I made him captain on occasions, although it would usually be Dean or Andy Porter when they were available. Both Aspin and Glover have gone on to coach and manage Port Vale, which gives me enormous pride to think that my influence has continued for so long and in fact my relationship with Neil was reignited more recently, as I will explain later.

Centre-halves were crucial for me and so it should come as no surprise that I spent good money on them. They are the fulcrum of any team and I was to spend big again when signing Peter Swan from Hull for £310,000 in 1991. Now I had three great centre-halves, I sometimes played with all three, either with Glover as a defensive midfielder, or with Aspin at right-back, or with all three as centre-halves, utilising wing-backs, depending on how I saw each game. It gave me great flexibility.

Later on, I signed some younger centre-halves who did very well for me, although we didn't spend big money on them. They were very raw and so came via my old-school scouting routes. The first was Gareth Griffiths, who I signed from Rhyl in February 1993 for £1,000, plus another £6,000 based on appearances, which was paid once Gareth proved his worth to us, which he did fairly quickly once he broke into the side in February 1994 to play a part in the end of that season's promotion. Gareth became a regular in our First Division team in the mid-90s and I regularly had to fight off big-money approaches to take him off us. However, a succession of injuries, including a difficult groin problem, then restricted his first-team appearances and scuppered any chance of a move.

During that time, Gareth served on the management committee of the Professional Footballers' Association, reporting directly to chief executive Gordon Taylor and other senior members of the management board, later becoming a trustee. Whilst playing, he obtained a first-class honours degree, a post-graduate marketing certificate, and qualified as a financial consultant. He's a smart lad, so Gareth is actually now my financial advisor, who I see regularly.

The other young centre-half of note I signed cost us nothing as he was developed through our apprenticeship and reserve team route. Anthony Gardner was a quality young defender, good on the ball and great in the air; a perfect combination. It didn't take long for his talent to attract suitors and it was clear we couldn't hold on to him as he would go on to play in the Premier League for Spurs and Hull, whilst earning an England cap in March 2004 versus Sweden.

Anthony signed pro aged just 17 and I gave him his debut a few months before I lost my job. He was eventually sold to Tottenham after the Vale were relegated in 2000, earning Vale £855,000. I'm claiming at least part of that profit too.

* * *

In midfield, Paul Kerr arrived from Millwall in July 1992 for a £140,000 fee. Paul was a firebrand who needed careful handling, but he could prove the difference in winning matches with his inspired runs from midfield, never better exemplified than in scoring that fantastic opening goal in our 1993 Autoglass Trophy win.

Another goalscoring midfielder was Ian Bogie, hero of those mid-90s Potteries derbies, who also scored at Everton in the 2-2 draw and in the replay when we beat the FA Cup holders. Ian was a very good player with a vicious shot. He wasn't the biggest, but his ability on the ball was excellent. I spotted him playing in Newcastle's reserves, although didn't sign him until March 1995 by which time he was at Orient. My mate Hugh Gallagher cracks on to me constantly that it was he who actually spotted Ian. Hugh occasionally used to keep me company on some of the long journeys and we'd have conversations whilst watching games in which I'd ask Hugh, 'Come on then, who do you think is any good?' Hugh claims that in response he put Ian Bogie in my mind in answering that once.

But perhaps I am most associated with signing a series of foreign players to patrol the midfield in the 1990s, which was another complete change of tack in Port Vale's transfer dealings. Previously the most exotic signings were Paul Millar and Gary McKinstry, who both arrived from Portadown in Northern Ireland. However, the first of the overseas stars, Robin van der Laan, only arrived at Vale Park due to a unique combination of circumstances.

Over the years, my networking meant I had developed great contacts overseas, one being Piet Buter, who was manager of Dutch clubs like Wageningen and FC Eindhoven (not their more famous neighbours PSV) in the early 1990s, and another called Jan de Koning, who had been a good enough player in his time to appear as a forward in the same Ajax team and Dutch under-21 side as the likes of Johan Cruyff, Johan Neeskens, Ruud Krol and Johnny Rep. Jan had become renowned for his eye for talent and both became good friends of mine and helped me a lot, starting with the arrival of van der Laan.

I got a call one day from Piet, who was manager of Wageningen at this point and had a bit of a situation he needed some help with. He told me, 'I've got this player who has just been suspended as he broke someone's leg and can't play in Holland for four months, but he could play in England.'

So, I said to send him over.

Robin turned out to be strong, powerful and both good on the ball and in the air. I could see immediately he would be able to cope with the demands of the English game. In fact, I felt he was better suited to England than the continent as he was so powerful. He came on loan at first, but then we signed him permanently in February 1991 as he was a snip at £80,000.

Once Robin had worked out so well, I used that route on regular occasions in search of more stars, bringing in the likes of midfielders Nico Jalink, Mark Snijders and Rogier Koordes, defender Jermaine Holwyn and goalkeeper Arjan van Heusden, for combined fees of just £84,500, so it bore great fruit for me. Swedish midfielder Jan

Jansson then arrived from Norrkoping in Norway for £200,000 after a loan spell in 1997, as I sought to take advantage of the growing pool of talent in Scandinavia.

* * *

Up front, I had a settled, in-form striker in Martin Foyle who I was constantly trying to find partners for. Nicky Cross was nearing the end of his career. He had scored 12 goals in 1992/93 and then 13 as we won promotion the following season, but that was the right time to move Nicky on, so I gave him a free transfer to Hereford United and in July 1994 brought in Lee Glover from Nottingham Forest for £200,000, plus an extra £25,000 based on appearances. Lee, though, struggled to hold down that second striker's spot as another new arrival, Tony Naylor, an exceptionally good goalscorer, built an effective partnership with Foyle.

Tony was tiny at 5ft 7in, but he had pace and tenacity and could finish clinically. I paid £150,000 for him from neighbours Crewe and he scored nearly 90 goals for the club in just under 300 appearances. Signing Tony was a no-brainer as far as I was concerned as he'd proved himself in helping the Alex to promotion from Division Three the season before I signed him. He became a mainstay of the team that kept us in the First Division (as the second tier had been renamed) throughout the rest of the 1990s. In 1996/97, Tony bagged 20 goals, including a wonderful hat-trick at Charlton in a 3-1 victory whilst playing as a lone striker. He finished as top scorer both that season and the one before, as well as, after I left, in 2000/01, when the club won the Football League Trophy once again. I remember one particular brace he got against Sunderland in August 1997 when his sublime skill and ability to turn on a sixpence using his twinkling feet turned their defence into statues.

Just after we signed Tony, there was one famous occasion I remember when I missed out on some fabulous young talent I'd spotted. We drew Alex Ferguson's Manchester United in the second round of the 1994/95 League Cup. With United having won their first double under Fergie just a few months before, both our fans and theirs expected their manager to field the likes of Ryan Giggs, Eric Cantona and Steve Bruce. But for the first leg at Vale Park, Fergie didn't play his usual first team, instead opting to play the 'kids', as Alan Hansen was so famously to dub them shortly afterwards. When I saw the team sheet, I couldn't believe all these names I'd never heard of; Beckham, Butt, Gillespie, Scholes, Davies, two lads called Neville, for example, all making their first or second starts for the club. And the visiting supporters were going barmy about his selection. However, as per usual, Fergie proved he knew what he was doing. Despite us taking the lead after just seven minutes when Glover touched Bradley Sandeman's raking 25-yard shot past Gary Walsh with a deft headed deflection, United won 1-2, with Paul Scholes scoring both goals, the first two of his 155 for the club. Late on van der Laan was clean through on goal, but fired over from eight yards. He should have done better with that chance and it meant the tie was over. United beat us 2-0 in their home leg with a similar team to secure a 1-4 aggregate victory.

After that I tried to get Fergie to loan me some of those young stars to help their 'development'. He wasn't having any of it, although slightly annoyingly he did loan Beckham to Preston for part of that same season; and Fergie claims I was the one who was the pain in the arse!

Anyway, those youngsters had quite decent careers without my input, I believe.

* * *

When Martin Foyle began to fade out of the picture, Naylor became equally effective as the perfect partner alongside another new arrival, Lee Mills. They formed a fearsome attack for us through the mid-to-late 1990s, which proved to be one of the most successful periods in the club's history. But thereby hangs a tale of transfers and trading.

Rewind to 1989 and I had a problem with a bad-boy striker who didn't score goals; not a great combination, I'm sure you'll agree. He may have been popular as a local lad, but Ronnie Jepson gave me headaches. He started only 14 games and never scored a goal, yet the part he played in the development of the club was huge, albeit accidental. Although I had been told Ronnie had a reputation and was a bit of a nightmare, I signed him for nothing from Nantwich Town in spring 1989 just after he had managed to clear his name in a trial in Belgium for his alleged involvement in the Heysel Stadium disaster of 1985, being finally found not guilty. Ronnie was in and out of the team as he missed a couple of sitters, especially one against Stoke which he must still be reliving in his nightmares, and I sent him off on loan to Peterborough United for three months, where he at least found the back of the net five times. But he never did for Vale, even on his return. Strikers that don't score goals are, ultimately, not much good, no matter how much I liked Ronnie as a lad.

This coincided with the opportunity to sign Robin van der Laan permanently for £80,000, but I had precisely no money in the coffers. The answer? Sell Jepson for £80k, which I duly did to Preston in February 1991, effectively netting me my new midfielder for free.

Ronnie, by the way, is now a highly respected coach and during the writing of this book went back to Huddersfield under Neil Warnock.

Then, because van der Laan performed so well for me, there was plenty of interest in him and, in July 1995, when a bid of £350,000, rising to £475,000 with appearances, came in from Jim Smith at Derby, I knew I would lose him. I tried to get Jim to pay more, but instead he offered to throw in his own unwanted striker, Lee Mills, who he didn't see as part of his own plans to win promotion to the Premier League (which Derby did that season).

Lee had started at Wolves and scored six goals in 33 games before moving to Derby the year before he became available to me.

In that season he had only played 16 games, many as sub, but he'd scored seven goals, almost one in every two games. He seemed good to me, so I agreed to Jim's excellent suggestion, took the money on offer, with Mills as the 'makeweight'. So, effectively, I got Lee for nothing.

I then used that van der Laan money to fund the vast majority of the £450,000 fee I paid to sign Jon McCarthy from York City. Jon would be sold to Birmingham City in September 1997 for £1.5 million, although £200,000 of that had to be paid to his previous club York to fulfil their sell-on clause.

So, starting with a free transfer in Jepson, who then funded the arrival of van der Laan, the pair of whose sales netted me just under half a million, I now had Lee Mills and Jon McCarthy. I got three great seasons out of my new striker, who bagged 44 goals for Vale alongside Naylor, before selling him on to Bradford for £1 million in August 1998, plus two fantastic seasons out of McCarthy before he was sold on for £1.5 million to Birmingham.

In pure cash terms, I spent just £75,000 of the club's money to generate a profit of £2.3 million.

How to turn dust to gold in three steps.

* * *

Mills proved the perfect partner for Naylor and cemented his place in Vale fans' hearts when, in October 1996, he came off the bench to score that injury-time equaliser in a Potteries derby game at Vale Park. He finished 1996/97 with 15 goals and was voted Player of the Year, before finishing as top scorer with 16 goals in 1997/98.

Around that time, full freedom of contract came in following the Bosman ruling. I realised very quickly that it would present me with a significant problem as we couldn't barter as well with big clubs when they came calling for our best players. Just before the ruling became law, I negotiated a 12-month contract extension for Lee, while he was on the treatment table following a bad injury, for which he was very grateful at the time. The thing was, I knew something he didn't; that I was delivering this extremely generous gesture so he wouldn't be out of contract and thus able to leave for nothing at the end of the season. Lee signed the extension at 11.45am before the Bosman ruling was made law at 2pm. The players thought I'd completely stitched Lee up with that and I took a lot of stick. I told them I was completely unaware of the Bosman ruling coming in. They didn't believe me.

The following season we were clearly going to lose Mills, not least because Bradford City, who were building a team which won promotion to the Premier League, made a £1 million bid for him. Bill Bell bit their hand off for the cash and Lee's head was turned with becoming the Bantams' first million-pound signing and chasing the big time, as we had only just avoided relegation after being a promotion-chasing team the season before. When Lee gave an interview to the press saying, 'Three years at Port Vale is enough for anybody,' it was clear he would be leaving. Thank heavens I had 'organised' that contract extension as Lee still had that one year left and so we could benefit from the fee when otherwise he could have just moved on for nothing. Perhaps fuelled by me 'stitching him up', Lee scored twice in a 0-4 thrashing his new club dealt out to us early in the 1998/99 season, as he went on to score 24 goals to propel Bradford to promotion. Lee also scored on his return to Vale Park in a 1-1 draw later in the campaign, perhaps having been given a point to prove after a matchday programme article described him as 'poor' and his touch as 'frequently awful'. Unwise, but nothing to do with me as I wasn't around by then.

* * *

Playing the way I did and having those great strikers to feed meant I needed and loved wingers. As I've mentioned it was a position I had a particular affinity with and I felt I could spot a good one, having signed the likes of Jon Jeffers, Ian Miller and Gary Ford early in my managerial career.

I signed my next winger, Kevin Kent, in March 1991, a few days after he had put in a superb performance against us for Mansfield, including scoring a great goal. I paid £80,000 and threw in Gary Ford, who by this time had hit 30, was carrying an ankle injury, and had cost me only £35,000 four years earlier. Kevin became a mainstay of the team that won the Autoglass Trophy and then promotion over the next three years. Sadly, injuries brought his career to a halt after he fractured his hand in October 1994 and his kneecap the following February, before being hospitalised in May 1995 with a back problem; this final injury brought about his early retirement at the end of the 1995/96 season, but I recruited him on to the coaching staff.

My mid-90s Vale team is associated with a pair of wingers I unearthed who delivered the goods for me consistently; Steve Guppy and Jon McCarthy.

I had been tracking Steve since he burst on to the scene with Martin O'Neill's Wycombe. He was such hot property that Kevin Keegan paid £150,000 to take him to Premier League Newcastle in August 1994, but, just three months later and having made one, sole League Cup substitute appearance for the Magpies, I managed to persuade Kevin that there was no point keeping Steve in the reserves, so I paid £225,000 for his services in November 1994.

Steve tells a great story about arriving in the Potteries and seeing the local newspaper headline 'Vale sign Premiership star' and thinking, 'Great! Who have they signed?' But of course the headline was about him, despite the fact that he had never played in the Premier League.

Steve was a very tricky left-winger who had great crossing ability. Not surprisingly, given his talent, he became a firm fan favourite and is now classed as a club legend after his memorable performances. I remember in particular how he caused Everton so many problems in that classic cup giant-killing. He was one of those utterly committed players who goes above and beyond. I recall one day we had finished training and because we still hadn't got great facilities at the club I went over to Keele University to see if we could borrow theirs. Lo and behold, who should I see there doing extra training into the late afternoon/early evening but Steve, working on his own with a couple of balls. When he saw me, he pleaded with me not to tell the other players as they would think him a bit of a swot. I told him how proud I was of him, 'Steve, it just shows how dedicated you are.'

I tried desperately to hang on to him, especially as we were gunning for promotion in 1996/97, but the temptation of finally getting into the Premier League proved too much and Steve was tempted away in February 1997 to join his former boss O'Neill, who paid £950,000 to take him to Leicester, where he won a well-deserved full England cap.

On the opposite wing McCarthy arrived in July 1995 for that club record fee of £450,000, mostly funded by my Jepson/van der Laan/ Mills scenario. He won Player of the Season in 1995/96, helped us reach the Anglo-Italian Cup Final, then come close to the play-offs in the following 1996/97 campaign. I thought that record fee was a great investment and so it proved both financially, given how much we made on his sale, but more importantly on what he gave to the team. He scored the winning goal in that Everton FA Cup victory after putting in an incredible performance that night, finishing off Guppy's cross. Jon's style was to drive at his opponent and beat them with pace. Like Steve, he became an international, winning 18 caps for Northern Ireland, for whom he qualified through his father.

McCarthy and Guppy were a smashing pair of wingers and their sales, while inevitable, brought in a total of £2.45 million. My problem was replacing their talent and dedication.

I struggled to find a left-sided alternative for Guppy, but, after Jon left, I replaced him with Gareth Ainsworth, who I signed from Lincoln for a new club record transfer fee of £500,000, which is still to this day Port Vale's record fee paid for any player. Gareth was a great replacement for McCarthy, with pace, power, strength, aggression and the ability to score goals. I had to shape his play away from the long ball that he had been educated in to passing to feet and playing one-twos, but he was another who practised and practised and became a fabulous player for us and I still keep in touch with him. In fact, during the writing of this book, just before he left Wycombe to move to Queens Park Rangers, he agreed to speak at a special dinner arranged to raise funds for the statue this book is also raising money for. It was a wonderful occasion and I wish Gareth all the best with his career.

However, Gareth would eventually play an unwitting part in my departure from the club, the whole episode of which I will reveal later.

* * *

Despite all those amazing players and great tales of transfers and what it takes to be successful in recruitment, my favourite story from my time managing Port Vale is the one surrounding the signing of dynamic midfielder Ian Taylor.

It all started in May 1992, when I sent Ray Williams to watch a striker I'd heard a lot about called Darren Roberts, who played for Burton Albion and would later sign for Wolves. However, the report Ray handed me told me not to bother going to see Roberts, but to go and watch this young midfielder who was playing for Southern League Premier Division opponents Moor Green instead, as he was a player of considerable potential. It had proved to be extremely difficult to replace Robbie Earle's industry and goals from the middle of the field when he left, so stumbling on Taylor, who was a forklift truck driver by day, was a real bonus.

We became aware that Notts County were also hot on his heels, so I rang the Moor Green manager and asked if Taylor could come and train with us, but he said no as the player was due to sign for County fairly shortly and in any case his club had a Midlands Floodlit Cup Final at West Brom to prepare for later that week. I had to see Taylor for myself, of course, but knowing that the Magpies were intent on signing him I had to move fast and smartly. A plan began to formulate in my mind.

Come the night of the cup final, Notts County's manager Neil Warnock was unable to attend as he had taken his squad away to Spain on an end of season jolly. Instead, his chairman Derek Pavis had been detailed to complete the deal after the game if he was satisfied with what he saw.

Pre-match, Ray Williams and I lurked in the pub near the Hawthorns and listened in to Pavis and his acolytes talking about their transfer target. Then, at the game, in the directors' box, I made sure Ray and I sat next to Pavis, who, being totally inexperienced in this recruitment lark, told me he was looking at the Moor Green number 10 (Taylor). I said I was only interested in the number 8 – whoever he was! I knew if he thought I was interested in Taylor, then he would snap him up immediately.

I spent the entire game tutting about the standard of play, placing as much doubt as I could into Pavis's mind and then, in a predetermined move, left the game 15 minutes early, claiming the player I was looking at was poor … along with everyone else. I then hid in my car, which was still parked in the pub car park across from the ground. About an hour after the match, Pavis and his entourage left in his Rolls-Royce as I cowered behind the wheel so as not to be seen. As they departed, I overheard them discussing that they had not made a deal as Pavis, being typically mean, would only offer £10,000 instead of the £15,000 Moor Green wanted. When Ray returned to me, he confirmed this as he had been left behind to be my eyes and ears.

We were in with a chance.

Knowing that Neil would still want Taylor's signature, but being able to take advantage of this being well before mobile phones were a thing, I rang Moor Green's manager the next morning to confirm I would pay the £15,000 to match their valuation, plus another £10,000 based on appearances in the next two seasons, outbidding the stingy Pavis. Deal agreed with the club, I now had to convince the player and lured Taylor to Vale Park the day before Neil returned. Ian remained adamant he would not commit himself to a deal until he had spoken to Warnock. He had principles and had given his word.

Worried we could lose him just when everything seemed set fair, I excused myself and rang Bill Bell from another room to ask for another £5,000 cash as a signing-on fee for Ian. I could hear Bill was in a pub and was hopeful, as lubrication often mellowed him. Even I was surprised at the speed with which he replied, 'You can have what you want, Stoke have just got beat in the play-offs' (to Stockport on 13 May 1992) and so, after agreeing to that sweetener on the grounds that if he went home without signing it was off the table, at 11.20pm Ian Taylor signed a hand-written contract, prepared by the club secretary who had hung around all evening just in case.

The next afternoon I got a call from Neil Warnock.

'Alright, Rudgie? What's happening?'

'What do you mean, Neil?'

'What's this about you being interested in signing Ian Taylor? I sent my chairman to look at him and he is signing for us.'

'He won't be,' I said. 'He's already signed for us.'

Neil's reply is unprintable.

But that's the dog-eat-dog world of lower-league football management. You have to be one step ahead if you are going to succeed.

Although Warnock was annoyed with me, he was absolutely furious with his chairman and phoned me later on in the season to tell me that every time he saw Taylor had scored for us on the results service in the boardroom after their games, he would tease Pavis about it!

Ian was the replacement for Robbie Earle I had been searching for, becoming the hub of our team. In his first season he top-scored with 15 goals and earned himself the Player of the Year accolade as well as a place in the PFA Second Division team of the year, but that was the ultimately disappointing 1992/93 campaign, which may have seen Ian part of the Autoglass Trophy victory, a memory of which is Ian's stunning overhead kick against Fulham in an incredible 4-3 victory in our opening round, but ended in defeat in the play-off final. The following season he was once again selected in the PFA's divisional team of the season as we won promotion with Taylor starring.

There was no holding on to Ian once the Premier League came calling that summer in the shape of Sheffield Wednesday and he moved for a tribunal-set fee of £1 million, with Moor Green receiving another £50,000 as their sell-on clause money. Getting two excellent seasons and over £900,000 profit from the deal, plus the way it came about in the first place, actually getting one over Neil Warnock, means that for me, not only was that another £30,000 well invested, but it remains my favourite Vale transfer tale.

There was one sour note, though. Great though Bill Bell had been in agreeing to that deal-making signing-on fee, he greatly disappointed me when I asked the board if they would pay Ray Williams a bonus for his 'million-pound find' after Taylor's sale, but they would only agree to a small fee and a set of tracksuits, which led to Ray being disgruntled and eventually leaving the club over a row about having to pay for cup tickets. That was one of many annoying sideshows which surrounded many of these transfer tales, more of which anon.

* * *

One signing I never made was a young, local lad, whose parents kept the pub by the ground. He and his mate used to constantly hang around outside the club. One of them, now star of stage and screen Jonathan Wilkes, signed as a schoolboy for Everton, so I really missed out there. The other never made it in football, but went on to have a decent secondary career in popular music. Yes, of course, I am talking about the legend that is Robbie Williams!

I've known Robbie since he was knee-high to a grasshopper. I remember in my early years as manager we were invited to a party in Burslem and his mum, who I knew from the pub, told me her son was going to sing. He was only about 15 then. After he'd done a couple of songs I turned to his mum and said, 'Hey, Robbie isn't a bad singer, is he?!'

Simon Cowell I am not.

Not only did Robbie become world famous as one fifth of Take That, but he did so whilst often wearing gear from the Port Vale club shop, thus making the club known around the world. Once he moved on to develop an even more starry solo career, on stage Robbie would always bang on about supporting Vale and he now has a suite named after him at the ground.

I remember, when he was in Take That, Robbie used to creep into Vale Park with his latest girlfriend and sit next to Del and his mum some time after kick-off, to avoid being mobbed. Needless to say, when we went to his concerts, unlike Robbie's method of entry into Vale Park, I didn't have to sneak in with my cap drawn low down over my head. Del and I became big friends with Robbie's mum and we went out with her and her partner a lot and our daughter Lisa got to know Robbie so well he came to her wedding.

Despite never formally signing the young hopeful, I managed Robbie on a couple of occasions when he and Jon asked me to. The first occasion arrived when the pair persuaded me to manage a team of Potteries celebrities versus a Variety Club team made up of celebs from around the country, which included the likes of Ant and Dec. Den Siegertsz, the legendary BBC Radio Stoke DJ, reminded me recently that he played in that game, but got injured ten minutes before half-time after the actor Philip Olivier, who played Tinhead in Channel 4's *Brookside*, flattened him in a tackle, buckling his knees backwards as he fell on him. Den was pleading with me to take him off as he could barely walk – 'Gaffer, you're killing me 'ere!' I remember him pleading – but I kept him on as there were only a few minutes to go to the break. As Den hobbled off at half-time never to return, I 'sympathised' with him, saying, 'This football lark is a bit of a tougher world than spinning records, isn't it, Den!' He rarely misses an opportunity to remind me of that!

Just after I was sacked in 1999, I also managed Robbie and Jon's team in the first Sports Aid charity match, called Soccer 6, which was held at Chelsea's Stamford Bridge. This was the precursor for what is now the major international Soccer Aid UNICEF fundraising game which takes place each summer. We thought we had done well to get 25,000 fans to come to a fun day out for that first game – nowadays it is a total sell-out at Old Trafford with over 75,000 fans and an accompanying TV show beamed around the world, featuring international superstars such as Usain Bolt, Paddy McGuinness and Liam Payne.

After that game in 1999, Robbie went on to Kylie Minogue's celeb-filled party, while I took Del out for an Italian in Chelsea. How the other half live, eh? I bet he still regrets me not signing him for the Vale, though.

* * *

I am extremely proud of my record of buying and selling players. Port Vale could not have progressed without the money generated from those deals that, over 15 years, yielded more than a £5 million net profit. I have a list of all the signings I made and one with all the players I sold which you'll find in the photo section that show how the £5 million profit was made; not bad when you consider the parlous state of the club when John McGrath and I arrived in January 1980.

I used to feel a huge sense of achievement in making a good deal that would benefit the Vale. In fact, I spent the club's money as if it were my own and never liked to think I had paid through the nose for a player, always considering the investment and what could be realised when the player was sold. Perhaps I may have been too cautious at times, but I was always mindful of the club's financial situation and aware of how easy it was to throw money away on bad signings. Ultimately, though, what I would like to say is that there were very few players I signed who ever let me down. In fact, quite the opposite; they were mostly magnificent.

I am often asked, though, of all these great players, who was the best signing I ever made? The answer to that question is easy; my wife, Del. I simply wouldn't have been able to do any of it without her.

Chapter 11

The Wonderful World of Bill Bell

'Bill was Bill; irrepressible, indomitable and true to his entrepreneurial spirit. But my God he was a pain in the arse.'

John Rudge

AFTER SPENDING all that time toiling to drag Port Vale up the league, to even be higher than Stoke City, how could I ever leave them? And yet, here I was in the summer close-xcccdcflooooop;season of 1997 verbally agreeing with Stoke chairman Peter Coates that I would take the job, succeeding Lou Macari, who had just resigned.

On the positive side, I really liked the idea of taking charge of a big club, entering a new era at the sparkling new Britannia Stadium high up on the hill at the new Trentham Lakes development, but, the fact that I gave the offer such serious consideration shows how fed up I had become with the bonkers lunacy that I had been suffering at Port Vale over the intervening, if mainly glorious, years. It was, quite frankly, a ridiculous soap opera which if scriptwriters penned, would get rejected as too outlandish, weird and downright absurd.

And yet it happened and nothing I had learned in all those sessions at Lilleshall could have ever prepared me for dealing with a chairman like mine.

This is the story of my often-tempestuous relationship with Bill Bell.

* * *

Bill was an archetypal, old-school northern businessman, streetwise like a market trader, who knew how many pounds made five. I have to be fair to him from the outset, Bill always backed me in the transfer market, as I've shown, and I had a lot of support from him over many years after he took over the chairmanship of the club from Jim Lloyd in May 1987, when Jim resigned due to his deteriorating relationship with the rest of the board. But – and this is a very big but – Bill was Bill, a one-off in many ways; irrepressible, indomitable and true to his entrepreneurial spirit. But my God he was a pain in the arse.

Simply put, Bill and I were like oil and water. He was shrewd to the point of being underhand, bullish, aspirational and a showman. Coupled with my rather less combustible personality and financial prudence, for many years, this proved very much the right mix to be successful.

Bill was Vale through and through. As a young man, he had actually been one of the construction workers who built Vale Park in the 1940s. After becoming a self-made man, he had joined the board in early 1984, then became the club's second-highest shareholder in April 1986, before taking over from Lloyd after what I now understand was something of a coup.

In order to understand my relationship with Bill, you need to know how I became manager. After John McGrath's sacking in 1983, with the club having less than no money, I did well enough during my caretaker spell to be considered for the job. By March we were looking as if we might survive, which had initially seemed impossible. Jim Lloyd wanted me, but Bill Bell and his two sidekicks outnumbered the chairman and his one supporter, commercial director Mick Cullerton. Bell wanted an external appointment, but partly because I'd done well and partly because it was cheaper (and,

I'm sure, partly to annoy Bell), Lloyd was determined to appoint me. So, instead of having a vote on the lines of numbers of board members, he proposed a vote based on shareholding. As he held 51 per cent of the shares at the time, he won instantly and I was appointed.

Cut to summer 1987 and, as his first act as chairman in front of the media, Bill stated that he was 'not afraid to cut loose any dead wood'. I wondered whether this may be a not-particularly veiled threat towards me, although at that stage he was nothing but pleasant to my face. I realised then, though, that I was in for a bumpy ride, not least because I was never really his man, having been appointed by the previous chairman. That we lasted another decade or more together is quite remarkable.

The thing was, due to our success, he couldn't really get rid of me, despite our tempestuous relationship. He nearly did, as I later found out, when we had that poor run in late 1987, early in his chairmanship, and almost went out to Macclesfield in the FA Cup before the glorious win over Spurs in January 1988. Perhaps the fact that came so early in his reign saved me as I was most certainly far more popular than him and the supporters backed me then as they did throughout my time at the Vale. In fact, the supporters kept me in a job on many occasions as their backing kept the board from pulling the trigger. They were so good to me over the years.

But Bill hated that; he couldn't stand me getting all the glory and wanted plenty for himself. I'm sure he often had his friends in his ear telling him it was his money I was spending to make myself look good. Well, as you've seen, nothing could have been further from the truth. I made the club over £5 million in transfer profit alone, let alone the gate money three promotions and all those cup victories brought in. Don't forget that the supporters raised half the money to sign Darren Beckford when Bill wouldn't dip his hand in his pocket for more than £7,500 either. And there was always an underlying attitude that the signings had to be right and the buck stopped with me, which was, of course, fair enough. Managers live and die by the success of their transfer dealings, and rightly so. I felt, though, that my record was as good as any in the game and yet I still had to suffer various issues and ignominies along the bumpy way.

* * *

You won't be surprised to hear that Bill's car dealership was eponymously titled 'WT Bell' and he would use his second-hand motors to lure players to sign for the club; a typical sweetener to seal a deal, like Bob Hazell's free transfer signing from Reading and Andy Hill's arrival from Manchester City. That wasn't unusual and, indeed, I myself had been enticed by that Lada offered by a different director back in 1980, so I knew how that worked and made the most of the benefit that the chairman allowed me to offer to players to capture their signatures.

However, ever the typical second-hand car salesman, Bill was renowned for sharp practices such as 'clocking' those cars to make them seem a lot more attractive than they should have been. How do I know this? Let me tell you the tale of Ian Miller, who I was in the process of signing from Blackburn after winning promotion in 1989. While I was negotiating wages and suchlike with Ian, he told me he wanted a car as he would have to commute from Manchester and his wife needed their own vehicle to take their kids to school.

'Well, that's lucky,' I said, 'our chairman can help with that.'

So, we found ourselves down at Bill's garage and I left Ian there discussing which car he was going to have in order to get him to sign on the dotted line.

The next day, deal done, I introduced Ian to the rest of the lads as our newest recruit and asked him how he had got on with the chairman. 'Very well,' Miller said. 'He got me a smashing car – a red Rover and it's only got 23,000 miles on the clock.'

There was a snort from amongst the players and one piped up, 'What's the registration plate?' Ian told them.

'That's funny because I had that red Rover last year and drove at least 48,000 miles in it … !' Bill's garage was down a longish hill in Burslem and his showroom was packed full of such cars. Almost always you would find him in full view out the front with a fag or cigar, blowing his trademark clouds of smoke. Always, that was, until he observed my car coming down the hill. Quick as a flash, he'd be off. Gone. I'd go into the garage reception and his staff mysteriously couldn't find him. I knew where he'd be; hiding out the back finishing that smoke, avoiding me because he knew I'd be asking for money to spend. That wasn't exactly a sound basis for a relationship between manager and chairman from the start and it didn't really get much better.

No manager is ever going to agree 100 per cent of the time with their board, but we have to respect their right to run their club as they see fit and get out of the kitchen if it becomes too hot. I have to say, not just myself, but pretty much everyone often disagreed with Bill, but his passion for Burslem and for the Vale was never in doubt. There were, however, many odd things which happened. For example, I remember once a car went on fire at his garage, but Bill didn't seem too concerned. That confused me. Then there were instances when Bill would go to an auction and buy a load of stuff for pennies, which he then brought into the ground. I asked him, 'What's all this?' and he told me he was going to auction it off to raise funds. Innovative, but odd.

In the 1980s most supporters paid cash at the turnstiles to get in, rather than by card in advance on the internet as it is now, and consequently the club collected a lot of cash. Bill would often be seen carrying boxes of it to who knows where. It could have been the bank, but I wasn't aware of any branches open at 7pm on a Saturday night.

Bill was always trying to get away with things; for example, avoiding paying what he owed. I've already mentioned the board's attitude to the great scouts who found us all those wonderful players, which I found totally unacceptable, not least because it eventually meant they upped and left, fed up with the treatment. I always remember Ray Williams being made to pay for tickets for cup ties by Bell; atrocious considering the millions of pounds worth of talent he scouted for us over the years.

But it could be players too. Bob Hazell had battled gamely with a back injury until he could go on no further. He was an inspirational figure in the dressing room and if he said it was Christmas in the middle of July, the lads would start singing carols! Sadly, midway through the 1988/89 season, Bob had to quit the game and retire. He departed, like so many others, with a sour taste in his mouth as the club tried to avoid paying him his just rewards, despite his efforts in beating Spurs and helping to pull us from the bottom of the league when he first arrived, but there was no recognition for his services, not even a thank you.

Then there was the nonsense surrounding the ticketing arrangements for the 1993 play-off final against West Brom at Wembley. Players and club officials had a certain allocation to use for family and friends. Not surprisingly, those got snapped up extremely quickly. On the day of the game, as we arrived at the stadium, I discovered that our team coach driver David Durber had, unbelievably, not been given a ticket. I would have given him one of mine, but I had run out of my allocation and, try as I might, couldn't get Dave a seat in the stands, despite there being thousands available as the attendance was a healthy 60,000, but there were over 25,000 seats available.

My answer? I sat Dave on the bench at the side of the pitch with us, making his day.

That whole ridiculous affair saddened me and added to the feeling of desolation when I sat in that dressing room, contemplating having to do it all over again the following season. Mixed in with those 'could I do it?' thoughts were, 'Do I have the energy to fight my own board over these petty situations?'

* * *

Somehow, throughout my time at Vale Park, despite having great times, promotions, Wembley visits and huge giant-killings against top clubs, the board of directors were never a happy ship and never easy to get on with as we swung from one crisis to another. I was very grateful for what they did, but they proved very difficult to work with and for. Bill could be particularly problematic. Our relations would be up and down like a yo-yo and he was often very frosty. It became very stressful, especially as often it was difficult to see why. It was always about money in many senses, but over the years we went from having absolutely none, to at least having some. So, it wasn't as if the club could go bankrupt anymore; thanks to my transfer dealings.

Looking back, I can now clearly see that almost all my major problems stemmed from the fact that the board simply did not get on with each other. It was never stable at all, despite having many incarnations during my almost two decades at Vale Park. They all had one consistent characteristic; infighting, featuring constant friction, discord and disharmony, which was why Jim Lloyd left as chairman. I quickly realised that the only thing I could rely on was that I couldn't ever rely on them doing what I wanted or needed when I needed it. Consequently, I found myself having constantly to play political games as a self-preservation mechanism, which became more and more draining over the years as they escalated. The comparison between the current Port Vale owners, the Shanahans, or indeed the Coates family at Stoke City, could not be more stark.

One example of this is that I always made sure Bill was intrinsically involved in signing players, just in case he tried to blame me for some kind of problem or failure. Once a deal was fundamentally agreed, I'd go to him and say, 'Right, these are his wages, this is his bonus structure, this is his length of contract, do you agree?'

Ensuring I got board sign-off was crucial for me because, certainly with Bill, you never knew when he would turn that against you and say, 'Crikey John, how much are you paying him?'

Note the word 'you' not 'we' at that point in a conversation.

So, I always had Bill there at the final stages to agree to the deal. That safeguard meant I could always say, 'Hang on a minute, Bill, you agreed it.'

On the one hand Bill didn't really interfere with my day-to-day running of the club. He probably only telephoned me five or six times in his entire chairmanship period and didn't ever say to me, 'Oh you should be playing him' or 'Why are you picking him?' That wasn't his style at all, unlike many chairmen.

On the other hand, he seemed to want to deliberately make things more difficult for me out of mischief; at least that was what it felt like. For example, there was the small matter of him interfering with my coaching team.

Alan Oakes was my first-team coach after I took over from John McGrath and was integral to our promotion in 1985/86. However, because he was my man, Bill was never happy with Alan being in post and, when that poor run of form saw us slump to the bottom of the Third Division table at Christmas time 1987, just a few months after Bill had taken over as chairman, he made good on his promise to 'cut loose any dead wood', sacking Alan and promoting youth team coach Mike Pejic, a former Stoke City legend, into the role. I had no say in this and no choice but to accept the situation and get on with it.

We turned that situation around thanks to that famous FA Cup run and our league form improved on the back of it. Did Bill Bell help by sacking Alan and promoting Pej? Perhaps. But he also risked undermining me entirely with the players as I looked like I couldn't organise my own management team. It was one of those situations in which I either had to bite the bullet and get on with things or walk out in protest. I was far too dedicated to my job at that stage to contemplate resigning, so I stayed. But it was the first of many instances of that kind of interference which would eventually lead to total implosion over a decade later. In fact, history would repeat itself in 1992 when Bell sacked Pejic, installing Bobby Downes as his replacement, again without asking me.

Bill and his board were always keen on the idea of a player-coach; it saved them some money, don't forget. Time and time again the subject would crop up on the agenda, but I never wavered in my opposition to the idea. It may sound like two for the price of one (which is why it sounded attractive to the directors), but my argument was always that if the man appointed was a player – and had to train hard as such – then when would he have time to coach? I just could not see it working. Yet Bell always fancied a big name and, in the mid-1990s, without asking me, tried to talk Manchester United's Brian McClair into joining us as player-coach. I am convinced Bill would have actually paid McClair more money than me in a bid to bolster the crowd and raise the profile of the club. Thankfully, it never came to anything.

The biggest issue surrounding my coaches would arrive in 1998, when the board took exception to my choice of first-team coach Phil Bonnyman, but more of that later.

* * *

It was perhaps refreshing that Bill Bell wouldn't interfere in team selection and actually coped with some poor runs of results at times, especially in early 1988, just before we turned things around, but there was one infamous occasion when he went ballistic about a poor defeat we suffered in the FA Cup at Division Three strugglers Scarborough in December 1994.

This was an unusual season because, despite us being in the First Division, we entered the FA Cup at the first round stage because the number of teams in the top two divisions was being reorganised as the Premier League moved from 22 to 20 clubs. Ourselves and Burnley were the two unlucky second-tier clubs to have to start in round one and we defeated Hartlepool 6-0 before being drawn away on the North Yorkshire coast. We were fairly lacklustre that day as we slumped to a 0-1 loss, which came amidst a run of only two wins in 16 league games, which wasn't exactly pleasing the board, although we had just won promotion a few months earlier, so were readjusting to life in the First Division and would eventually finish 17th.

We looked a sorry sight trooping on to the coach after the match. As I clambered aboard for the long trip home, I was given an envelope by our new physiotherapist, Rick Carter. Instead of coming to see me to express his understandable displeasure, Bill had handed a letter to him (not me, you'll notice). When I opened it, I read that Bill was directing us all to be in the following morning for extra training because we had embarrassed him. He never cleared that with me, but again I had no choice but to comply.

Bill publicly stated that defeat was 'unacceptable' and then, finally fronting up to me on the Monday, told me he'd heard that the players had sneaked out to go drinking in the pub across the road from the hotel we were staying in on the Friday night before the game on the Saturday.

'Who told you that?' I asked.

'Never you mind,' Bill replied. 'Were they?'

'That's a load of bollocks, Bill. We were all in there because there was a match on and the TV in the hotel lounge wasn't working, so we went to watch it. No one drank alcohol and I was there the whole time.'

He didn't believe me.

Remarkably, Bill's next move was to hire a solicitor to investigate the circumstances leading up to that FA Cup defeat. This was because the information about our activities in a public house had reached him via the travelling supporters' liaison police officer, who he trusted far more than my innocent explanation.

So, astonishingly, he sent his lawyer to Scarborough to look into the allegation.

It turned out not to be proven and I was extremely unhappy with the chairman's intervention – players do not need to be told when they have a bad game. I just about avoided having a showdown between him and the entire squad, who were livid at being falsely accused.

The aftermath of that incident could have gone one of two ways. It actually went both. We lost four of the next five league games and were struggling, with disaffected players at war with the board. But then Martin Foyle hit form and I tightened the defence up hugely to win four of the next five, conceding only two goals. We got through it, but the scars were beginning to mount. Bill and I ended up regularly not being on speaking terms, bizarrely leading to communication between chairman and manager being conducted solely by letter via club secretary Bill Lodey.

It wasn't just myself and other board members Bill fell out with, though. He regularly had huge and public spats with supporters. On 26 April 1996, the club announced that a deal with the council had been reached to joint-finance a £1.6 million outdoor sports complex at Bycars Park, but that never happened, which led to a huge wave of protests and, in October 1996, Bell put the entire squad up for sale and threatened to sell or liquidate the club if he received any further abuse from critical fans. No one came forward to buy the club, as the debt was revealed to be £1.5 million at that point as work to improve the stadium had swallowed up all the remaining profits on my transfer dealings that hadn't been reinvested into developing the squad. Remarkable then that this was the season in which we came so close to winning promotion to the Premier League.

* * *

One of the biggest problems I had to face at Port Vale came in the shape of one-time director Don McGrath. He was no longer on the board, but was appointed by Bell as 'supporter liaison officer'. McGrath set out to answer the supporters' queries as to where all the money had gone that had been accumulated from selling players, wanting to justify the club's claims it had gone on signing-on fees and wages. Prior to the meeting, I caught him red-handed in the secretary's office rummaging through player contracts, claiming he needed the figures as a shareholder. He had obviously been given permission by Bell to pry, but I was worried that he planned to present them to the supporters, which would be a clear betrayal of confidentiality in my opinion.

Sure enough, he spilled the beans on Andy Hill's contract, a player we had signed from Manchester City to cover a long-term injury to Neil Aspin. Andy was on a vastly greater wage than the other players, otherwise we would have not have been able to persuade him to sign. Through McGrath making this public, it duly became a big talking point in the dressing room and I now had a massive issue to manage where previously there had been none as everyone had been oblivious. I wrote to McGrath telling him he had made my job very difficult with re-negotiating players' contracts now they knew how much we were paying Hill. The other players naturally wanted to be treated the same and refused to take part in any of the club's commercial activities in protest. They also approached the Professional Footballers' Association to investigate McGrath's disclosure of private and confidential information.

I requested a meeting with him in which he denied my allegations that he had been given permission to examine contracts, but it backfired anyway on the board as, en masse, all the players demanded improved terms. Crazy.

* * *

So, with all this going on, you might wonder why on earth I stayed at Port Vale?

The simple answer is that I loved it there. At all times the Vale fans were just wonderful with their ongoing support for me. Add to that my family were settled in Stoke-on-Trent and I didn't want to uproot them and you will understand why I turned down almost all of the approaches that came my way.

Preston, Barnsley, Plymouth Argyle and my old club Bristol Rovers all approached me with interest, but I turned them down. I even took a call from the West Bromwich Albion chairman with an attractive-looking proposition, but knocked him back after having a chat together whilst away on holiday in close-season, another occasion when Del had to allow me to 'choose' our destination based on footballing reasons.

Compared to many of the Vale supporters who earned their money in the pottery industry, I had a good living working for Port Vale at a wage most locals would have been grateful to receive. But compared to other jobs in football management, my salary was modest and I could have increased it considerably had I opted to take a fresh challenge. However, being fortunate enough to have supporters who backed me through thick and thin was worth more than money to me. Not many clubs' fans would shout 'sack the board' rather than 'sack the manager', but that was always the cry from the terraces in times of trouble. Normally in football the crowd gets the manager the sack. In my case, Port Vale's wonderful fans kept me in a job.

Being in demand meant I always had a relative amount of security, if there can be such a thing in football management, as I knew I would get another job. But I wanted to stay at Vale. However, as the relationship between Bill Bell and myself became increasingly combustible, even that became more difficult. For example, in the mid-90s, I was happily attending a board meeting at which we were due to agree my new contract, but Bill quibbled over so many minor details I got totally fed up and stormed out, jumping into my car and speeding past a group of fans who had camped out with banners pleading for me to sign the new deal and stay. As I drove angrily away, I calmed down a bit and eventually decided it would be best to turn around and go back, as those fans had made me realise everything I had that was good at Vale. So I did. I parked up back at the ground and was approached by a reporter from *The Sentinel*, Martin Tideswell, who asked me, 'What's going on, Gaffer?' Martin always called me Gaffer, even though I wasn't his actual boss.

'Bill Bell has annoyed me so much that I'd decided not to sign my new contract,' I told him, getting my media message out there before the chairman could. 'But thanks to these wonderful fans, I have changed my mind.' It had actually happened before.

In summer 1994, Bradford City rang me to ask if I would be interested in taking over as their manager. We had just won automatic promotion to the First Division, but I was reeling at Bill Bell refusing me my manager's promotion bonus money, which had been agreed the year before. Instead, I was given the same bonus as the players – this was justified, apparently, because our agreement had not been put in writing the previous summer. Not surprisingly, I was deeply unhappy with the lack of gratitude shown, so welcomed the approach.

I spoke with the Bradford chairman Geoffrey Richmond, then plucked up courage to ask Bell for permission to meet them to discuss terms. To be fair to him, Bill told me to go, so I drove up to Bradford and met with Richmond and Allan Gilliver, my old mate from my Huddersfield days who I had made my debut with and who I was in digs with as a young lad and had been best man for. Alan had gone on to have a great career at Blackburn Rovers, but now was working at Valley Parade and had suggested me to his chairman as the perfect person to fill their vacancy. They offered me £25,000 a year more than I was on at Port Vale – a 25 per cent increase in salary – and were quite clear about spending serious money to gain promotion to the Premiership. In fact, I would receive a bonus ten times that I had just received from the Vale if I got Bradford promoted in the next three years.

The press got wind of what was going on and the news broke, creating further pressure around an already intense situation. I had a huge decision to make. On the one hand, we were settled in Stoke and had just bought a plot of land on which we were building the house we now live in, while our kids loved the area. But I also had to take into consideration that I had been at Vale Park a fair amount of time. True, we had just celebrated promotion to Division One, but I had to question how much further we could go together. Equally, Mr Richmond was renowned as being a much more 'hands-on' chairman, while, in fairness to Bill, he rarely bothered me in that sense, and I wondered if I could deal with a chairman peering over my shoulder every moment when I had been used to working on my own 24 hours a day, seven days a week. Bill seemed quite happy for me to go to Bradford and Brian Horton might have become the manager of the Vale five years earlier had I done so. The local press and radio were fuelling this maelstrom by asking, 'Will Rudge stay or will he go?', whipping up a fervour amongst the fans who were on my side.

Once I returned home, Del and I spent a sleepless night agonising over the decision, but by the time the sun came up, we had decided that, all things considered, as I was yet again at loggerheads with my own chairman, and had been hugely disrespected following winning promotion, my time at Vale was over and I'd go. I had simply had enough of the nonsense and fancied a fresh start; as much for my sanity as anything.

So, I set off for work that morning intent on handing in my resignation, having a letter in my briefcase, but when I got to Vale Park there were around 300 supporters outside pleading with me to stay. Despite my intention to leave, the supporters made a huge impact on me and ultimately it was they who changed my mind as they had been exceptionally good to me through all the ups and downs and I was very grateful to them and needed to repay them.

When I went in, the board were very conciliatory and listened as I told them I didn't particularly want to leave the Vale, especially after winning promotion, even though financially it would have been far more beneficial. I accepted that on Vale's gates they were not in a position to offer me a huge amount of money, but I told the board I felt there were other ways they could have rewarded my considerable success on the field via the profit from sales of players. Dario Gradi, at Crewe Alexandra down the road, was on double my basic salary plus a percentage of outgoing transfer fees, while I currently received nothing from all those player sales I had engineered that made the club millions of pounds of profit. So, we negotiated a change to my contract; although I didn't get a pay rise, I was offered improved terms, which included a proportion of profit on transfer sales over a three-year deal.

My feelings for the supporters were a governing factor in staying, despite many people in the game telling me to leave as I had taken the club as far I could. I emerged from that board meeting all smiles and back slaps from the chairman, having signed the new contract and facing a difficult call to Geoffrey Richmond to inform him of my decision to stay. Telling Del we weren't having to pack up and move lock, stock and barrel to West Yorkshire wasn't much easier; I had left the house that morning with the intention of resigning and heading north, but returned still the Valiants' manager, without an increase in salary, with that letter still in my briefcase.

It could only happen at the Vale!

* * *

My final link with a move from the Vale was to be the unthinkable; to cross the Potteries to join Stoke City. In the 1994/95 season Bill Bell reacted to being tipped off that there was interest from the red and white side of the city appointing me as manager by getting on the phone to *The Sentinel* to report my contract extension following that Bradford near-miss scenario. The back page headline that night screamed 'Hands off Rudge!' which killed any speculation or rumour at that point.

Then, when Lou Macari left Stoke in 1997, there arose the fateful second opportunity to cross the divide. The way that came about was that my friend Hugh Gallagher ran a plumbing company and was doing some work for Peter Coates, who was then the Stoke chairman, at his daughter Denise's terraced house. When Peter realised Hugh was a good friend of mine, he used him to get a message to me to ask if I would meet to discuss the job. I had met Peter at a football do once previously and, interest piqued, as the impressive Britannia Stadium was just opening, the salary offered was very lucrative and my Vale contract was again in dispute, with wrangling over pension contributions and other benefits being removed without my consent, I met Peter, initially at Denise's house under the guise of helping Hugh. Then, I met with board member and property developer Stan Clarke, who also ran Uttoxeter racecourse, under the cover of a race meeting, and, finally, at Stan's own home, where I had the pleasure of seeing his winning owner's trophy from the 1997 Grand National, won by his horse Lord Gyllene.

The negotiations were detailed and prolonged and I felt I was being pulled one way by sentiment and the other by better prospects; now in my early fifties, my pension was beginning to play an important part in my plans for the future, so was a major issue for me. Stoke's offer would solve all of that and secure my family's future, whilst simultaneously ending the soap opera of working under Bill Bell.

The biggest problem I faced, though, was that the Port Vale crowd had been so good to me. Could I do this to them? I had been at Vale for so long it would be very difficult going to Stoke, as the rivalry was so very real at that time. The clubs were in the same division and Del was deeply worried that we may have problems, as it would be so explosive to up sticks to join the local rival team. She was rightly concerned about the kids being bullied or vandalism and the like too. Who knew how both sets of supporters would react?

However, I would never have contemplated any of this had I felt appreciated by Vale's chairman.

This whirlwind of subterfuge and scheming came to a head when Peter Coates sent me a contract, accompanied by his solicitor to ensure I signed it. I was still a Port Vale employee, but the plan we had hatched was to play on Bill Bell's ego to get what we wanted. My contract at Vale contained a six-month break clause on both sides, but the ploy was that, when I handed him my notice in a stage-managed showdown scenario, Bill would get the hump and just throw me out, paying me up instantly, so much did he hate Vale's rivals. I could then just join Stoke.

I picked the pen up, but the question whirled around my head; could I, should I, sign that contract?

Chapter 12

Managing to Survive

'It was like a lower league Becks and Fergie incident, just with fewer man-buns.'

John Rudge, recalling an incident with midfielder Paul Kerr

FOOTBALL MANAGEMENT is a wonderful profession, but it can also be infuriating, stress-inducing, and lonely. As a figurehead, everything rests on your shoulders; from the hopes of the supporters, to the careers of your players, the futures of youth team starlets, the welfare of your own family and the pressure placed upon you by your board to be successful for your club. You set the strategy, sign the players, select the team and on your head be it; that, they do teach you at Lilleshall.

I loved it. Every last second.

I was involved in four promotions, three Wembley appearances, countless giant killing-triumphs and sold players to the tune of £10 million. So, it went well enough, but the day-to-day, nitty-gritty has nothing to do with those glamorous days and nights and everything to do with sheer hard graft.

Managers may not be on the pitch, but we have a very heavy influence on what happens on it. We can employ good coaches, improve tactics and fitness and analyse opposition strengths and weaknesses to counter and exploit them more effectively over time, thus some are better and others fare less well. Ultimately players need to win their personal battles out on the pitch and so much of that is to do with desire, mentality and fitness, both individually and as a group. Talent can only flourish if all of those facets are working to their optimum level, ideally at a higher level than your opponents. So, in selecting your players, you have to also consider all of those factors, which means doing your research, hence all the long trips to unromantic places to watch new talent I undertook.

You can be lucky on the odd, specific occasion, but generally speaking very little depends on what fans call luck. I worked extremely hard along with my staff to achieve what we did at Vale Park. We were renowned for playing good football, even in the depths of the old Fourth Division where many teams were, shall we say, more agricultural in their approach to the beautiful game. My style was based on quick, simple, one- and two-touch football; control, pass and move on. The more direct method – route one – is OK until you come up against better quality defenders who can read which ball is going to be played and adjust accordingly.

I generally deployed a core 4-4-2 formation. I think it is an attractive way to play and is difficult to compete against, but it does call for players who have a fair amount of skill. It is simple if you adopt a method in which players are disciplined to play the ball in a certain area all the time; for example the right-back to play the ball to the inside-right channel so the front players can make their run accordingly. This can be effective with those of lesser ability because the thinking is done for them, but I liked to put the onus more on the players themselves, instead of using robots, giving the player in possession the choice of which ball was on. The better the player, the more freedom you can give him because he will make the right choice most of the time.

I always had very good wide players like Jeffers, Kent, Ainsworth, Guppy, McCarthy and going back, of course, Mark Chamberlain. Their job was to get the ball to the strikers, either early to play them through to run in on goal, or to get to the byline and get crosses in. I gave them freedom to create. I much preferred players who were capable of springing the element of surprise because it is a creative and attractive way to play, rather than being stereotyped and unimaginative. I like the thinking man's game and a game that flows.

However, I did occasionally use three centre-halves, one a sweeper, rather than two. In the Autoglass Trophy Final at Wembley which we won, I did this with Peter Swan, Neil Aspin and Dean Glover. Each player was slightly different; Dean was a ball-player, Neil a marker and Swanny could sweep. When we played 5-3-2, I liked the left- and right-sided centre backs to bring the ball out of defence, like Dean Glover could, because then you could push the wing-backs further forward. This is crucial to the success of the system, otherwise you are always going to be short in attack and the opposition will push the strikers on to your centre-backs to stop them coming out with the ball. In that case you need somebody like an Ian Taylor with the energy to surge through the middle.

Tactics and systems can either be chosen as a preconceived notion of how you want to play and fit players into that system or you can look at players in the squad and opt for what you feel would suit their strengths. I had a style and the players who arrived were brought in to suit. Sometimes I had to be flexible, dependent upon injuries, as we were rarely able to afford to carry like-for-like replacements within our squad of the same quality as my first-choice team. For example, in 1987/88, I switched from 4-4-2 to 4-3-3 and only one defeat followed in the next 13 league games.

All of that comes before the teams walk out in front of the fans to kick off – the other key job of the manager is to adapt in-game. You select what you think is your best team, but, if it doesn't work and you fall behind, then you have to change in an effort to salvage the game. I remember, in the Anglo-Italian Cup Final against Genoa at Wembley in 1996, I made a tactical change after about 35 minutes because they were outnumbering us in the middle of the field, so we switched from 5-3-2 to 4-4-2 and it helped to combat their main strengths even if it failed to alter the result (we lost 2-5, although from that point we drew 2-2).

In the 1980s and 90s in England, the majority of teams played the same way. This traditional style of play was seldom tested by new methods and there was a lack of originality tactically. If players were confronted by something out of the ordinary, they would look across at the bench appealing for help because they were not conditioned to working out problems for themselves. In Holland, especially at Ajax, players as young as eight were instructed how to react to a variety of circumstances and other international teams did the same. Ossie Ardiles played a diamond shape when manager of West Brom and we had to counter that several times. In fact, I played a similar way myself on occasions, playing Ray Walker behind the front men. Other sides struggled to cope with that.

There is always a division of opinion on whether you should change to accommodate the opposition or let the opposition worry about you. Alex Ferguson's brilliant Manchester United team of the era rarely altered their pattern because they felt they were good enough to take on all comers, but if you are Port Vale preparing to play Arsenal you have to adjust. It is all very well to say you are not going to worry about the other team, but, if you cannot get hold of the ball, it is better to go man to man because then at least you are going to compete. In that case, players know what is expected of them and you are not going to be pulled from pillar to post.

I enjoyed making the tactical decisions when playing particularly good opponents in our FA Cup runs. I thought we got the upper hand a few times and was pleased with our tactical triumphs against teams such as Arsenal in 1998 when we held them to a goalless draw at Highbury, only being beaten by the last kick of a penalty shoot-out in the replay.

Generally speaking, I always felt I had a good team and didn't want to change it unless I had to. I sometimes got stick from Vale supporters for not making substitutions quickly enough, but back then I normally only had one to play with, later it would be any two from three, not the five from eight they have now. I took my fair share of criticism and a manager's decision who to take off will often be greeted with derision from at least part of the crowd because not everyone is on the same soccer wavelength, but substitutions can be a lottery. You can throw someone on and all of a sudden it can work, but I would say that there is more good fortune than good planning in the art of making substitutions; there were even times when I subbed a sub, for example.

Substituting players can upset the balance of a team significantly, even when you are well ahead, but so can not making the right change. I didn't always get it right by any means. One game that sticks in my mind for all the wrong reasons was on Sunday, 19 January 1997 when we were leading QPR 4-0 halfway through the second half at Vale Park and somehow contrived to draw 4-4. In fact, we could have lost the game. We hit Rangers with four in 21 first-half minutes with some wonderful play. Jan Jansson was outstanding as creator of two and scorer of one, following a brilliant four-man move.

You really shouldn't fail to win when you have a four-goal lead, but this was the archetypal game of two halves.

Debutant right-back Jermaine Holwyn, one of my Dutch recruits who I'd had to bring on after just seven minutes due to an injury to centre-half Gareth Griffiths, scored an own goal halfway through the second half to give the visitors hope. But we still looked comfortable, despite that upset, until three devastating goals in the last five minutes brought Rangers level. The first was an outstanding volley by one of their substitutes, Andy Impey, and the latter two were created by another sub, Danny Dichio, who caused havoc in our back four, with Impey providing the cross for Dichio to nod down for John Spencer to lash home the injury-time equaliser. I was undoubtedly out-subbed that day by Rangers boss Stewart Houston. To make matters worse the game was live on TV which means people regularly remind me of it.

I can't recall what I did at the end of that game. Cried into a whisky, I should think.

* * *

Football management demands utter commitment. No holds barred. Football is 24/7 with me; always has been and always will be. That was part and parcel of my success I believe. I rarely treated myself to a day off and usually took just two weeks' summer holiday even though the terms of my contract allowed four. I am not saying that a day off now and again would not have done me good and I was always being urged to escape to the golf course more often. I actually joined Barlaston Golf Club, but played just twice one year, which worked out at about £200 a round!

From the day I arrived, the club ran on a skeleton staff from top to bottom and little changed from the old Fourth Division to the newly named First; I had one first-team coach, a youth coach and part-time physiotherapist. Each individual would be responsible for up to four jobs and as the manager, I would be cast in the role of chief cook and bottle washer, gaffer, chief coach, chief scout, press officer, psychologist, psychiatrist and chief negotiator of all manner of things. Why, people would ask, did I not delegate, but delegate to whom? At a club like Port Vale there were always too few hands on deck. I accept that, to a degree, I liked to do things myself anyway.

My car might as well have been on auto pilot for the daily journey from my home in Trentham to Vale Park and life was invariably hectic because there was always something that needed attending to. The daily routine would begin with my arrival at the ground just before 9am, although I was frequently called at home on business before leaving for work. Once at HQ, it would not be long before I was fielding the daily calls from the local media, eagerly hunting news for their early editions and bulletins, especially if there was a transfer in the air. *The Sentinel*, BBC Radio Stoke and Signal Radio were the chief outlets of publicity for the club; unless we were involved in a big cup tie, the national media barely recognised our existence. I felt it was important to establish a good rapport with the local newshounds because it was to our mutual advantage and I was fortunate to get along with *The Sentinel* journalists Chris Harper, who I worked with for many years, and, later on, Martin Spinks. Others I dealt with regularly were Signal's redoubtable George Andrews, Ivan Gaskell, with whom I used to do regular Thursday morning recording sessions in his role as sports editor of BBC Radio Stoke throughout the 1980s and 90s, and the BBC's commentator Gerald Sinstadt, who lived locally.

At 10.30am I held a meeting with my staff over a brew to discuss the day's training schedule, while the physio updated me on the situation with the wounded, walking and otherwise. Training facilities – or rather lack of them – were always a problem, especially when it rained, so the players would bundle into cars, taking towels with them in case it was wet and muddy, do their work and return to the ground a couple of hours later for a shower. It was pretty primitive.

After training, I would return to the office and deal with other matters like correspondence. With no personal assistant, I would draft out my letters and hand them to the staff in the main office for typing; no computers in those days. The evenings would inevitably mean taking in a game somewhere and on my occasional nights off I would sit at home feeling guilty, wondering if I might be missing out on something. I would usually work out the scouting trips whilst at home on Sundays with the aid of the fixture list for the week, as provided by a national press agency. It was an invaluable source of information as it covered all major leagues including non-league and I had many an argument with the chairman as to its value of £350 a season. There were several times when the sheet did not arrive because he refused to pay for it.

You have to be ready to do almost anything as a football manager. I've already told stories of getting washing machines fixed so we had a clean kit for a massive FA Cup tie and painting the Vale Park dressing rooms, but you also have to look after players as a kind of concierge when travelling abroad. Whilst in northern Italy for the Anglo-Italian Cup competition, we once got lost in incredibly foggy weather as the bus transported us from the airport to our hotel. We seemed to be going round and round in this pea souper for ages before finding another hotel which we ditched in and I had to negotiate rates for 15 rooms for the night!

I coped quite well with the workload in my early days, but, as time went by and we climbed the divisions, it became more of a strain, especially with arriving back home from a game late at night and then having to prepare what we were going to do in training the following morning. I gave myself what was really an impossible task, but I got into a routine I found hard to change. Some people may say I fell between stools in acting as manager, coach and chief scout, but I could dismiss that theory by pointing to our record in rising from the old Fourth to the new First Division. It was all about hard work and the willingness to tackle it.

The role of a manager's right-hand man is not to be underestimated. He may, as Brian Clough once said, suffer three fewer heart attacks a season than the man in charge, due to the lower level of responsibility and accountability, but you need someone you can trust as your right-hand man. It's fundamental. I could trust my fantastic coaches with my life as they always had my back, although the board weren't always so keen on them.

As I've mentioned, my first coach was Alan Oakes, a nice genuine fellow who had an impeccable pedigree as a player with Manchester City. Even in his early forties, Alan could outrun and outplay many of the Vale players, still being blessed with skill well above the level of the Third and Fourth Division. Alan was easily contented with life and preferred staying in and watching *Coronation Street* than going out. A little later, I brought in Mike Pejic part-time as a youth coach and he proved a different kettle of fish. He had been an outstanding full-back at Stoke and had been working in a fruit and veg shop in Biddulph, whilst running his farm up in Leek. Keen to get back into the game, Pej worked morning, noon and night with the Vale kids at Staffordshire University to secure a full-time job. He had some bright ideas and the youth team gained shape and organisation under him, but there were concerns amongst some parents who didn't like his ways and I did have to reprimand him on one occasion for grabbing a youngster by the throat. Pej had been tough as a player and would sometimes adopt that same attitude as a coach, as if the only way to crack a nut was with a sledgehammer.

Courtesy of Bill Bell, Pej was promoted to first-team coach in controversial circumstances, without my blessing, and I had no choice but to accept that. Our partnership worked for a while, and he did very well when we gained promotion in the 1988/89 season. However, his confrontational methods with players such as Bob Hazell and Ron Futcher led to problems and the senior pros came to see me after one training session to tell me things couldn't carry on the way they were going. At that point, I backed Pej and told them to get on with it, knowing in the back of my mind things were not good. In a football club you need a keen nose to smell whether things are right or not and, clearly, they were not. The touchpaper to the powder keg was ignited after a reserve game. Our goalkeeper, Trevor Wood, made a mistake and Pej took issue in an aggressive manner which ended up in fisticuffs. That was the final straw and I decided I couldn't carry on with this and decided I had to move him on. Unbeknownst to me, Bobby Downes, the youth team coach, demanded a meeting with the board and told them a few home truths and, as a result of both factors, Pej was sent on his way, after our four years together, crossing the city back to his former club to be coach to Lou Macari at the Victoria Ground.

The chairman asked Bobby to step up, once again failing to ask me if I agreed, just steaming on in and promoting Bobby. Once again, I had to accept it. However, with him as my right-hand man, we had a fantastic time with two trips to Wembley and automatic promotion. With Bobby, I didn't have to wade in to calm down heated situations as I had with Pej. He did extremely well in what was a much happier camp, although with seasoned pros like Peter Swan and Keith Houchen in the squads, we had to be on our toes.

After our promotion in 1993/94, Bobby was tempted away by a better deal at Wolves and it was difficult to replace him because as usual money was tight. Billy Dearden, coach at Mansfield, was highly regarded in the game as being trustworthy and genuine, although some at the club questioned who he was. When I employed Billy, one of Vale's directors, Don McGrath, was particularly critical and mockingly told me that Billy was even older than I was (he was by eight months and we were both just 50 at the time). But I asked the board who they expected me to attract on the poor wages on offer for an assistant manager of a First Division club to win that argument. I won and Billy proved to be an excellent assistant who I could trust with my life.

Once I had generated more funds by the mid-1990s, I was allowed to recruit a second coach to relieve me of some of the weight and pressure, so I brought the recently retired Mark Grew back and he did very well with the kids before coming into the first-team picture alongside Billy. Mark has had several spells as a coach at the club, first under myself then with Brian Horton, Micky Adams, Jim Gannon and Rob Page, being a caretaker-manager, alongside Geoff Horsfield, between various changes of manager. Mark rightly had a testimonial game to mark 25 years' service at Vale as he was a tremendous servant.

The most crucial thing my right-hand men were for me was my eyes and ears. Things happen at football clubs, as I've already indicated. Keeping the players in line can often be challenging and as they are young men who like having fun in life, whilst also being professional athletes, who should be keeping themselves at peak fitness to perform. Those two things don't always sit together perfectly.

I never really had any disruptive players, but that wasn't because they didn't have the opportunity, given all the various shenanigans which went on at Vale during my time there. It was because I chose them carefully and was always honest with them. I gave them responsibility to run their own dressing room and they knew if I had to get involved then someone had stepped way over the line. That meant the players kept the atmosphere vibrant, making the club, generally speaking, a happy place to be.

Some players would get the hump over contract negotiations, but you just have to do the best you can as a manager, who mostly has his hands completely tied by the club's finances. The worst moments used to come towards the end of a season when I was deciding who would be going on the free transfer list, which meant you didn't want to offer them another contract. That might be because of age, injury, ability, or, in our case, sometimes because we couldn't afford them. Some took this better than others.

But any manager in any industry will tell you the same: workers won't agree with everything you do, but you have to do what you think is right, not try to be everyone's friend, or try to get in certain people's good books, although I have to admit that one great motivator I came up with was the players' bar. Our then goalkeeper Mark Grew used to act as the barman and if we got a clean sheet, as it was £1 a pint, I gave the players £20 out of my own pocket so they could have a drink each. That went down very well.

I did have a few ups and downs with some players, but you are always going to get that. Especially as you are always leaving someone out of the team; it is impossible to keep everyone happy.

Paul Kerr was a very good midfielder, who scored that fabulous goal at Wembley for us, but he was also a bit of a prima donna. I had a couple of incidents with him. At Stockport's Edgeley Park, after I took him off early in the second half, by the time we got back in after the final whistle, Kerr had flounced off home. Fines ensued. He also once chucked his boot at me in the dressing room at Burnley after I told him I was subbing him at half-time. It was like a lower-league Becks and Fergie incident, just with fewer man-buns. When you are a manager you have to stick to your guns, no matter what others think, and eventually Paul had to go. Many managers would have gone public after an incident like that to court publicity and bring attention to themselves in dealing with players, particularly in today's media circus, but I always preferred to keep things 'in house'.

I tried to keep a rule of not criticising or blaming individual players in the press. I would prefer to say we defended badly as a back four when an individual had cost us a goal and would talk to the player individually about the mistake, rather than make an example of him in the media; a manager has to recognise that different players respond to different treatment. This is the art of man-management. Some need a kiss and a cuddle, others a boot up the backside.

I had other players who came to blows, although on one famous occasion that was with each other. Despite being a fantastic player for me, Peter Swan was an extrovert who liked a drink and a practical joke, including an incident in which he pretended to be dead, with Keith Houchen driving him round Burslem in a hearse, supergluing shoes to the dressing room ceiling which meant we had to replaster it, plus various socks, shirts, trousers and underpants getting cut up. Fun was constant, fines were regular. In his autobiography, Swanny wrote about how he got drunk with Houchen the night before the Autoglass Final at Wembley, although the lads covered for him and I was unaware otherwise I'd have dropped him. Good job I didn't as he was voted Man of the Match! That was Swanny all over.

The incident I'm referring to came when he and Bernie Slaven came to blows during a training session in autumn 1993. It seemed fairly innocuous, but the pair were both fairly combustible and, suddenly, Slaven was punched in the face by Swan. Ironically, the pair would eventually make up and become friends, but I had to move them on as they became a problem for me because they had become far too pally and disruptive as a trio, along with Keith Houchen, who for some odd reason decided I wasn't using him enough so stopped speaking to me. I gave Houchen a free transfer in June 1993 so he could return to former club Hartlepool United, Slaven joined Darlington on a free transfer in February 1994, so he could be with his family, while in July 1994 we sold Swan to Plymouth for £300,000.

People would not have seen me as a tough disciplinarian. I tried to win players over with reason, treating them like men, but I didn't suffer fools gladly and just occasionally needed to step in and wield the axe. You just can't let players get away with things. You have to set an example and say, 'hold on a bit, you've been collared'. So, I became more of a quiet assassin in moving players on and bringing others in who believed in me.

No matter what the managerial style – rant and rave, throw cups around the dressing room, be calm, be a disciplinarian, be flexible, be soft, call it what you will – ultimately being a successful football manager is all about achieving results, which can lead to differing approaches. Some managers like Kenny Dalglish, who had the reputation of being a disciplinarian, never fined players. Similarly, Harry Redknapp told me that he found fines for big players at West Ham did not have any effect, as they were on so much money. That was never the case at the Vale and there were set fines for misdemeanours like reporting late. The money – and we were only talking a fiver or tenner at the time – would go into the players' kitty and they would have their chosen representatives on the club's disciplinary committee. The fines could prevent confrontation if all players were subject to the same rules and the system helped relieve the pressure on me because every day a new problem of some sort would be added to the pile. We had internal disciplinary procedures for bookings and red cards because I found that losing players from a small squad for foolish behaviour could be detrimental to the team and me. For example, in my last season at the Vale, suspensions cost me Manager of the Month for October 1998 as both centre-backs got suspended and the weakened defence, featuring a youth team centre-half, Anthony Gardner, lost to Sheffield United after we had been on a run of four wins and a draw.

I played for a number of managers in my career and each one made an impression on me, but the important thing is to take aspects from them to learn from, then be yourself, rather than try and merely copy others. Some intimidated players and, in some respects, fear can be quite a useful tool, but in others it can be detrimental and prevent players from realising their true potential. I wasn't a ranter like John McGrath by any means, but I had my moments. For example, in October 1988, I kept the team in the dressing room for 45 minutes at Brentford after a particularly poor performance saw us slump to a 1-2 defeat early in our promotion season. Some home truths were told, but the players responded brilliantly. We won seven of the next nine games and I won Manager of the Month for November 1988. That was despite losing Mark Grew to a thigh strain and having to play several games without Ron Futcher, who got sent off against Swansea for arguing with a linesman, although only after he had scored the opening goal and we hung on for a 2-1 win.

Talking of sendings-off, in January 1989 Bob Hazell was red-carded after an altercation with Chester's abrasive striker Gary Bennett, who had a real attitude on him. He wound Bob up so much that, after being dismissed, Hazell walked to the side of the pitch and stood there for the last few minutes, ignoring all of our shouts from the bench to go into the dressing room. When the game ended, we all trooped down the tunnel, but I quickly realised Bob hadn't followed and hared out to find out what was going on. Bob hadn't moved and was still waiting for Bennett, who was by now stranded alone out on the pitch. It was a proper Mexican stand-off. Bob was adamant he was going to 'sort Bennett out', but I finally convinced him that wasn't the right way to go. I knew Bob could have faced a long suspension if he got his hands on Bennett, which I didn't need as he was so crucial to us.

Managing a football club also means facing some odd scenarios. I once had to deal with Ian Griffiths needing a skin graft after getting his hand trapped in a toilet door at Northampton, while Chris Banks had his nose broken in an altercation with a gang of youths whilst waiting at a chip shop, which begged questions about his diet amongst other things, and Alan Webb suffered second-degree burns putting in a sliding tackle on Preston's state-of-the-art plastic pitch at Deepdale. No coaching manual prepares you for those situations.

There is, ultimately, no blueprint for success in football management, no manual from the League Managers' Association to read for those venturing into the game's most hazardous occupation, no course put on at Lilleshall to run you through how to cope with these kinds of things. You are completely on your own.

* * *

I may have had my share of run-ins with the players, but I did not hold grudges. I was always aware I needed to be able to call on them at all times, not back myself into a position whereby I would not select them because of something they may have said or done. That said, they could do some bloody stupid things sometimes ...

At the end of the 1993/94 promotion season we flew to some lovely apartments in Spain to celebrate, but, as soon as we arrived, I sensed a problem. There was a welcome pack of provisions in the fridge that included bacon, eggs, sausages and milk. We were in multi-storey buildings and, within half an hour of our arrival, the players were bombing the staff below with eggs. That was the last time I went away with the players on a post-season club trip. After that they made their own arrangements for an end-of-season fling.

I liked to get the players away for a few days for pre-season training, play a couple of matches and enjoy a game of golf. I also felt it was important they went out together for a drink on one evening on the trip. It was a great bonding experience, but sometimes led to the odd shenanigan here or there of the kind I've already mentioned which led to us winning both promotion in 1993/94 and a tidy sum from a bookmaker. That was by no means the only occasion things went awry, however.

In 1986, to prepare for our first season back in the Third Division after winning promotion, I took the squad to Exeter, travelling down in the rickety club minibus and several cars. We beat Exeter 4-1 and, in the evening, went to the local nightclub and bar to celebrate and for some team bonding activities. About midnight I called time and insisted everyone returned to our university accommodation (we couldn't afford anything as stylish as a three-star hotel in those days) for some rest. As I was getting into bed, I heard the pitter-patter of feet going past my window. Four of the players were heading off out again in a taxi, so, with Alan Oakes, I gave chase back to the bar, footballers being mostly predictable beasts. Sure enough, the miscreants were huddled in a darkened corner trying to be inconspicuous. Without wishing to cause any fuss, Alan and I ordered a drink, raised our glasses to the players, who were by now cowering behind their pint glasses hoping we hadn't seen them, drunk up and returned to the university. Within ten minutes I heard their taxi drive up and the pitter-patter of feet going back past my window. I collared the four the following morning and told them they had let me down. For me, it wasn't the extra drink they'd had, but the fact they had gone against my instructions, so I told them to pack their bags and get off home; leaving them to find their own way back, which would have tested their knowledge of Britain's transport system to the limit, I suspect. I have no idea how they made it. I next saw them back at Vale for training a few days later. The disgraced players were also fined a week's wages, but I chose never to advertise their misdemeanours and promised I wouldn't tell their wives why I had sent them back early, so I can't reveal their identities even now. They know who they were.

On another occasion we were up in Scotland for pre-season and, knowing the players were all tucked up asleep in our accommodation at Stirling University after a hard day's training, one night I headed off to bed around 11pm. It was a baking hot evening, so I couldn't really sleep and lo and behold, around 1.30am, I heard a taxi roll up outside and the sound of inebriated voices, shushing each other.

'Ay, ay,' I thought and up I got, drawing a chink in the curtains Poirot-style.

As I suspected, two of our players got out with a couple of Scotland's finest young ladies in tow. Knowing the players' rooms were on the top floor, I made my way to the staircase, which was shaped in a square, with four small flights between each floor, meaning those coming up couldn't see me lurking in the shadows towards the top. I was enjoying this.

As they turned the corner, I jumped out into the light and said, 'Oh yeah, what's all this then?'

You should have seen their faces. They were caught red-handed. I got rid of those lasses straight away as the players, who shall also remain nameless, were already attached, then packed the miscreants off to bed with a flea in their ear.

The next morning, I let Mark Grew, then coach, but who had witnessed me send the players home in 1986 as a player, run the legs off the entire squad in training, then, in front of everyone, I grabbed the night owls and told them to make their own way home as they had let me down that night, making an example of them so others would not follow in their footsteps.

They asked me how they were going to get home. I said, 'I dunno. That's your problem, not mine. Now piss off.'

And off they pissed; footballers having to think for themselves venturing out into the real world. It took them a while to get back, I believe.

There was many a time I said to players that if they wanted to ruin their career that was up to them, but I would not let them ruin the careers of me and my staff.

* * *

The other type of 'man-management' which fans don't realise is so crucial in a manager's life is managing your family. In my case, I had a wife and two girls, so 'man-management' is a complete misnomer. We would head off somewhere warm for that annual fortnight's break – however, I couldn't resist steering those choices of destinations to where I knew there might be an inkling of a signing or a contact that I could make. I 'accidentally' bumped into people like Derek Monaghan or a West Brom director who wanted to talk with me about their managerial vacancy, or to watch a potential signing like Andy Jones or, in later years, Mikael Hansson whilst on holiday in Sweden (Scandinavia was a popular holiday destination for me as their season goes from spring to autumn due to the climate). In fact, my wife always says I got very good at selecting beaches based on who might be on them, but not in a George Best way.

I don't know how Del has managed to survive. I owe my family everything.

Talking of survival, the financial health of the club began to come under more and more pressure in the late 1990s, hence the pressure to sell our best assets mounted. Clearly, when your biggest stars leave, the rest of the team will suffer and in 1997/98, instead of having built on nearly reaching the play-offs the previous season, we found ourselves in a situation on the last day of the campaign whereby we had to win at Huddersfield in order to avoid relegation. We had been on a run of gaining one point from 27 either side of Christmas which plunged us into trouble and were scrapping for our lives.

To freshen things up towards the end of that season, I brought in an additional coach, Ray Graydon, who I knew from the circuit. I felt that as a coaching team we were getting a bit stale and I needed something different to stimulate the players as I'd been at the club for 17 years, 13 as manager at that point. Ray brought different ideas and a new voice and I enjoyed the sessions he took for me. It worked brilliantly and we had a great March, winning 3-0 and then 2-1 against relegation rivals Reading and Manchester City in successive games, before thrashing Oxford at home 3-0. But we then lost three on the bounce, leaving us in the perilous situation of having to win our final match to be safe; draw or lose and the calculators came out for some complicated maths. Better just win, eh? I sent the team out to attack, attack, attack.

The futuristic McAlpine Stadium was a happy hunting ground. Port Vale had never lost there in its short existence and we had the backing of 4,000 fans crammed into the away end for a match that proved to be one of my most memorable. To their delight, we opened the scoring in only the second minute when Jansson's corner was cleared, but Bogie returned it to him and his cross was headed back by Dave Barnett for the evergreen Foyle to turn and stroke the ball into the corner of the net. Three sides of the ground, including the end where the goal had gone in, were silent; there was pandemonium in the fourth.

That goal helped to settle the nerves and our second arrived when Foyle headed on Gareth Ainsworth's cross for Jansson to volley in at the far post. After half-time Jansson bent his free kick wickedly under Harper's crossbar and into the net. I remember a policeman from Stoke-on-Trent, who had travelled up with the supporters, joining in the wild celebrations as, at 3-0, we were now in the clear.

Despite Paul Musselwhite having to make a couple of superb saves to maintain our clean sheet and Delroy Facey's header being disallowed for offside on the hour, we rounded things off when Mills headed home with ten minutes left to complete a wonderful and vital victory in the sunshine.

As well as being engrossed in our game unfolding before us, both ourselves on the bench and the supporters had ears glued to the radio keeping track of what was happening at the Britannia Stadium, where two of our relegation rivals faced off. The fact that Stoke lost 2-5 to Manchester City – a result that sent both clubs down alongside Reading – added to the supporters' delirious celebrations. That feeling was as good as winning promotion. The atmosphere in our dressing room was fantastic and the chairman brought in champagne. Bill Bell must have been a mighty relieved man, for he estimated the victory had saved the club £1 million in revenue.

Happy days. We had survived. Just like I did for almost two decades at Vale Park. Almost.

In fact, the original title of this book, when I began writing it in 1999 with *The Sentinel* journalist Chris Harper, was going to be *Managing to Survive' – a celebration of 20 years at Vale Park.* The irony that I didn't last more than a few weeks after we began working on it is not lost on me.

Chapter 13

The End of the Beginning

'My loyalty was ridiculous and arguably self-defeating as it was inevitable that the Port Vale board's would run out at some point.'

John Rudge

ENGLAND WORLD Cup winner and legendary Republic of Ireland manager Jack Charlton always reckoned five years at one club was plenty, so heaven knows what he made of my 19 years, 15 as manager, at Port Vale. The thing was, by early 1997, I myself had begun to wonder if I had become a bit rusty and stale. I was only 53, but had already considered that I could groom someone like a Robbie Earle or a Ray Walker to become the next manager by working alongside me at first, then becoming first-team coach, while I eventually became director of football when they were ready to take over.

But it never came to pass and I began to lose my best players, leading to results suffering, and had to concentrate on rebuilding the team, as maintaining the standard of players required to play the Rudge way became increasingly difficult. I was under severe pressure, but my loyalty was ridiculous and arguably self-defeating as it was inevitable that the Port Vale board's would run out at some point.

This is how events unfolded prior to my departure from the job I had treasured for a decade and a half.

That victory and survival party at Huddersfield in May 1998 proved merely to be the precursor for a particularly difficult summer that left me with my poorest squad for years. We lost striker Lee Mills to Bradford, while, over the previous year or so, we had also sold both of my talented wingers, Jon McCarthy and Steve Guppy. Those three sales brought in almost £3.5 million in total.

I also had some key players reaching their natural end; Tony Naylor and Martin Foyle were by now 31 and 35 respectively and Dean Glover, also now 35, moved on that summer. Neil Aspin had turned 33 and was in what would prove to be his last season, while Ray Walker had left the previous summer and his replacement Jan Jansson had done OK, but wasn't Ray.

I'd had a good run, but there also just wasn't the talent around to suitably replace those I lost as the expansion of Premier League squads and all the money in that division meant players were scooped up and would often not be farmed out on loan anymore to the likes of Port Vale. I would have to admit that the quality in the squad undoubtedly suffered.

It clearly wasn't a good thing for the rest of the squad to be seeing all the best players leaving and not being replaced, but my hands were tied as Bill Bell had this bee in his bonnet about completing Vale Park, making it a 20,000 all-seater stadium, as it had never actually been 'finished'. This probably stemmed back to the fact that he had, as a youngster, worked on its construction back in the 1940s as a mechanical engineer. It was an itch he had to scratch. I, however, felt that, as we didn't fill the ground as it was each week, we would be far better served spending that money on replenishing my threadbare squad. This was to become a major bone of contention, which ground me, and many others, down.

Vale Park had, in fact, become so near-derelict that there was a period of time in which the ground's capacity was reduced to 12,000, as parts of it were deemed unsafe. To complicate things, nearby mine shafts also had to be filled in at a cost of £175,000, while further problems emerged when the council opened a market in Burslem town centre and, in an attempt to eliminate the competition, closed Vale Park's market, which had been making the club £100,000 a year; that didn't increase Bill's humour.

Bill spent hundreds of thousands on improving Vale Park over the years, purchasing an electronic scoreboard for £20,000 at the Hamil Road end of the ground and installing executive boxes bought cheaply from Newcastle United. The Bycars End was renovated at a cost of £90,000 and, in 1989, he opened an £80,000 48-seater disabled stand, the first such purpose-built construction in the Football League, and a new 600-seat family enclosure. In compliance with the Taylor Report following the Hillsborough tragedy, the ground became all-seated and all-covered at a cost of £250,000. To achieve the latter, in June 1992, Bell bought Chester City's old main-stand roof and transported it to Burslem at a cost of £300,000, with half that sum coming from the Football Trust. In March 1995, as befits Bill's vision of Vale Park as 'the Wembley of the North', a phrase he kept alive from its opening publicity from 1950, £750,000 was spent on resurfacing the pitch and the purchase of a giant cover to protect the grass from frost.

After decades of neglect, this had been much needed, but now, for me, the decision to expand the stadium to 20,000 was a mistake, which I often pointed out to Bill, as our average gate was around 12,500, but he was always thinking of the big games when the stadium would be full, but, of course, those don't come along that often. We could always build temporary stands for those games and put an extra few quid on the ticket prices, I argued. But he wouldn't have it, eventually becoming totally blinkered in wanting his completed stadium. It sucked the club dry.

The tipping point came in September 1997 when plans were drawn up for a 5,000-seater stand on Lorne Street, with 14 executive boxes and a 300-seater restaurant, which would cost £1.8 million, with a further £1.2 million being pledged by the Football Trust. Bell told the press, 'It is my ambition to see my job completed. We have decided to develop our own stadium fit for the Premiership.' You have to admire his desire and determination. My point was, how could we ever get to the Premier League if we didn't have a competitive squad?

Something would have to give.

* * *

With our differing viewpoints on where money should be spent causing regular flare-ups, my relationship with the board plummeted to rock bottom and it was at this point that communication became solely by letter, with club secretary Bill Lodey as the 'postman' going between us.

Were he here to make his case, Bill would argue that in September 1997 he had allowed me to break the club's transfer record yet again, spending £500,000 on Gareth Ainsworth from Lincoln, while I also splashed out £200,000 on Jansson. But that still left £2.8 million in the coffers, or rather being spent on the ground. In the summer of 1998, I was only allowed to spend £300,000 on striker Peter Beadle from Bristol Rovers and £100,000 on defender Mike Walsh from Scunthorpe United. My other signings – Simon Barker, Brian McGlinchey, Paul Beesley, Neil Brisco and John McQuade – were all free transfers, while Stephane Pounwatchy joined on a monthly contract from Dundee and I took Scott Mean from West Ham and Andy Clarke from Wimbledon, both on loan.

'Who?' you might say … the experienced Barker aside, it wasn't my best summer's work and I knew it. In fact, the only recent addition I had made who had improved the team significantly was Ainsworth, who I spent many hours coaching to learn to adjust his position so he received the ball on the turn ready to use his pace to run at full-backs, get to the byline and cross into the box. Was I losing my touch at unearthing diamonds?

That question floated around in the back of my mind, but the proof of the pudding could only be in the eating. Pre-season

1998/99 did not get off to a good start when we embarrassingly lost our traditional opening friendly against Newcastle Town, which reinforced my view we needed to strengthen the squad. The problems were to escalate a couple of days before kick-off when Lee Mills departed and we entered the new season well under-strength. At the same time our best remaining player, Ainsworth, was being affected by all the speculation linking him with a move to Leeds United (I turned down a £1.3 million bid) and for the first six games of the season he was a shadow of his former self. He was a key figure in the side and, with Foyle and Naylor injured, we had a poor start, failing to win any of the first seven matches, including a dreadful League Cup exit against Third Division Chester. We were struggling.

Open warfare had been brewing for 14 months or more and, in mid-October 1998, the major ruck which was symbolic of the issues around the club at the time erupted when I was handed one of Bill Bell's many missives by Lodey. Despite those millions I had made them, the board wanted to save money and the letter listed five players that had to be sold, headed by Foyle, Aspin and Naylor. As manager, I felt these sorts of decisions were my prerogative, as detailed in my contract, and not those of the board. Furthermore, the letter instructed me to replace Phil Bonnyman, who I was apparently to sack, with a player-coach – that old chestnut again.

There was no discussion, just a diktat handed from on high … in writing … with no wriggle room. I couldn't believe what I was reading. I was so frustrated and disappointed to receive such a letter after so long with the club that, after reading it through a couple of times, I ripped it up in front of Lodey, saying, 'You know what you can tell the chairman to do with that – stick it right up his arse.' Bill reported my actions back to Bell. I later pieced the letter back together, photocopied it, and sent it to the League Managers' Association, as I sensed it was the beginning of the end for me and Port Vale. I had got to the stage where I thought 'Bloody hellfire, I can do without all this.'

We had now entered feud territory and, infuriated, I tracked Bill Bell down to his garage. As I entered, Bill was talking with a client and he went on for ages, not breaking off to even acknowledge me. So, I left it, waiting in my car outside until the client departed. I then stormed back inside and accosted Bell.

'Bill, what's this letter? This is ridiculous. I've been here nearly 19 years, can we not sit down and discuss things together? And you ask Bill Lodey to give me a letter like that, demanding me to do all that.'

He took one look at me after I had ended my rant and just said, 'You're finished, you are.'

The chairman also denied my request for a meeting with the board to discuss the situation. I had to reply to the letter to cover myself legally, and did so, telling Bell I did not think it was a satisfactory way to do business and requested regular weekly meetings – but none were arranged. The letter, ostensibly, was from the full board of directors, although I knew three out of the five were in the dark and the demand saw director Stephen Plant resign, as he sided with me, not Bell.

It probably did not suit the board that the team then embarked on an unbeaten run of five games with four wins and a draw that almost landed me the Manager of the Month award for October 1998. What it did achieve was Phil Bonnyman being given a new contract!

Having just beaten Norwich at home, we won away at Barnsley in a live TV game, but returned to the Potteries to find that the directors had for some reason informed a local radio reporter that they were very concerned and upset by the team's performance. Clearly that was a premeditated and pre-written press release to a tame reporter which hadn't taken into account the fact that we had played brilliantly and won and would go on to actually win the next two games as well. But this sort of nonsense was typical of the board at that time and the row escalated over the next two days until they climbed down and issued a press release that 'current staffing issues would remain' but were 'keeping an eye on the situation'. I'd won that battle, but the war was still ongoing.

During all this we were getting through players like hot cakes. When Richard Eyre came on as a substitute at Oxford on 21 November, he was the 32nd player I had used in the first three months or so of the campaign. That came after I gave 18-year-old youth team centre-half Anthony Gardner his debut against Sheffield United at the end of October due to those suspensions to my first-choice centre-backs. The lithe, lanky Gardner showed great promise, even if his inexperience did contribute to conceding a couple of goals, resulting in a lot of groans from the supporters, although a year later there was total uproar amongst fans when he was sold to Spurs.

This was all during a run of losing nine of 11 games. Clearly, we were very up against it, although we beat Bury thanks to a Simon Barker penalty to record our first win in ten the Saturday before Christmas as we scrapped for survival.

* * *

In the midst of all this, in late October/early November 1998, I took the opportunity to head off to Sweden to watch a couple of potential transfer targets I'd received good scouting reports about. While I was out of the country, the board, powered by Bill Bell, took matters into their own hands and, in my absence and without contacting me, agreed to sell Gareth Ainsworth to Wimbledon for a club record outgoing transfer fee of £2 million. I only found out when I took a call telling me Ainsworth had been sold. I was livid.

Of course, Gareth wanted to grab his chance of playing in the Premier League and he did, with both hands, doing very well for the Dons. I understood that and am still in touch with him as he is now the manager of Queens Park Rangers, having done fantastically well at Wycombe Wanderers, taking them to their first ever promotion to the Championship after winning the 2020 play-off final at a sadly empty Wembley, due to the Covid-19 pandemic. When he left, as I never got the chance to say goodbye in person due to being abroad, I wrote Gareth a letter wishing him well and pointing out to him that he needed to remember to receive the ball on the half-turn as much as possible; ever the coach.

Had I agreed to or even known about this deal, I could have coped, despite being disappointed at losing my best player, but the board totally sidelined me. It was desperately disheartening and saddening; not least because I had actually come across Alex Ferguson by chance whilst in Sweden, as he was also scouting over there, and we chatted whilst at a game in Gothenburg. I asked if he had any youngsters he might be able to let me have and Alex offered me Terry Cooke, his young and exciting right-winger, but I said no because I knew he wouldn't play due to Gareth being the first name on my team sheet. By the time I could get back to Alex once I returned to England, Cooke had been loaned out to Wrexham. I was kyboshed, hands tied behind my back by my own board.

I was also angry because both Leeds and Fulham had shown interest in Ainsworth and I felt I could have played them off against each other to increase his selling price, a trick missed by the board. Then, just to stick the knife in, Bill Bell declared publicly the £1.5m profit from Gareth's sale would go towards the new Lorne Street stand project, not on new recruits.

It didn't end there; in his contract, Ainsworth had a clause which stated that if he didn't ask for a transfer he would get the value of the signing-on fee paid to him by Vale. As he hadn't asked for this move, this fee was due to him, but Bell refused to pay it. Angered once again, I told Gareth I would fight to get that for him. It went to a tribunal and, backed by the PFA, Gareth did eventually get his money. In fact, Bill knew he'd have to pay it, but he just wanted to try his luck to see how far he could push things. Typical Bill all over, wanting to renege on his obligations.

I had now lost my best remaining attacking player to add to the long list of departures, but the team was suffering in all sorts of positions. To solve a problem at right-back, my Scandinavian scouting trip resulted in me signing Robin Berntsen, but it turned out he wanted to play in midfield, not right-back, which had always been his position and we fell out swiftly over that, so instead I signed Des Lyttle on loan from Nottingham Forest to plug the right-back gap, while to solve my chronic goal shortage I signed striker Christophe Horlaville on loan from Le Havre and 23-year-old Derek McGill from Queen's Park in Scotland. Neither worked out, although Horlaville's signing would also play a part in my departure from the club.

By the turn of 1999, we were struggling around fourth or fifth from bottom of the Championship amidst a dreadful run of one win and two draws in 13 league games. Even then, there was no supporter revolt against me as manager, nor any chanting of 'Rudge out'. I can only say how grateful I was to the fans for their support. Perhaps my loyalty at not leaving was being repaid.

* * *

The period surrounding my 19th anniversary with the club and 15th as manager should have been joyous and celebratory, but instead turned into one of mourning. They say bad things come in threes. First there was the funeral of John McGrath, my former boss and the man who had been responsible for bringing me to Burslem, who had died on Christmas Day; then the funeral of six-year-old Jakob Lee, a Vale supporter who had died just days before we played Liverpool in the FA Cup third round. We then lost 0-3 at home to Gerard Houllier's Reds, thanks to two goals from young England star Michael Owen and one from veteran Paul Ince, so there would be no great cup run to generate funds either. Those events all came within about a week, but the defeat was only a professional disappointment, nothing to compare with the two funerals.

In the midst of this, I was trying to make the crucial signings to get us out of trouble in the First Division as we were slipping slowly into the abyss. Having been rejected by Burnley's Glen Little and

Coventry's Paul Hall, on Friday, 15 January 1999, just before the midday deadline so they could play on the Saturday in a vital home game against Swindon, I signed Marcus Bent, a promising 20-year-old striker from Crystal Palace for £375,000, and Hibernian's experienced Trinidadian international Tony Rougier for £175,000. I wasn't so keen on signing Tony as I had heard a few adverse things on the grapevine, but I thought he would be as good a replacement for Ainsworth as I could secure at that time. Bent had been on my radar for some time after doing well at Brentford, but had a price tag of £1 million. Mark Goldberg, the Palace chairman, was dealing with transfers at that time as the club were in turmoil following their previous season's relegation and heading for administration, so I managed to reduce his initial suggestion of £600,000 to £375,000 with a further £25,000 based on appearances.

Two signings for £550,000; a significant investment and Bell was in agreement with the signings, being all smiles at the press conference in which we paraded our expensive new recruits, happy to take the glory by posing with them for the photoshoot. So, I did not get the impression on the Friday night that I was under any immediate pressure, even though I appreciated how badly we needed a win.

I put both new signings on the bench in order to ease them in as they had barely trained with the rest of the lads. On a cold, snowy day, Swindon scored after nine minutes and made it difficult by playing five at the back. We had chances, but lacked quality, so I brought Bent on as we searched for an equaliser. We lost 0-1; an 11th defeat in 14 games which saw us slip to 23rd in the league table.

After the game, Bill Lodey told me the usual Monday afternoon board meeting had been brought forward to the morning. That didn't bode well. The plot then thickened on the Sunday, when I received a call from a national newspaper reporter telling me that Brian Horton, who was at Brighton at the time, had been lined up as my successor and that my sacking was imminent. That afternoon, Del and I went to an art gallery in Stoke for an exhibition opening and a local newspaper journalist there said to me that he'd heard I was going to be sacked too.

'Really? Have you?' I was all smiles on the surface, but seething inside.

I wish I had put a bet on – Brian had often been linked to the club during periods of unrest, he was an ex-Vale player and the chairman's wife thought he was a 'nice guy' (wives often have influence!). I had nothing against Brian. I had always got on well with him and had tried to sign him in the twilight of his career. He had even attended my testimonial luncheon at the Potters club in Stoke, but all this clearly did not bode well.

After receiving the tip-offs, I went to the ground on the Sunday evening with Del and cleared out the majority of my possessions from my office because I didn't know in what circumstances I might be leaving the following morning, assuming I was to be booted out.

* * *

Monday is never a good day after you have been beaten on the previous Saturday, especially in an important home game. This Monday, 18 January 1999, dawned cold and dreary – just right for an execution. I waited in my office for the Grim Reaper and there duly came a knock on my door. It was a stony-faced Lodey.

'They want to see you now,' he said.

'This is the end then, Bill, is it?'

He did not reply, so I knew the game was up.

The execution was done in typical Port Vale style; in the not-so-plush surroundings of the Portakabin on a building site that was serving as a boardroom while the ill-fated Lorne Street stand was under construction. What more perfect metaphor for the situation could there have been?

As I entered, it went through my mind that we had a First Division club in a better financial state than at any time in its history, with over £2 million nestling in the bank, and a great new striker bought just four days earlier for a bargain £375,000. Of course, our league position of second from bottom was one of concern, but players were returning from a run of injury and illness that had been incredibly disruptive to us, I had two new signings to improve the team following recent sales of five of my best players and was confident that I could dig us out of this hole to escape the bottom three. I had done it before and I could do it again.

I was pretty calm as I entered the Portakabin, unwilling to enter any slanging match. Bill Bell sat in his chairman's seat, joined by his son-in-law Andrew Belfield, who was clearly in an awkward position and wouldn't want to cause a family rift. Next round the table sat Ian McPherson, a genuine Port Vale supporter and nice guy, but who was not in a strong position as he had to raise cash for his failing business and so had recently allowed Bell to buy the majority of his Vale shares at a cut-rate price. Making up the quorum was Neil Hughes, the club shop manager and marketing director. Neil did not have any shares in the football club and, to my mind, had only been co-opted on to the board merely to side with Bill Bell.

These then, were the four men sitting in judgement on my career at Port Vale. It was, in my opinion, a feebly constituted board that was about to make a knee-jerk decision on my future after 19 years of blood, sweat and tears at Vale Park and 40 years in the game. In the past, when we had hit lean times, there had been people on the board who had acted thoughtfully, but at this moment I felt the gun had been loaded and was pointing at my head with the trigger ready to be squeezed.

The chairman kicked off by mentioning results – admittedly we had won just one out of the last 15 – and said we were going to have to do something about the situation. The next thing Bell said wasn't what I expected. The conclusion the board had reached was that it was time for a change – Bill actually said, 'You've been here 19 years now, you're getting a bit stale' – but that they wanted me to become director of football.

'Is that so Brian Horton can become manager?' I asked directly.

Unflinching, Bell flatly denied that he had Horton poised for the manager's job. 'We haven't spoken to anyone, have we?' he said, casting around the room.

'No,' replied the board members, not that any of them would have told me the truth if it went against what the chairman wanted.

He then went on to tell me that they were going to sack Phil Bonnyman, who Bell had had his knife out for from the day he arrived. I was acutely aware that my earlier, successful fights to save my number two now counted against me. I may have won the battle with the chairman previously, but I would never win the war.

Somewhat shocked at this turn of events, despite being as informed as I was, I decided I wasn't going to make a song and dance about it and remained calm. Over the years I'd had my share of shouting matches with Bell and his board, but in this situation it was pointless. It was clear that I had come to the end of the road as manager of Port Vale.

I asked for time to reply to their official offer of director of football, which was made in a three-paragraph letter I was handed. I knew I couldn't work in that position with Bill in charge, nor would it work with Brian Horton, because he was a well-established, experienced manager who didn't need a director of football figure. That would only have worked with a new manager at the helm who needed guidance, as I had been considering working towards. Not only that, but I hadn't even spoken with Brian to find out if he wanted me to have the role. It just didn't add up.

I left the meeting and told Phil Bonnyman that the chairman was going to sack him. Phil seemed quite relieved, while Mark Grew and Billy Dearden were called in to the board meeting and informed they were taking over and the chairman had compiled a list of players he wanted to unload, which I assumed Horton had had a hand in. Meanwhile, I called the squad together to let them know what had happened, but didn't say my farewells, as the offer of a new role in the club was still technically in the air.

I did not hang around, leaving Vale Park for the uncertainty of my future. I had never been sacked before and wasn't quite sure I'd been sacked now, but effectively that was the upshot of what had just happened. I drove home in a sort of stunned shock.

Within the hour my departure was announced, although the official statement released by the club didn't even say 'thank you'. *The Sentinel*'s evening headline that Monday read simply 'All Over Now For Rudge' and the story carried a quote from Bell saying it was 'the most difficult decision in my 15 years as chairman', although he hadn't said that to me.

As soon as the news broke, my home phone started to ring and ring all day long. Over 200 disbelieving callers telephoned me, starting with Robbie Earle, then Alex Ferguson, Kevin Keegan, Alan Ball and Graham Taylor, along with countless other members of football royalty. Those calls were wonderful and I appreciated them all. Many told me how bizarre it was that any chairman would sack their manager within days of sanctioning a club record deal for a striker and bringing in another player without giving them a chance to see if they made a difference. I could only agree.

Robbie Earle then met me to present me with a framed 1998 Jamaican World Cup shirt with the words 'To the gaffer, with thanks for all the help all those years ago' on it. It sits proudly in my office at home as you'll see in the photo section.

When Robbie Williams rang, he vowed he would never set foot in Vale Park again while Bill Bell was still there – a promise he pretty much stuck to as the only time he did was for Vale legend Neil Aspin's testimonial, but that was while Bell was away on holiday. I'll let Robbie off with that one. Robbie also sent me tickets to see him in Coventry and when he came on stage he was wearing a flat cap! Safe to say, most of the fans there to see him that night were oblivious to its meaning!

I was overwhelmed by the tidal wave of supportive messages and cards I received. I even had flowers. Well, I suppose it was my funeral, figuratively speaking.

* * *

Reflecting back, you simply cannot keep selling your best players and think you are going to improve the team. But those were board decisions, not mine. Perhaps I was naïve in thinking my record afforded me some sort of protection. I had 18 months left on my contract and if the chairman had called me in to discuss the situation and whether I felt it was time to groom a younger man to the manager's job, maybe I would have been more open to the offer of director of football on those terms.

I had requested a letter outlining what my responsibilities would be in the new role, but Horton was appointed just 24 hours later without a word of consultation, and the job description, when it arrived, included the brief of finding the new manager. No surprise there, it was all a façade anyway. The director of football role was entirely fictitious. It was, frankly, merely a ploy by the chairman to avoid paying compensation to me. I didn't fall for it.

I actually met Bill Bell at a hotel later that week to find out more about the supposed role, which he really couldn't clarify at all. It was a new concept in the game and I would have to work out how it would fit in with the new manager. I didn't think it was remotely a starter. In any case the club had effectively sacked me by moving me from my job into this position as a *fait accompli*. In my eyes this was now a clear case of constructive dismissal; Bill was being Bill yet again. The board even tried to hide it by advertising the manager's job in a national paper for the next three days, even after Brian had formally taken over on the Wednesday. Brian tells me he didn't receive a phone call from Bill until that morning, so I have to take his word on that. And to be fair to him, Brian did a wonderful job in keeping Vale in the First Division on the final day of the season. However, the manner of my departure and the deceit of the board will never be forgotten.

I could have taken up the offer and stayed and there were plenty of fervent admirers urging me to accept it. Had I remained, however, I would have resembled a general without an army, after being removed from the office I had occupied over the last 15 years and I really do not think it would have worked.

There were a few fan protests at the next game at Ipswich, with some wearing flat caps in my honour, as they went on to do for many years, but then on Saturday, 6 February, before the first home game following my departure, there was an organised protest which has become known as the 'Flat Cap March'. Over 400 Vale fans, some as young as three, bedecked in my trademark flat caps, trudged from the Queen's Theatre in Burslem to Vale Park to express their disgruntlement with the board's decision, arriving a few minutes after kick-off. There they released 843 balloons – black with the white digits '843' printed on them – to symbolise the number of games I oversaw as Vale manager. I believe that wonderful tribute could not go ahead without the fans getting permission from air-traffic control at Manchester airport in case they drifted out of Burslem and into the flight path above. Simultaneously, in a show of solidarity, Vale fans in Australia released balloons into the bush in the dead of night.

Supporters often get managers the sack, but in my case those wonderful Vale fans kept me in the job. I would have not stayed for as long as I did, had it not been for them. We enjoyed many great times together, which I like to think is why they did not turn on me when things got tough. In that way the supporters, at least, expressed their appreciation for what has been achieved. So, while I left Port Vale with a sense of sadness and disappointment, I also felt overwhelmed by the fans' support.

The protests were carried out in a more cowardly manner elsewhere. On the Friday night the windows of 18 cars on the forecourt of Bell's garage were smashed, which I simply cannot condone. In response, Bill, not for the first time, put the club up for sale. The £50 left over from money raised for the balloons was slapped on the National Lottery in an attempt to raise the £3 million or so needed to buy Vale off him, but the ticket didn't come in.

* * *

There was another incident which took place around my dismissal. As I mentioned, French centre-forward Christophe Horlaville had signed on loan from Le Havre. The lad did alright, but, in early January 1999, while everything was going wrong, his agent, the infamous Willie McKay, rang me to tell me another club, Metz, would take him back to France and pay us £125,000 to release him from his loan. However, for brokering this deal, Willie would be due £25,000 of that. I agreed, but Bell refused to pay Willie's commission, despite the move going ahead; another ridiculous reneging on his dues. I feel that at that point Bill was already calculating that he could use that money as part of my compensation pay-off.

By the time this came to a head, I had departed, so I didn't know the board hadn't paid that fee until Willie rang me, irate; and Willie McKay angry is a sight for sore ears. I listened to his tirade of abuse, before managing to get a word in edgeways, telling him, 'Willie, it's nothing to do with me anymore. I'm no longer in post, so I can't do anything about it. But I can give you Bill Bell's business address.'

So I did. Apparently when Willie turned up at the garage it was a fearsome sight. Bill paid up.

* * *

As I believed I had been constructively dismissed, and Bell had only offered me a settlement of one year's salary, not the 18 months of my contract which was remaining, I told him I would be meeting with the League Managers' Association (LMA) to discuss my options. Before I knew it, Bill had got himself a barrister to defend the club. The LMA's chief executive John Barnwell was brilliant, helping me to engage a lawyer who represented me and the dispute became formal as part of an employment tribunal. That was an incredibly stressful period as the hearing wasn't held until summer 1999.

In order to assist my claim, I had to put together two lists of players – one of those I had bought and their costs and one of those I had sold. The two show that overall in my 15 years as manager I had spent £5 million, but recouped £10 million, making Port

Vale Football club a cool £5 million project; imagine what that would equate to in the modern transfer market in which selling a winger like Gareth Ainsworth to a mid-table Premier League team could net you £15-20 million alone.. You'll remember that I had renegotiated some clauses in my contract after turning Bradford down which meant I was also due some money from outgoing transfer sales. All this added up to a compelling case and, eventually, I was successful at the tribunal. I'm not going to tell you how much I got as I don't want Vale fans to think I milked the club at all, but it was a lot more than the initial offer.

It was a very traumatic time, including some extremely difficult days as Vale hadn't been just my job, it had been my way of life. I had loved every minute of it. When I was sacked, my daughter Lisa was getting married that summer, and we had also just bought a plot of land in Trentham on which to build our new house which we now live in, so I didn't need the stress of the dispute at all as I had plenty going on.

To keep me from going completely doolally, while the tribunal situation was ongoing, at his request I helped the England Under-21 manager Peter Taylor as I knew him from Lilleshall, assisting with some training and at some games for a few months, but then he got sacked and replaced by Howard Wilkinson, ending my involvement.

* * *

As the scenario around my departure had been so divisive, subsequently Bill Bell and I never spoke for 14 years. We only saw each other once in that time, when we sat at the same table at a cup final at the Millennium Stadium, but we never exchanged words; stony silence from my former employer. To give you an idea of his continuing animosity towards me, I later learned that Bill said that had he found out I was going to be at Neil Aspin's testimonial match, he would have prevented the game from going ahead.

In early 2013, by chance I was at the Nuffield hospital in Newcastle-under-Lyme for some routine tests, when I saw Bill was there with his son. I'd heard he had developed stomach cancer, so I plucked up some courage, went over and said, 'Hello Bill. Look, we had fantastic years together and I'd just like to say I hope you are going to be OK.' So, I was happy to put that to bed and I very pleased that I did as Bill died within a few weeks, aged 81.

* * *

On Saturday, 15 May 1999, some weeks before my tribunal with the club was settled, Del and the girls told me to get a good suit on as they were taking me out for a meal to cheer me up as it had been a very difficult time. We were going to a restaurant at nearby Trentham Gardens. I duly complied, expecting to have a lovely, relaxed evening out with the family.

Little did I know when I walked through the door that I was actually heading into the main venue room, which was full of 750 Vale fans. As we entered, the whole place erupted into an amazing, emotional outpouring of noise. I'd felt many things as manager of Port Vale, but that was one of the most magical and memorable moments for me. How Del, Lisa and Deb had managed to keep the secret is beyond me. I must say a huge thank you to them and all the supporters who worked so hard to put such an incredible tribute on. Thank you all.

It was a wonderful event; a *This is Your Life*-style evening hosted by Ray Stubbs, which featured hordes of my former players and colleagues. I can't name them all, but ones that spring to mind immediately are Don Megson, both Chamberlain brothers, Mark Grew (who turned up despite still being employed by Bill Bell, thus risking his job), Phil Sproson, Ray Walker, Andy Porter (who, that afternoon, had played for Wigan in the play-offs and then driven down to Stoke to attend the dinner), Robbie Earle, Neil Aspin and, via video link, the signing that got away; Robbie Williams.

I later learned that Swedish midfielder Jan Jansson, who had scored to save the day at Huddersfield in May 1998, couldn't come to the dinner as, when he was contacted by the organisers to ask if would attend, he'd told them he had been kicked out of the club and was leaving the country as the new manager didn't want foreign players.

Wonderfully, Alex Ferguson penned the foreword to the programme for the event. The Manchester United supremo wrote: 'Nineteen years of hard work, self-sacrifice and service to one football club borders on disbelief – especially in this day and age. John Rudge's negotiating skills were almost an art form. I know his knack for begging and borrowing players was one of the modern wonders of the football world and I am not sure that this remarkable attribute has been truly recognised over the years.'

There was quite a lot of money raised as a bucket collection, which we donated to Douglas Macmillan Cancer Support, and I still have the video of that incredible night now, which we occasionally watch. It was a truly magnificent occasion.

* * *

I am writing this almost a quarter of a century since all that happened and I now wonder if Bill Bell did me a favour by ending my tenure at Vale Park and allowing me to move on. Looking back at that horrible period now, I have to ask myself a series of questions:

Was the development of Vale Park to the detriment of the team a good idea?

No, absolutely not. It ultimately led directly to the club's relegation in 2000. It is especially poignant that Bell never got to see the stadium completed in his time in charge as the club fell into administration in late 2002, following the collapse of ITV Digital, and the stand was only completed several years later, which begs the question – was his original Lorne Street stand plan too expensive and too ambitious for Port Vale?

I would say a whole-hearted yes.

All that being said, I have to admit that Vale Park is now as good as any ground in the lower divisions.

Another question is, were those last two high-profile signings the failures which doomed my reign?

Well, of course, neither played a full game for me, with Rougier not even making it on to the pitch in anger. I'd point out that, 18 months later, Rougier was sold to Reading for £325,000, while Horton apparently never really fancied Bent, playing him out of position on the left wing and, not surprisingly, he went 15 games without a goal. Darren was transferred for £375,000 to Sheffield United in October 1999, before being sold on to Blackburn for £2 million and going on to star at Ipswich and Everton. Marcus later described moving from Palace to Vale as 'my dream blown up in my face' as he struggled to adapt to life outside London, referring to the culture shock saying, 'Someone said, "All right, Duck," which put me on my toes. I thought, "Why are you calling me Duck?"'

Not everyone adapts to life in Burslem like I did.

So, within a few months the board had sold those players for £700,000, a £150,000 profit. My gripe is that they handed £640,000 of that to the new manager to fund five new arrivals, while I'd had my hands tied behind my back for a couple of years due to prioritising finishing the ground.

Another question that it is fair to ask is, was I at Vale too long? Maybe, but I wouldn't change it for the world. I do think I needed a fresh impetus and the stress was taking its toll as the issues with the board really ground me down. I do wish I had been able to execute my own plan to work with a Robbie Earle or Ray Walker to groom them to become the first-team manager, with me eventually moving upstairs. If only Bill Bell and the board had given me that chance.

I can look back now at Port Vale with great satisfaction, thinking of the journey I took them on from the bottom of the Fourth Division to the new First Division, with great giant-killing cup runs and Wembley trips. I like to think I gave Vale's fans something to be really proud of; not least, being able to stand their ground against their rivals across the Potteries; Stoke City, in my 843 games as Vale manager.

I never got a letter of thanks or recognition from the board when I left. That wasn't the case from the rest of football and, of course, from the incredible Vale supporters. In fact, the most emotional moment that very black Monday when I was effectively sacked arrived when an elderly, lifelong Vale fan found my door and cautiously knocked on it in tears. When I answered, he told me how sorry he was, thanked me for all the wonderful times the club had enjoyed under my leadership and gave me his black and white scarf, which he'd had since he was a child. My relationship with the Vale fans was as strong on that day as ever, despite my misfortune.

Little did they realise what a test for that bond lay just around the corner.

Chapter 14

Restoking the Fires

'You bottled it, John!'

Deidre Coates, wife of Peter

SO, THERE I am in 1997 with the contract in front of me to become the next manager of Stoke City. I was about to make the most seismic shift in Potteries football history.

I know what you're thinking. Surely there was no way that the long-serving manager of Port Vale could, in all conscience, become the manager of their deadly city rivals. That would go against all that is right in footballing loyalty.

You're wrong.

I signed it.

Partly because I was so fed up with Bill Bell, partly because I felt that with chairman Peter Coates' backing Stoke City could win promotion to the Premier League which I had never managed to achieve and partly because I thought the new stadium could suit me nicely.

As this was the second time Peter Coates had tried to get me to become his manager, I also felt wanted, whereas I was constantly at loggerheads with Bell and his board.

I had always got on very well with Peter and respected him as he had worked his way up from very humble beginnings, starting a company called Stadia Catering in the 1960s, whose speciality was catering events at football grounds that would eventually merge with competitor Lindley Catering. He was also involved in founding Signal Radio in 1983 and used the profits from the success of these ventures to purchase a chain of betting shops in the early 1990s that he dubbed Provincial Racing, employing his eldest, Denise, as first a cashier and, from 1995, the managing director.

In 1997, however, his involvement at Stoke City as chairman over the past 11 years had culminated in the huge decision to leave the ancestral home of the Victoria Ground for the new Britannia Stadium up on the hill at Trentham Lakes after deciding it would be too costly to upgrade the old stadium to meet the all-seater requirements of the Taylor Report.

So, now I was in the enviable position of being the manager of Stoke City, with a wonderful, sparkling, brand new stadium to revel in.

The problem?

I hadn't actually yet left Port Vale.

As I mentioned earlier, we had developed a plan which would see me hand in my resignation to Bill Bell expecting that, in a fit of pique, instead of requiring me to work my six months' notice, he would throw me out immediately.

After signing the contract under the supervision of the Coates' solicitor, I left the house with a letter of resignation in my pocket to see Bill. As it happened, first I had to go to the Town Hall to give some prizes to young people of the Potteries. This would be my final duty as manager of Port Vale.

But, I could feel the doubts already nagging at the back of my mind. As I handed out those prizes, I went over and over it; Del's concern that supporters from both sides, but especially Vale, would not react well, the abuse our daughters may face, the concern about our property and particularly my car being damaged. Most of all, after expending all that effort to get above Stoke, I realised I couldn't then be the person to reverse that trend, while I also was desperate to complete 20 years' service with Port Vale. All of these thoughts began to bubble up. Del and I had spent long hours discussing them all before I put pen to paper, but now this was real. It was actually happening.

By the time I drove across to Vale Park after the prize-giving, letter still in my trouser pocket, I had worked myself into a lather. As it happened, Bill was in a far more phlegmatic mood than usual – at least he was speaking with me – so the letter never emerged, despite my fingers reaching for it as we talked.

I could tell you that I came to a considered decision that my future was best served at Port Vale, but the truth is, in that moment, I bottled it; not least because of the wonderful Vale fans who had kept me in that job when times had been tough for me. Their support had been everything and I didn't want to ruin my relationship with them beyond repair. I just couldn't do it. It would have felt like cheating on a partner.

Letter still in pocket, I finished the meeting, drove home, told Del and took a deep breath before phoning Peter Coates to give him the bad news. To be fair to him, Peter didn't take it as badly as I expected. He understood my reasons, especially that moving to be the manager at Stoke was just too much of a switch too quickly, although he told me to go on holiday first before making a firm decision. I did and it merely served to cement my decision. It was definitely the right one.

So, I remained the manager at Port Vale until January 1999.

* * *

By 1999, Stoke City had fallen on very hard times, at least for them, being ignominiously relegated in the club's first season at the new stadium, before then failing to even reach the play-offs in the following season under Brian Little, despite a great start which had seen them win eight of their first nine games. The situation felt familiar.

This time, when Peter Coates came calling for a third time, I needed no persuading. I was itching to get back in; firstly, I was out of work, secondly, I was no longer at Vale, thirdly, the bitter separation was fresh and, fourthly, I had a family to provide for. All the barriers which had prevented me from making good on that signed contract two summers earlier had been removed and now my loyalties lay on the red and white side of the city as I was appointed as director of football, although I still had to suffer Deirdre Coates, Peter's wife, telling me in no uncertain terms how I had 'bottled it' back in 1997. I made it clear to Peter that I still didn't want to be manager of Stoke. I probably hadn't had enough rest after 19 years at Vale. If I'd had 12 months out, I might have said I wanted to be a manager again, but, after the trauma I'd been through, I wanted to take something of a back seat for a while. You may think I took the easy way out and that may be true, but it proved to be an excellent decision as I would remain in post for 14 years through plenty of thick and thin.

So, ironically, I accepted at Stoke the very position I had, in theory at least, rejected at Vale. You may think this strange, but actually there were a range of factors in this making sense for me. Firstly, I wanted to stay based in the Potteries. Secondly, being director of football at Stoke, a club where I had no history, would be entirely different than at Vale where I had been the man in the hot seat. Thirdly, it would give me the opportunity to work with a younger manager, helping out where I could.

Peter may no longer have been the official chairman of the club – that was now Keith Humphreys as Coates had taken a step away from being the figurehead after taking a lot of flak for the club's struggles to concentrate on his new company Bet365 which had grown out of those betting shops – but he still effectively made the key decisions. His first choice was the Gillingham manager Tony Pulis, who had come within a few minutes of defeating Manchester City in the 1998/99 season play-off final before losing on penalties, but he opted to join Bristol City instead. Peter then asked me to travel across to Sheffield to speak with Gary Megson. Gary was the son of my former manager at Bristol Rovers, Don, and had been an apprentice while I was at Rovers as a player, so I knew him. Gary had just finished a couple of years as manager at Stockport, who were in the same division as Stoke and he had done fairly well in the first of those, finishing just short of the play-offs. Gary was very keen on joining, but wanted to know how he would work with me, so I explained that I had turned the manager's job down, so he had nothing to worry about there and gave Gary my guarantee that I would only be looking to support him, not stab him in the back. Concerns placated, we shook on the deal and Gary, along with his coach Nigel Pearson, who had just managed Carlisle United to the most dramatic of survivals at the foot of the Football League thanks to an injury time goal from goalkeeper Jimmy Glass, joined the club for the 1999/2000 season to make what I felt was a fabulous triumvirate to win Stoke City promotion. I knew there were lots of good players such as centre-halves Nicky Mohan and Larus Sigurdsson, although he would shortly be sold to West Brom for £350,000, midfielders Graham Kavanagh and Kevin Keen and striker Peter Thorne, so Gary had good building blocks for a decent side. But he was the manager. My role was as a support mechanism, coordinating scouting for new players and of the opposition.

Being director of football meant I was involved, but it wasn't me on the touchline, tearing my little-remaining hair out. There isn't that innate fear as when you're the manager. You're anxious, yes, but it just isn't the same pressure, especially on a matchday when your role is fairly negligible as most of your work is long term or in preparation, so you are nowhere near as tense during a game or its build-up, nor are you the focus of supporters' gripes anywhere near so much.

I found that a relief and took to the role as a more strategic and planning discipline, which I could approach calmly and methodically, knowing that, ultimately, it wasn't my head on the block. I thrived on it. Having said that, I never said never to taking a manager's job somewhere else, but the only opportunity which came along was when Bristol Rovers offered me the post in February 2001 when Ian Holloway moved to QPR, but my former club were struggling in the relegation zone and I didn't fancy ripping up my life only to find myself in the bottom tier again, so I resisted their overtures. I just focussed on the job in hand at Stoke, returning us to the First Division.

Key to my role was the recruitment of players. This started with identification, ran through contacting the player either directly, or, more and more, through agents, and then negotiating the contract and drawing it up, all of which I'd done in my role as manager at Vale. I would then be involved in keeping players happy or, if the manager wanted it to happen, seeking to move them on. One problem I faced on that front was that the training ground was dreadful. The Michelin centre had only just been purchased from the tyre company and there were only basic facilities, which created great difficulty in attracting players. We thought about moving to a site near Yarlet, south of Stone, but I'm glad we chose to develop the training facilities where they are as it is a very good spot just off the M6 junction 15, making it very accessible to players who live anywhere from Birmingham up to Lancashire.

I now had a very different, and much shorter, journey to work, turning off the A500 on to the A50 to get to the Britannia Stadium, instead of continuing on several miles to get off at Burslem for Vale Park. This felt very strange and quite difficult at first, but I soon settled in. Vale fans obviously thought I was something of a sell-out as I was now working for their sworn enemies, but I felt that they treated me exceptionally well in the circumstances and Del's fears never came to pass. Certainly, being director of football and not the manager helped hugely and I am very happy that I made that choice and thankful for the Vale fans' reactions. Equally, the Stoke fans were very good to me and there was never a situation where I felt they held my Port Vale past against me. They understood that I was on their side now and I would like to thank them for that as it could have been far more difficult.

Gary, Nigel and I bonded brilliantly, an example of which I can give you from our extremely competitive golf days. This particular one was to celebrate Gary's birthday, which had come in May, but we took a belated opportunity for a team-building round after pre-season training, which soon became a dogfight between Gary and myself as to who could finish second behind Nigel, who, as a very good golfer, was well ahead of us. Come the last hole we were dead level, but I won it, making Gary the 'rabbit' in golf terms.

Next morning, I drove across to my mate's house and asked if I could borrow his pet rabbit. Hutch duly secured, I drove the unsuspecting bunny across to the Britannia Stadium and left it on Gary's desk for him to discover when he arrived for work. He didn't take it well, but I am happy to confirm no rabbits were hurt in the taking of this piss.

Despite having no finance behind us, we were doing OK, in and around the play-off zone as the season unfolded, but behind the scenes there were lots of ructions. Peter Coates was seeking to sell the club to an Icelandic consortium who had approached him and Keith Humphreys on the recommendation of national team manager Gudjon Thordarson, who had been a regular visitor to Stoke to watch first midfielder Toddy Orlygsson and then cousin Larus Sigurdsson.

At this time, Peter was struggling a bit to put money into the club as Bet365 was still but a foundling business and the conflict between the current board and supporters had intensified over the previous two seasons as life at the Britannia Stadium had started badly. Peter negotiated a deal whereby the English directors relinquished control, but still retained what were to become known as 'golden shares', effectively meaning that if the Icelanders wanted to sell in the future, he and his colleagues would be the only people they could sell to.

It turned out that there were people in Iceland who had a lot of money sloshing around and they wanted to have a British football club to invest in and have some fun with. We never really got to find out who all of those involved were, but the figureheads were the manager, Thordarson, the chairman, 33-year-old Icelandic businessman Gunnar Thor Gislason, and major backer Magnus Kristinsson, a fishing magnate, although the consortium in full comprised eight principal shareholders and around 350 other minor ones. Iceland literally bought into Stoke City in a major way. They were ambitious and spoke of winning promotion to the Premier League as the club's finances were now on a sound footing and there would be money for new players. 'We will make Stoke City great again' was the headline in *The Sentinel*. It all sounded marvellous.

However, Gary, Nigel and I had known nothing of the £3.5 million deal negotiated by chief executive Jez Moxey, who stayed for six months or so after the deal was completed before moving to Wolves. At the time of the takeover, we stood seventh in the league, one place outside the play-offs and Gary had been named Manager of the Month for September 1999. When we were told, we all thought we'd be leaving. The whole point of the Icelandic consortium, known as Stoke Holdings, buying into British football was for them to build success based around a mix of Icelandic and British talent, but they were to very much be the leaders and decision-makers. That became apparent when Gary was sacked after just 22 games in charge, going on to become a very successful manager at West Bromwich Albion, winning promotion to the Premier League twice. I do wonder whether we would have had our success sooner than we did had he been allowed to stay longer than the handful of months he had at Stoke as we were really building something.

* * *

Gary was replaced by Gudjon Thordarson, who had taken Iceland close to qualifying for Euro 2000, despite being in a strong group which included world champions France and Russia. Both Nigel and myself also thought we would be out of work, but, when he arrived in mid-November, Gudjon told us he wanted us to stay as he knew nothing about the English league.

Phew.

The new era started brilliantly with a 4-0 thrashing of Wycombe on a windy night in late November and quickly saw the introduction of a range of Scandinavian internationals such as Einar Danielsson, Sigursteinn Gislason, midfielder Brynjar Gunnarsson for £600,000 from Swedish club Orgryte IS, Arnar Gunnlaugsson on loan from Leicester and the manager's own son, Bjarni Gudjonsson, recruited for £250,000 from Belgian side Genk. They joined Anders Jacobsen, who had been at the club since the summer, while I recruited Mikael Hansson, after taking Del on holiday to see him play in Sweden in the summer of 1999, and Frode Kippe on loan from Liverpool. The Icemen truly had cometh.

My role changed completely after the takeover as the board operated largely from Reykjavik, with myself and Jez Moxey liaising with the remaining English minority shareholder/directors. Also, Gudjon wasn't joking about his lack of knowledge of English football and needed a lot of guidance. I was more or less doing a co-manager's job alongside him, but was out of the limelight and didn't feel the pressure as much as he did. We just divided up the tasks and got cracking. I developed a good relationship with him and we agreed a gentlemen's challenge; each seeking to out-recruit the other to bring in the best players for the club, so I spent many hours every night milking my network of both national and international contacts, back to the old days of trying to find some diamonds and pearls.

Chris Iwelumo was a big strapping striker who had moved from his native Scotland to play in Denmark at Aarhus Fremad but now wanted to come back to the UK. In March 2000, I received a phone call from David Moyes' brother Kenny, Iwelumo's agent, telling me his client was trialling at Preston, where his brother was manager, and I said I would watch him play in a reserve game at Vale Park, which Preston won 3-1, with Chris scoring. I offered him a contract the next morning and persuaded Iwelumo to sign it after he sat in the Harvester car park in Kenny's car mulling it over, with Chris telling me that he chose Stoke because of me and how I had treated him. David offered him a contract that night. My speed of action had secured the player once again. I'm not entirely sure how the brothers reconciled that particular issue between them! I also got the price down to £40,000 from the initial £100,000 his club wanted by negotiating hard as I knew Iwelumo wanted the move.

We also promoted the likes of Clive Clarke, Robert Heath, Paul Connor and James O'Connor from the youth and reserve set-up and snuck into the play-offs thanks to a brilliant run at the end of the season, powered by the goals of Peter Thorne, who suddenly hit one of the richest veins of goalscoring form I've ever had the pleasure to witness. Thorne was a brilliant goal poacher and netted 15 times in the final 13 league games to finish with 30 in 55 appearances that season, including scoring the winning goal in that season's Autoglass Trophy Final at Wembley as we defeated Bristol City 2-1.

That was a wonderful spring afternoon. The old stadium was in its last days, but the twin towers witnessed a great game in front of over 75,000, around 40,000 of whom travelled from the Potteries. For me, it was a very different experience to being the manager for such a great occasion, but I was really happy for Gudjon. A trophy in your first season at any club is not to be sniffed at, especially given the circumstances of how he had taken charge.

We had a wonderful open-top bus tour through the city, ending up back at the Brit in the pouring rain with fantastic celebrations and the supporters were a wonderful sight, with so many happy faces. However, we were still very focussed on winning promotion, although we ended up in the play-offs, facing Gillingham, managed by Peter Taylor, the man who had so kindly asked me to help the previous year while I was fighting my case against Port Vale.

We won the home leg 3-2, but conceded a last-minute Andy Hessenthaler goal to halve the deficit and in hindsight, that was a massive momentum swing. However, it didn't prepare us for the utter disaster at Priestfield four days later when two ridiculous refereeing decisions by Rob Styles sent us crashing out.

The first saw Styles issue a second yellow card to Clive Clarke for throwing the ball down angrily after a throw-in decision went against him when the ball clearly came off the Gillingham player.

If that wasn't ridiculous enough, then a scuffle in the Gillingham penalty area at a corner saw Kavanagh red-carded, even though he had actually been cut on his face and had blood running down him. Styles had completely lost the plot and was reacting solely to the baying of the home fans. It was 0-0 at the time, so we were still 3-2 ahead on aggregate, but now only had nine men. A few minutes later Barry Ashby headed home a corner and eventually, despite heroics from our remaining players, Gillingham ran out comfortable 3-0 winners to go through 5-3 on aggregate, although we did have one great moment when a shot from Paul Connor hit both posts before bouncing clear; that was at 0-2 and would have levelled the tie on aggregate. The football gods, as Gudjon said in his post-match interview, were not with us, while it's fair to say that Stoke fans didn't welcome being officiated by Mr Styles after that.

To make matters worse, Del had driven down with the manager's wife, Ran, along with the mother of one of the directors, Phil Rawlins. They had a horrible journey, couldn't find anywhere to eat in Gillingham and so went into the ground, only to find there were only portaloos as the stand was being rebuilt, which didn't go down well. When they got back to the car, Del realised she had got a puncture, which just topped off an awful night. The ladies managed to flag the team bus down and some of the players and coaching staff, including Dave Kevan, got off and changed the tyre in the pouring rain. They didn't arrive home until gone 2am.

Gudjon was beside himself after that defeat and the pressure was very much on for 2000/01 as promotion was now an expectation. With his blessing, that summer I signed Tony Dorigo, a classy left-back who had won the league title whilst at Leeds, but was nearing the end of his career, and centre-half Wayne Thomas from Torquay United for £200,000. Marvin Robinson joined on loan from Derby, but broke his leg in only his third appearance, while I then missed out on Stockport's Michael Ricketts, who would go on to success with Bolton and win an England cap. I reverted to my contacts again to persuade Andy Cooke to sign from Burnley. I had played with Clarets boss Stan Ternent at Carlisle and persuaded him to let Andy, who was a mad Stoke fan, join for a fee of £300,000. Andy scored 23 goals in two and a half years with us, including ten in the 2001/02 promotion season.

Alongside my signings, Gudjon recruited more Scandinavians; Henrik Risom, Stefan Thordarson and Birkir Kristinsson arrived that summer, while we had to wait until the Norwegian season finished in October for the arrival of striker Rikhardur Dadason, who was built up by Gudjon and the press as the Messiah. Dadason had scored 47 goals in 69 games over the previous three seasons for Viking Stavanger in Norway and then seemed to secure cult status by scoring with his first touch after coming on as a substitute in the League Cup as we defeated Barnsley 3-2 thanks to his last-minute goal. I had been over to watch Dadason that summer and was concerned about him adapting to English football, but the decision to sign him was left entirely down to the manager, who was insistent he would be the difference, although failed to persuade the board to spend £150,000 to get him released from his contract early, which was why we had to wait for what then felt like the second coming.

Looking back, I feel that was the beginning of the Icelandics finding it hard, running out of money and not being able to make it work. In addition, there was tension between them and their manager, who had wanted Dadason for pre-season training.

This was also really the first time I saw how Gudjon reacted under pressure. Different to Gary, Gudjon had a fiery temperament with the players, being very boisterous and aggressive in the dressing room, which didn't always go down well and I became a shoulder to lean on again.

That season proved very taxing at times. Despite knocking both Charlton and Barnsley out of the League Cup, we then got hammered 0-8 by Liverpool, although Thorne hit the post after rounding Liverpool goalkeeper Pegguy Arphexad with the score at 0-0. As if suffering a record home defeat wasn't enough, the week beforehand we had got knocked out of the FA Cup first round by non-league Nuneaton Borough. Those were truly terrible results.

League form was also up and down. Dadason netted only eight times and it was left to Thorne's 25 goals to scrape us into the play-offs once again, where we faced Ray Graydon's Walsall in the semi-final. Again, the first leg was at home, but ended goalless. We took the lead in the second leg, through a trademark Kavanagh volley, but, after Dadason missed a good chance, which I felt Thorne, who was left on the bench by Thordarson, would have scored, we succumbed to a four-goal salvo. That started after goalkeeper Gavin Ward dropped a corner into the net unchallenged and we capitulated to lose 2-4; one goal coming from a poor-back pass and another a tame free kick which beat everyone to hit the net.

The result was devastating, and did not help Gudjon's mood, which had become tetchier as the pressure built that season, being especially noticeable in the dressing room, but also with the board and even in front of the press. In time, he would grow a beard, which became more wild as the pressure increased.

* * *

After that disappointment, I looked to add quality to our squad to make that little bit of difference in games. That summer of 2001, two opportunities presented themselves to me which I worked hard to get over the line.

I first became aware that Dutch international winger Peter Hoekstra was available when my contact over in Holland, Piet Buter, who had helped me at Port Vale, alerted me, telling me Hoekstra, who had been released by Ajax after struggling with injury, could be interested. I didn't think for a moment he would sign, but when I spoke with him, Peter said he fancied the challenge. He didn't have an agent, so in an effort to woo him, I brought him over to England and took him for lunch in Stone at an Italian by the canal. I honestly thought there was no chance that we would be able to attract an international to come and play in the third tier of English football where he would have to turn out at the likes of Bury, Tranmere and Oldham, but somehow, we talked him into joining. I maintain that the meal was that good at La Dolce Vita that Peter simply wanted to keep going back for more! Perhaps he felt playing in England would be good for him. Whatever the reason, Peter signed in August 2001 and became an integral part of what would prove to be a promotion-winning squad. He may have been getting towards the end of his career, but Peter's ability on the ball was incredible and he was wonderful around the group and with supporters. He provided thrills and entertainment, with fantastic tricks, which also meant he attracted a lot of agricultural tackles. He had a wand of a left foot with which to put in crosses, through balls and hit thunderous shots, such as his turn and volley at Watford in the successful battle against relegation in 2002/03 and the second in his memorable hat-trick against Reading in December 2003. He was undoubtedly one of the best players to put a Stoke shirt on in my era; a quality signing I am proud of. The crowd loved him.

My next transfer coup was Sergei Shtanyuk, a Belarusian international defender who had just moved from being club captain at Dynamo Moscow to Royal Antwerp, but hadn't taken to his new club and was looking for a move. This time, my Belgian contact called me to ask if we might be interested and we invited Sergei over and put him and his wife in a house two roads from mine so we could look after them as much as we could, which included having to go to a Home Office appeals panel to get him a work permit. We did have one incident early on when Shtanyuk's wife got lost in London, which ended up with the police knocking on our door and Del had to sort her rescue out, but Sergei proved a very good centre-half who was the bedrock of our successful 2001/02 season. He then played almost the entire 2002/03 season and won Player of the Year as we stayed up on the last day of the campaign. Eventually, though, his wife just could not settle and wanted to go home, so we sold him to Russian club, Yaroslavl, in 2003.

Sergei played alongside Peter Handyside, who I recruited from Grimsby after the best part of a decade at Blundell Park. We got him on a Bosman free transfer in the summer of 2001 and I persuaded Gudjon to make him club captain. Peter was a Scot who took no prisoners, but could play too, being very aware of what was going on around him. He dovetailed exceptionally well with the solid Shtanyuk, who would compete for headers and look to win the ball, with Peter tidying up and looking to play the ball out.

With those three signings alone, I'm going to say I won the challenge Gudjon and I had shaken on and I'm going to make the case for a hands-down victory on that front.

All of that transfer activity was funded by the controversial sale of stars Graham Kavanagh and then Peter Thorne to promotion rivals Cardiff City for a combined fee of £2.7 million. The Icelandic consortium were feeling the pinch financially and needed to generate funds. Thorne was a hero who had scored 80 goals in 189 appearances and I remember having to take him to one side and tell him the club needed to sell him as we needed the £1.7 million fee Cardiff were willing to pay. I know he didn't want to leave, but Gudjon had his eyes on another striker he rated highly, Souleymane Oulare, a Guinea international, from Las Palmas in Spain.

Another significant change which came as a huge surprise to me was the board letting coach Nigel Pearson go, bringing in Dave Kevan instead. I don't know if Gudjon had any input into that. I didn't, that's for sure. Nigel was extremely disappointed and it hasn't surprised me in the least to see him go on to have a good career as a manager, notably taking Leicester into the Premier League and going on that tremendous run which averted relegation in 2015 and set up their incredible title triumph the following season under Claudio Ranieri. He has also done very well at Bristol City, where he took charge in 2021.

* * *

The 2001/02 season felt like Groundhog Day; a third successive campaign under the consortium with no actual progress in the league as we still couldn't win automatic promotion. The pressure was extreme and Gudjon got tetchier and angrier as we once again finished in the play-offs, facing, guess who? Cardiff. Would those sales come back to haunt us?

There was an air of gloom around the place, especially after the Bluebirds, who had gone undefeated under manager Lennie Lawrence since he had taken over three months earlier and featuring those two departed stars Thorne and Kavanagh, went 2-0 up in the first leg at the Britannia. Substitute Deon Burton nicked a late consolation, which meant we were just the one goal behind and, with away goals not counting until the end of extra time, in with a chance.

The second leg was tight and there were few chances, although I remember Iwelumo skying a good opportunity from close range and our keeper Neil Cutler making a scrambling save from a Peter Thorne header. Just as the game entered injury time and the Cardiff Tannoy announcer was telling their supporters to keep off the pitch, Clive Clarke chipped a cross in from the left, which Bjarni Gudjonsson knocked back at the far post and James O'Connor lunged in to prod home from six yards out to draw us level at 2-2 on aggregate. Deliciously, the ball went through Kavanagh's legs, unsighting the Cardiff keeper Alexander.

The gods were with us, as was the momentum, and O'Connor was involved again in extra time when his free kick from the edge of the box deflected in off substitute Souleymane Oulare's backside to wrong-foot Alexander and give us the most dramatic victory.

No one had believed it would be third time lucky, but somehow fortune had been on our side, especially as our winning goalscorer (if you can truly call Oulare that) had only recently made a comeback from a life-threatening blood clot on his right lung, which left him hospitalised for a significant period, after there had even been initial fears for his life when he was rushed to hospital with severe chest pains and breathing difficulties. We had initially ruled him out for the rest of the season as he was put on drugs to thin his blood, meaning it would be highly dangerous to play contact sport. For him to make such a dramatic comeback was astonishing.

* * *

Talking of luck, the build-up to the final was dominated by the fact that we would be changing in the Millennium Stadium's south dressing room and for all cup and play-off finals thus far played at the ground, which was standing in whilst Wembley was rebuilt, the winners had always changed in the northern one. It was clearly just a quirk of fate, but the curse was bigged up, although we felt we were going to be the ones to break it, as confidence surged following our victory at Cardiff and we knew we had Steve Coppell's Brentford's number, having beaten them at home in the league and only lost away after an early red card meant we were down to ten men for over an hour.

The final could not have gone better for us. Perhaps the need to keep up the winning tradition of the north dressing room weighed heavily on Brentford as they really didn't turn up in the first half. I had identified Deon Burton as a good goalscorer who wasn't playing much at Derby in February 2002 and it wasn't difficult to persuade him to come and help out. Deon bagged the opener from close range after Iwelumo flicked on a corner and then Bjarni curled in a wicked free kick which Bees striker Ben Burgess shinned into his own net; game over before half-time.

I was so pleased for Gudjon and we embraced on the Millennium Stadium turf, having come a long way together over the past three years. I have my play-off final winners' medal displayed with pride in my office around the neck of my bust, on which also sits the 843 cap from my time at Port Vale; you'll see a picture in the photo section. I was now building a new future at Stoke City and had indeed played a major part in winning Stoke promotion from a division in which Port Vale now languished. The two clubs have never been in the same league since.

Chapter 15

International Relations

'Tone, you've got to play your cards right here. Let them bring them over and take a look at them and when they are no good, just send the buggers back.'

John Rudge advising Tony Pulis
on unwanted Icelandic players

YOU WOULDN'T anticipate winning promotion and then getting the sack. I was quite happy for Gudjon to get cracking in the First Division the following season, but the board wasn't. The day after the promotion parade around the Potteries took place, his departure was announced.

That may seem ridiculous, and I'm sure it felt so to many supporters, but behind the scenes the relationship between board and manager had reached boiling point. Part of my role as director of football had been to link the manager to the board and vice versa.

To say that proved an interesting experience during that period is putting it mildly as I found myself as the go-between in an escalating conflict between the board, or more specifically chairman Gunnar Thor Gislason, and their own manager. In fact, Gudjon once told me he felt he received more support from the English directors, which was ironic, although perhaps explained by the continuing split along the lines of nationality that cleft the board throughout that time.

Over the years, I had been privy to several slanging matches between Gunnar and Gudjon in the corridor, although these were mostly in their native tongue, but they could go at it hammer and tongs in English, so sometimes everyone knew what they were having a barney about, other times we didn't have a clue. Either way, the words were extremely heated and provocative.

I had to tread a very fine line. At least I had seen how this operated when being in Gudjon's shoes whilst manager at Port Vale and having to deal with a far more difficult chairman in Bill Bell, so I tried to guide him whenever I could. Often, though, he had already made his mind up.

It all escalated in the 2001/02 season as the pressure was on and it looked like we were going to lose in the play-offs for the third successive time. I watched from my position on the fence as Gudjon took to criticising his employers in the press. That is never going to end well, but he did that because he thought he could survive, especially after winning promotion, when his stock should have been at its highest.

He had engineered a situation in which he felt he could oust Gunnar in a boardroom coup and began to manoeuvre himself so he could persuade some of the board to dispose of his problematic boss, but it was a miscalculation.

I remember, to celebrate promotion there was a dinner held at the ground. When I walked in with Del, I found myself faced with either turning left to sit with the chairman and the rest of the board or turn right to sit with Gudjon. The relationship had broken down that far, they wouldn't even sit together to celebrate achieving their aim. I stood there, frozen for a moment thinking to myself, 'What shall I do here?'

It was definitely a lose/lose situation, but I decided we'd sit with Gudjon, hoping that the board wouldn't hold it against me. I now believe that was the night that sealed Gudjon's fate.

I don't know exactly what happened as I wasn't privy to it, but, as I understand it, shortly afterwards, instead of the board voting on whether to change chairman, as Gudjon had proposed to them, they voted on whether to change manager. It ended up something like four to two in favour of sacking him and so Gudjon departed.

I remember when the announcement was made, I left the ground at the end of the day, passing a few supporters outside who wanted to know what on earth was going on. We'd won promotion and then sacked the manager. No one does that! It made no sense to the outside world, but made a world of sense to those of us on the inside. The situation couldn't continue, so it was best for the club that it was brought to a head. It was just that Gudjon didn't see what eventually happened coming; a victory for Gislason in an increasingly bitter battle.

* * *

Quite frankly, I don't think the Icelandic consortium thought winning promotion from the third tier with Stoke City was going to be as difficult as it proved. It sucked them dry of money, as would establishing themselves in the First Division, soon to be renamed the Championship. It had now cost them their talismanic manager and a lot of the interest from folk in Iceland went with Gudjon as he departed in tears. This time, Gunnar announced he wanted a British replacement and, thankfully for me, confirmed that my job and those of the coaching staff were safe.

At this point, Phil Rawlins, one of the English board members, who had bought in since the takeover, taking a 10 per cent stake for £1.2 million, showed an interest in buying the club. Consequently, his suggestion of appointing Steve Cotterill, who was doing well at Cheltenham Town, having won them the 1998 FA Trophy, promotion to the Football League in 1999 and then from the fourth to third tier in 2001/02, won favour. With the Icelandics considering selling up, they listened to his choice and appointed Cotterill, although Rawlins did not pursue the purchase.

The new manager was tasked with keeping Stoke in the second tier, although Steve being English meant he would need a lot less help from me, but I soon realised he needed me in other ways as he could be very aggressive and rash with the players, much like Gudjon. Not only that, but I had to bridge the gap between him and the Icelandic board, as none of them were in Stoke to speak to directly. He was severely tested as we won just three of the opening 12 league games and went out of the League Cup at Bury, whereas he'd been used to winning. During the October international break, I received a call from Steve asking for a meeting, which was unusual because he lived down south and it didn't make sense that he would come all the way up to Stoke during a time when so many players would be off round the globe.

Instead, he just carried on talking and told me he was thinking about leaving.

'You what?' I couldn't believe what I was hearing. I knew the situation wasn't great, but he had done OK in his first three months.

Steve said he wasn't very impressed with the Icelandic board, telling me he couldn't cope with the fact they were in Iceland and he struggled to communicate with them. Instead, he'd been offered an opportunity to be number two at Premier League Sunderland to Howard Wilkinson, who he had met at Lilleshall, and then take over as manager.

I couldn't change his mind and, just like that, he was gone.

I am sure Steve now views that move as a mistake as it didn't really work out for him. For Stoke fans, it meant the bizarre nature of Gudjon's departure was soon forgotten as Cotterill became known amongst them as 'Quitterill'.

So now, we were looking for yet another manager. The Icelandics wanted me to stay on for continuity, but I quickly made it clear I didn't want the job, being more than happy in my current role. First-team coach David Kevan stepped up as manager for four games, all of which were lost as Dave didn't relish the pressure of management.

One of the Icelandics had wanted George Burley, rather than Cotterill, in the first place, so now they put their foot down and tasked me with persuading him to join. George had just left Ipswich after eight years in charge in which he had finally got them back up to the Premier League and won the 2000/01 Manager of the Season accolade for taking them into Europe through a fifth-place finish, which was a fantastic achievement. They had then had a terrible season as they got too stretched with competing on so many fronts and been relegated, but I knew George would be a fabulous man to work with.

After George had agreed to come, the board invited him to watch our evening game against Watford on 30 October 2002. I drove him back to the North Stafford Hotel, where he was staying, after watching the fairly dismal 1-2 defeat and had a drink with him, chatting about the following day's press conference at which he was to be unveiled. However, while we were sitting in a quiet corner of the bar, his mobile was ringing nineteen to the dozen all the way up to about half past midnight. He would make his excuses and disappear off and answer it, so I couldn't hear what was being said. Eventually, I departed, saying, 'See you tomorrow.'

To which George replied, 'See you tomorrow.'

Except I didn't.

I realise now that those calls were outside influences persuading George that managing Stoke was not a good idea and led to him abruptly changing his mind. I don't know exactly what they said to him, but whatever it was, it led to him fleeing for the hills and the club had a huge amount of egg on its face. Especially as the press conference was due to be broadcast on Sky Sports News.

The major problem I had with this was that George didn't have the decency to ring me to explain that he had changed his mind. I had left the hotel thinking I would be working with him as manager. His phone, which he had responded to multiple times the previous night, remained solidly unanswered.

This caused carnage, as you can imagine. Suddenly, instead of a run-of-the-mill new manager unveiling, the press corps had a great story on their hands of 'will he, won't he turn up' as the board's and my faces got longer and longer. Sky TV were loving it, throwing live from Isleworth to the ground, while we hared around, trying to find out what was happening. Eventually, we had to make a statement that George was not taking the job and in the rather depressed meeting after we had disbanded the press corps, Gislason turned to me and said, 'John, what on earth are we going to do now?'

I had helped get Tony Pulis an interview in the brief round the board had held before agreeing on Burley, as well as him having been considered when both Megson and Cotterill were appointed, and he had impressed. However, because the Icelandics thought he was Peter Coates' choice as Peter had wanted him back in 1999, they had gone with Burley. I knew that if Peter made the suggestion of appointing Pulis again it would be ignored, so instead, in answer to Gunnar's weary question, I just said, 'Well, it looks like it will have to be Tony Pulis then.' And, so it came to pass.

Everyone was happy. Peter got his man, while the Icelandics thought they had made the decision.

Call me Kissinger.

* * *

Tony had chosen to go to Bristol City when he turned the job down in 1999. Being a former Rover like myself wasn't a good recipe, though, and his tenure only lasted to January 2000, when he had moved to Portsmouth, dragging them out of the relegation zone to mid-table safety by the end of the campaign before falling out with chairman Milan Mandaric and being sacked a few months into the 2000/01 season. He then spent much of the next two years fighting a legal battle against another former club, Gillingham, where he had become embroiled in a bitter scrap with chairman Paul Scally.

His appointment was not well received by supporters, who were worried about his style of football as Tony was, let's not beat around the bush here, happy to do whatever it took to survive; and if that mean playing big fellers and humping the ball long then that's what he would do. Tony's major boast was that he had never been relegated as a manager. The current scenario would put him severely to the test; Stoke had won just three games, and none in the last 16, losing the past four and he would lose his first four too. Eventually results started to improve, although it took nine matches to register a first victory; an epic 3-2 win over Sheffield Wednesday at Christmas thanks to a last-minute Brynjar Gunnarsson winner. That was Tony's tenth game in charge, so it pays to have patience sometimes. That period was a big test. You show your true colours when things are difficult and you're fighting against the elements. Tony was strong and came through with flying colours.

I remember his first game very well. It was a baptism of fire, not least because of the reaction of a significant number of Stoke fans. With the team 0-3 down at Walsall, Tony made two substitutions, replacing Iwelumo and Gudjonsson with Cooke and Chris Greenacre, only for the Stoke fans behind the goal to vent forth with a chorus of 'You don't know what you're doing!'

Both subs scored to pull us back to 2-3 and it looked like a remarkable comeback might be on, but then Thomas gave away a stupid penalty with a blatant push and we ended up losing 2-4, but Tony had made his statement and the fans, clearly upset at what had been going on at the club, began to respect him from then on.

Tony knew the lower divisions incredibly well, so my role changed and, rather than researching players, I would be given targets to hunt down. Tony wanted battle-hardened, experienced pros, so this led us to recruiting experienced loan signings, such as goalkeeper Mark Crossley, left-back Marcus Hall, centre-half Mark Williams and midfielder Paul Warhurst, as there was simply no money in the kitty. They dovetailed well with the likes of Thomas to form a sizeable and solid defence.

Another player who made a key difference was my old centre-forward from Port Vale, Lee Mills, who I persuaded to come back on loan from Coventry, where he had ended up after leaving first Bradford then Portsmouth, for whom he had signed when Tony was their manager. Lee hammered in a late equaliser in a crucial draw at Norwich and then scored the only goal in the return game against Walsall, deflecting in a Thomas shot which was heading wide. He may have only played seven games, many of those as sub, but those two goals secured four points, the margin we would eventually stay up by.

The final loanee who made a difference was Ade Akinbiyi, who we persuaded to join from Crystal Palace where he had become something of a pariah, after a similarly dismal spell in front of goal whilst at Leicester. We knew he was a good goalscorer as his spells early in his career at Wolves, Gillingham and Bristol City showed. Ade had played for Tony at both of the latter two clubs and he'd sold him to Wanderers for a club record fee of £3.5 million in 1999. Now, four years later, his stock was low, but coming to Stoke rejuvenated Ade. His powerful, workaholic running style was just what we needed up front and the fans took to him, even if his finishing remained a tad wayward at times. He did manage to score two crucial goals in his four games at the end of the season, the second securing a famous victory over Reading in the final game, heading home Lewis Neal's left-wing cross at the near post in a flail of dreadlocks, then taking his top off to celebrate in the sunshine in front of the Boothen End with just his vest on. Somehow, Tony had pulled us around and we avoided relegation, which had seemed extremely unlikely in late February when we had been thrashed 0-6 at Nottingham Forest.

One player on his way out was Chris Iwelumo, and thereby hangs a tale. When Tony arrived, he played Chris in a few games and the big striker finished up as leading scorer with seven goals in that first season as we avoided relegation, but, in summer 2003, Tony signed Akinbiyi permanently and also took Gifton Noel-Williams from Watford on a free transfer, meaning Chris was consigned to the bench, if he made the matchday squad at all. Tony asked me to move him on, as he also wasn't enamoured with his work rate, so I put together a video of Chris's best moments so we could tout him around to generate some cash that Tony could use to bring someone else in. When we were done, myself and the video guys at the club were really pleased with the highlights reel we'd put together, featuring Chris's best moments, including all of his goals, especially that fantastic volley against Wigan in the FA Cup, slamming a deep cross into the net first time from the edge of the penalty area, and his equaliser in the Potteries derby in October 2001. Tony and I sat down and watched the tape, along with a few other key staff, and, as it played, I realised the tape made Chris look like Pele, Alan Shearer and Zinedine Zidane combined. When it finished, Tony turned round and said, 'Hold on a minute, John, this is just the kind of player we're looking for!'

We used that video to persuade Brighton, who had just been relegated back to the third tier, to sign Chris on loan and he did well for them, before moving out to Aachen in the Bundesliga second division then returning to England to play for Charlton, Wolves and Burnley, as well as for Scotland, so it wasn't just my editing skills which made him look good, the boy could play! Chris tells this story on a regular basis now he is a TV and radio pundit.

Also moving on in summer 2003 was midfielder James O'Connor, sold for £250,000 to West Brom because we would have otherwise lost him for nothing under freedom of contract. To freshen things up, Tony signed experienced Dutch goalkeeper Ed de Goey, who had just been let go by Chelsea, and Carl Asaba, who he had managed at Gillingham. During the autumn, as we were still struggling, we brought in big Gerry Taggart from Leicester. Gerry had been a top player coming towards the end of his career, but could still do a fantastic job in the Championship and made the world of difference to our defence. I had signed another central defender, Clint Hill from Oldham for £120,000, but he was struck down by injury, hence needing Gerry. I had seen Clint play a few times and liked his commitment. In fact, Clint would tackle his granny if it meant saving a goal. He threw his body in front of everything, which was why he got injured a lot. Clint didn't really recover until the following season, but went on to be a fine player for us at both centre-half and left-back, when Tony deployed his often-favoured option of four centre-halves along the back.

Another arrival was talented midfielder John Eustace, although he would spend much of the next couple of seasons injured, while tigerish midfielder Dave Brammer joined from Crewe, where he'd moved after spending three seasons across the city at Port Vale.

That made us a tremendously competitive side and we finished comfortably in mid-table that season and began 2004/05 losing just one of the first 11 games, hitting the top of the table after defeating Ipswich 3-2 in mid-September. But we were competitive in other ways, none more so than Taggart, an abrasive Irishman who loved a drink and righting wrongs. He had been a clubmate with Dennis Wise whilst at Leicester and had a long-standing feud to settle with the now Millwall player-manager. Wise had broken the nose of Callum Davidson during a fight on a 2002 pre-season tour. Taggart was a friend of Davidson and took great exception to this, not least because Wise had inflicted the blow while Davidson was actually asleep on his hotel bed.

So come October 2004, the Lions' visit to the Brit set the scene for revenge. I had always known Gerry could be very aggressive, but sat in astonishment as he turned on Wise after a tackle and grabbed him, getting him in a headlock on the ground. It was like watching Giant Haystacks wrestle Jimmy Krankie. I'm fairly sure Gerry would still have Wise pinned to the ground now if the referee hadn't been Uriah Rennie, the much respected official, who also happened to be an expert kick-boxer and serving magistrate. Rennie hauled the two apart and, unbelievably, only issued yellow cards when everyone in the ground assumed they would be red.

In the dressing room after the game, Gerry said Wise had run his studs down the back of his leg, so he'd reacted and then assumed he'd be sent off. When he wasn't, he'd told Rennie next time he saw him at the dog track he'd buy him a drink!

* * *

At that time, Jez Moxey's successor, chief executive Jonathan Fuller, just allowed me to get on with things in terms of players and recruitment, especially where it concerned contracts. He was very hands off in that sense. This was very similar to how I had worked for all those years at Port Vale and suited me down to the ground, so I was very happy to get on with things, while Jonathan concentrated on organising the rest of the club, especially generating sponsorship revenue and through the various lounges and matchday hospitality routes. The club began to stabilise in the Championship under Tony and I enjoyed a celebration when I reached the age of 60 in 2004, as the club presented me with an engraved mug to mark the occasion and various colleagues gave me lovely gifts, followed by a little celebratory drink in the boardroom.

Tony and I were a great team and attracting some attention as a duo, so much so that we used to get various offers, one of which came towards the end of that season when the club was contacted by an American manufacturer of a new heart diagnosis machine to ask if we would help them with some publicity. Tony and I drove down to London to try out this new apparatus, which apparently could spot potential problems some ten years earlier than conventional methods.

Tony went in first and came out a few minutes later, beaming with pride, chest puffed out.

'John, I've scored 98 per cent. I've got a heart like Steve Redgrave's,' he gloated.

In I went and, lo and behold, after much muttering, I was given the diametrically opposite news – my score was something like 45 per cent. In fact, my heart was in a bit of a state, having dangerously high levels of calcium deposits in my arteries, and I needed to head to hospital for further tests.

Hooting with laughter, Tony drove me back to Stoke and I went to hospital. As you can imagine, I had the urine extracted from me for the entire journey. The more detailed ECG I then had gave the doctors some cause for concern, although I passed a treadmill test with flying colours, and I had a full exam every six months for the next few years. Thankfully, they never found anything, but it was a heck of a scare.

* * *

Just when it looked like the club was about to mount a promotion attempt a lack of goals caught up with us. That stemmed back to what had happened in the summer of 2004. Tony thought he could persuade striker Peter Crouch to sign from Southampton. He had been given a budget of £2 million by the board to have a serious go at promotion and that was how he wanted to spend just over £1 million of it. Rather bizarrely, the board never responded to Tony's request. In fact, when I tried to call Gunnar Gislason, I was told he had gone out fishing and was uncontactable, which tells you everything you need to know about how keen they were to sign Crouchy. The opportunity fell by the wayside and Peter was sold to Liverpool a year later for £7 million.

Another missed opportunity came just before Christmas after Tony and I had agreed another £1 million deal, this time with West Ham for Bobby Zamora. However, by that time the knives were out for Tony and the Icelandics said they would only let us have £800,000, so the deal fell through. It felt like they were deliberately blocking progress.

In fact, major shareholder Magnus Kristinsson had put Stoke up for sale in protest at Tony being given a new contract that year, but, when no acceptable bids came in, the club was taken off the market and instead, at the end of the season, the manager was removed.

But not before an infamous season unravelled, which has become known as the 'binary season' because, from the end of October to mid-February, all 17 league games resulted in either a goalless draw or a 1-0 victory to either team (in fact four of the previous seven games did too, and the match after the run ended with a 3-2 victory over Leicester ended in a goalless draw against Coventry, but who's counting?). Playing four centre-halves across the back, with Hill at left-back and Thomas at right-back, then Taggart and experienced new signing Michael Duberry from Leeds in between, didn't endear Tony to either the board or the fans. It meant we also didn't concede many goals and sat comfortably in mid-table, or marooned there if you preferred. The football was far from scintillating and the supporters vented their anger at the lack of entertainment. I felt sorry for them, but knew that Tony had his hands tied behind his back by the board's refusal to bring in the players who would score the goals.

Not only that, but the striker we did have wasn't happy either, as I found out to my personal cost in early February 2005.

Ade Akinbiyi may have been a cult hero at Stoke after his part in the 2002/03 survival campaign and his 17 goals in the season and a half since, but his contract was a problem as he had taken a wage drop to sign permanently, but only on the promise from the chairman that this would be reviewed the following season.

No review had been forthcoming.

Now 30 years old, Ade wanted higher wages and also a longer contract, so went round telling everyone he wanted to finish his career at Stoke if a deal could be agreed. He knew he had been the subject of transfer bids from Sheffield United and Wigan Athletic which had been rejected, so was in demand, which put him in a strong position.

No contract appeared.

Fed up with waiting for the board, who were once again hiding in Iceland, Ade came to me to try and unblock the impasse. The only problem was, I had not been given any authority to negotiate a new contract with him. The scene was set for one of the more bizarre episodes of my career.

After training, I heard a knock on the door and Ade entered. He clearly wasn't happy, which I already knew, but I told him I could do nothing about it. He would need to speak with the chairman.

Ade asked if he could stay and I told him he was welcome to, but it wouldn't change anything; only Gunnar Gislason could offer him a new deal, but I could never get hold of him myself, so ...

Ade made himself comfortable.

And sat.

After about an hour, I agreed to try and call the chairman and was surprised when, for once, Gunnar took the call, although I bet he wished he hadn't. Ade launched forth and spoke to (or should that be at) the chairman for an hour, making clear how he, and other players, felt about the atmosphere at the club.

Gunnar listened, but then just said, 'Goodbye.'

Frustrated, Ade remained seated. He never lost his cool with me at all, but he must have been seething inside to be treated like that, so I said, 'Look, it's no good you staying here, Ade. I can't make this decision without the board.'

He remained sitting there, staring impassively.

Half an hour later I said, 'Ade, listen, this is a waste of time. I can't sanction this deal.'

His silent protest continued.

An hour later, the same conversation repeated itself.

I carried on with my work and when five o'clock came I said, 'Ade, I've got to go now.'

'I'm staying here,' came the reply.

'Seriously, Ade, I'm going,' I said.

I headed home, leaving the frustrated Akinbiyi stuck on that chair. I don't actually know exactly how long he remained sitting in my office, but eventually someone persuaded him to go home.

Needless to say, word soon got around. The papers all wrote sizeable pieces about his sit-in, while the players were killing themselves with laughter over it. So much so, in fact, that we only went and won the next game at Wigan after losing the last five to the only goal of each game. It was without the injured Ade, but yes, you've guessed it, we won 1-0.

I've got a newspaper clipping about that incident which says: 'Apparently unruffled by the occupation of his office, Rudge said: "Ade is a very important player for us and has done exceptionally well here. He gets on very well with Tony Pulis, who gets the best out of him."'

Ever the diplomat. And boy, did I need those skills throughout that period.

Perhaps not surprisingly, a £600,000 offer from Burnley, now managed by Steve Cotterill (remember him?) was accepted shortly afterwards. When he left, Ade issued a statement, insisting he had never sought a move and had only left because the club's hierarchy wanted him gone. That wasn't myself and Tony, that was the board.

Ade wasn't the only one to go public with his grievances; Gerry Taggart and Wayne Thomas also went to the press, with Thommo claiming the club was treating him like an 'arse'. He eventually allowed his contract to run out in the summer of 2005, before joining Akinbiyi at Turf Moor. So, we lost another good player. They were disappearing like mirages in a desert.

Amidst all of this, the manager was also at loggerheads with the Icelandic board; not over his own pay, but over those transfer funds which had failed to materialise. To mask that, the board now accused Tony of failing to exploit the foreign transfer market. To bring things to a head, the Icelandics brought over two of their own players and basically insisted Tony play them. Tony was not impressed, not least because he didn't think they were any good. Tryggvi Gudmundsen, the ageing all-time leading scorer in Icelandic football, and Toddi Gudjonsson arrived instead of Zamora or Crouch, two of the hottest young English strikers at the time. Tony was seething at the funds having been withheld from him and now being expected to play this pair, who fans soon dubbed Triggy and Ziggy. I remember saying to him, 'Tone, you've got to play your cards right here. Let them bring them over and take a look at them and when they are no good, just send the buggers back.'

Tony was having none of it. He didn't see the point as they weren't up to Championship standard. His refusal to play ball seemed to be the straw which broke the camel's back with the board and it became inevitable that Tony would be leaving at the end of the 2004/05 season, no matter how well we did, for displaying far too much resistance to the board's wishes, backing himself into a hole.

When the firing came on 28 June, Gunnar publicly stated that Tony had not invested in the foreign market sufficiently, although the truth lay far more that their investment hadn't worked out how the Icelandics had expected, with many of the financial issues caused because they didn't understand English football.

I remember walking with Tony from the main entrance at the Britannia Stadium out to his car in the car park after he had told me he had been dismissed. I knew he'd get another job fairly quickly, which he did; at Plymouth. But I had no idea, as I said goodbye and watched him drive off, what would happen to me. The club was up for sale again. Phil Rawlins had once more explored a purchase, but instead opted to found a new club in Orlando, Florida. That left only Peter Coates and Keith Humphreys as interested or even viable buyers, given their 'golden shares', but in the end the Icelandics decided to give it one more go.

At that stage, I had no clue as to who would be given the manager's job for the forthcoming season and was in complete limbo. Little did I know that the devastating upset of seeing Tony sacked was merely the beginning of what would turn out to be one of the most tumultuous periods in my football career.

Chapter 16

Jesus Christ, Adolf Hitler and the Shit Guy

'I have no respect for the guy and want to kick him in the balls.'

Johan Boskamp, on striker Sammy Bangoura

THAT SUMMER of 2005 saw me in limbo. I wondered if the Icelandics thought I would leave as well, but I had no intention of moving on, so just kept turning up for work, trying to do my best for the club, wheeling and dealing for players as we hardly had any left. Clive Clarke had joined Premiership West Ham for £275,000, Wayne Thomas and Carl Asaba had left on frees, while the following January John Halls would be sold to Reading for £250,000 as the Icelanders needed to generate funds.

We needed new blood, but without a manager it was difficult, and we missed out on a young Kevin Doyle, signed by Reading from Cork City instead of us. I did have one deal to complete, but even that proved difficult. Before he left, Tony Pulis had agreed to sign Mamady Sidibe, the giant Gillingham and Mali striker. Now the manager had moved on, there was some uncertainty over whether the club wanted to go through with Mama's contract, which would start on 1 July. Without a manager, Mama was also unsure if he wanted to commit. I was left in the middle.

We really needed to appoint someone or we would end up with just the eight players we had signed on at that point.

Then news broke of who that new manager was to be and it was a totally left-field choice; Johan Boskamp.

Who?

* * *

The Icelandic consortium were throwing everything at making one last effort to win promotion in the 2005/06 season. Boskamp, it turned out, had pedigree, even if he was unknown in the UK. After a stellar playing career which had seen him make the Dutch squad for the 1978 World Cup alongside Cruyff, Krol and Rep, he had managed Anderlecht to three Belgian titles and into the Champions League, before leaving to coach Georgian side Dinamo Tbilisi, where for a while he held the dual role of also managing the Georgian national team. He'd returned to Belgium, where he won the 2000 FA Cup with Racing Genk, then managed clubs in the Middle East, as well as coaching the United Arab Emirates national team.

The way it came about was that the Icelandics had appointed Eidur Gudjohnsen's dad, Arnor, to find a new manager and he'd put forward Jan de Koning, the former Ajax coach who had provided me with Dutch and Belgian players over the years. But Jan didn't want to be the boss, so instead suggested his friend, Boskamp, who agreed to take the job with de Koning as his assistant. Jan explained to Johan that he needed to keep me on as I was the one who knew everything about the English Football League, so my job was safe and, as with Gudjon all those years before, my expertise was called upon working alongside a foreign manager.

Johan's appointment seemed something of a coup on paper, although it was always an over-reaction to the 'Englishness' of the Tony Pulis regime. The reality would prove to be somewhat different.

Speaking with him on the phone before he arrived in England, I got Johan to agree to signing Sidibe, who I told him would be a great signing for us and so he proved. I believe the fact that Mama played for Stoke for eight years, being crucial to us winning promotion and establishing us as a Premier League club, then only left due to injury, vindicates this. He is still involved in the club now as a scout in France and remains living in the area, with his son, Souleymane, playing at Stoke's academy. He and his wife, Bineta, even once opened a patisserie in the Potteries Shopping Centre in Hanley.

I remember getting far more involved in Mama's arrival than I would normally, as he phoned me to say his removals men had let him down. He was all packed and ready to go, so I arranged a new removal van to bring his family's furniture and possessions all the way from Kent. I met him at the club house we'd rented for him in Stoke, where I helped him and his family unload his belongings. They didn't teach you about humping players' furniture around at ten o'clock at night at Lilleshall, I can tell you, but it did cement a great relationship between me and the big man with the shining smile, who was incredibly grateful for my assistance.

Mama was a fantastic pro and wonderful with the fans. The other players loved him, despite his goalscoring not being the greatest. The thing was with Mama, you could absolutely rely on him.

Oh, and he was free, having reached the end of his contract at Priestfield.

I had also been briefed once again that we needed to be exploiting the fabled foreign markets, so signing a player who was in some senses both British, having played in England since 2001 with Swansea then Gillingham, as well as foreign, fitted the bill nicely. It soon became apparent that my local knowledge would be much-needed as Boskamp knew nothing about English football. And I mean nothing. That isn't to say he was useless by any means, but it didn't bode well right from the off.

It wasn't just his career that was unknown to me, even though I did my research when Johan's appointment was announced – I also didn't know what Boskamp looked like. As he was travelling from the continent and I wasn't sure when he would arrive on his first day, I popped downstairs from my office and passed this dishevelled, frankly tubby, gentleman asleep on the couch in the main reception. I could see this chap's shirt was untucked and his belly was hanging out as he lay there, but took very little notice of him as I walked across to the receptionists to ask if there was any news as to when the new manager would be arriving. I was shocked to be told, 'he's here', as the lady pointed past my shoulder to said Boris Johnson look a like, snoring away on the couch.

It was an introduction which set the standard for what was to follow.

Johan was ambitious when he first arrived, saying to the press, 'I like to play attacking, attractive football and I like fast football. I believe the bookies think we are on the way to the Third Division, but me, I'm hoping we make the play-offs.' However, he soon became disillusioned with the Icelandics, as all the previous managers had. Just a lot quicker.

Yes, even more quickly than Cotterill.

A mere three weeks later, during our pre-season in Germany, just after we had lost 0-1 to Hannover and were really struggling to sign players, Johan got very down as we had a late night drink at our hotel and blurted out to Jan and I that he'd had enough and was going to call the chairman and resign. We stayed up deep into the night and talked him round. I told him, 'Listen, we will be OK. You get a few more players using your Belgian contacts and I'll be able to find some more English ones. You can do this.'

This proved to be typical; with Johan there was always some crisis or other going on. We stumbled from day to day, up high then down in the dumps. Lurching from one thing to another just wasn't my way of doing things. I prefer slow and steady.

Much of the Boskamp craziness was to come. For now, we needed players; droves of them. I remember Gerry Taggart once asked during pre-season, 'What the hell are we going to do, John?'

Coaching from the sidelines. No wonder I had to don a cap to hide my quickly receding hairline!

Celebrating staying up at Huddersfield after a wonderful 4-0 victory in May 1998.

Turning on the Christmas lights at Ipstones with Brian Little, the Stoke City manager, in 1999.

The signing that got away, although Robbie Williams did recruit me to manage his team for Soccer 6, the initial predecessor of the now global annual event, Soccer Aid.

Developing the giant centre-half Anthony Gardner led to an £855,000 profit for Vale, my epiphany in Cannes when I realised I should have gone to work for his agent, Jonathan Barnett, and this ridiculous photo opportunity, which might give you the idea that I'm small. It's perspective, I tell you …

The pain and anguish as my time at Port Vale came to an end; managing can be a lonely business.

The sale of right-winger Gareth Ainsworth by the board behind my back was the catalyst for the series of events which led to me leaving Vale.

John Barnwell of the League Managers' Association helped me in my case against Bill Bell.

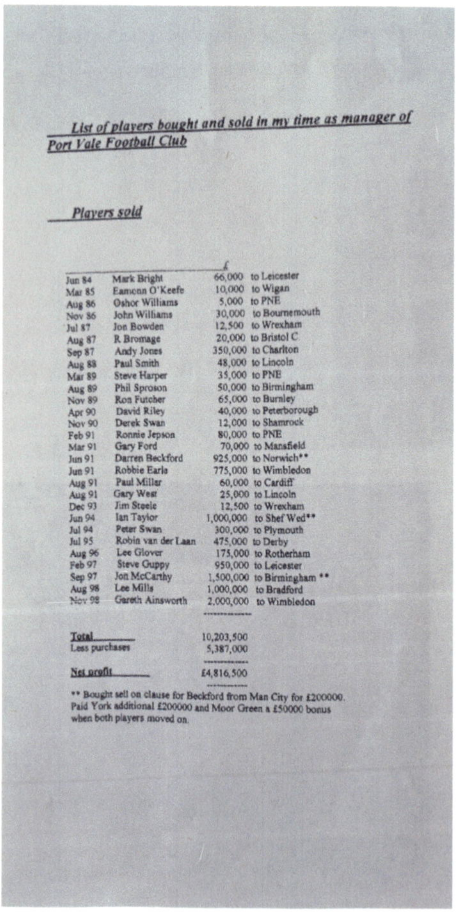

List of players bought and sold in my time as manager of Port Vale Football Club

Players sold

		£	
Jun 84	Mark Bright	66,000	to Leicester
Mar 85	Eamonn O'Keefe	10,000	to Wigan
Aug 86	Oshor Williams	5,000	to PNE
Nov 86	John Williams	30,000	to Bournemouth
Jul 87	Jon Bowden	12,500	to Wrexham
Aug 87	R Bromage	20,000	to Bristol C
Sep 87	Andy Jones	350,000	to Charlton
Aug 88	Paul Smith	48,000	to Lincoln
Mar 89	Steve Harper	35,000	to PNE
Aug 89	Phil Sproson	50,000	to Birmingham
Nov 89	Ron Futcher	65,000	to Burnley
Apr 90	David Riley	40,000	to Peterborough
Nov 90	Derek Swan	12,000	to Shamrock
Feb 91	Ronnie Jepson	80,000	to PNE
Mar 91	Gary Ford	70,000	to Mansfield
Jun 91	Darren Beckford	925,000	to Norwich**
Jun 91	Robbie Earle	775,000	to Wimbledon
Aug 91	Paul Millar	60,000	to Cardiff
Aug 91	Gary West	25,000	to Lincoln
Dec 93	Jim Steele	12,500	to Wrexham
Jun 94	Ian Taylor	1,000,000	to Shef Wed**
Jul 94	Peter Swan	300,000	to Plymouth
Jul 95	Robin van der Laan	475,000	to Derby
Aug 96	Lee Glover	175,000	to Rotherham
Feb 97	Steve Guppy	950,000	to Leicester
Sep 97	Jon McCarthy	1,500,000	to Birmingham **
Aug 98	Lee Mills	1,000,000	to Bradford
Nov 98	Gareth Ainsworth	2,000,000	to Wimbledon
Total		10,203,500	
Less purchases		5,387,000	
Net profit		£4,816,500	

** Bought sell on clause for Beckford from Man City for £200000. Paid York additional £200000 and Moor Green a £50000 bonus when both players moved on.

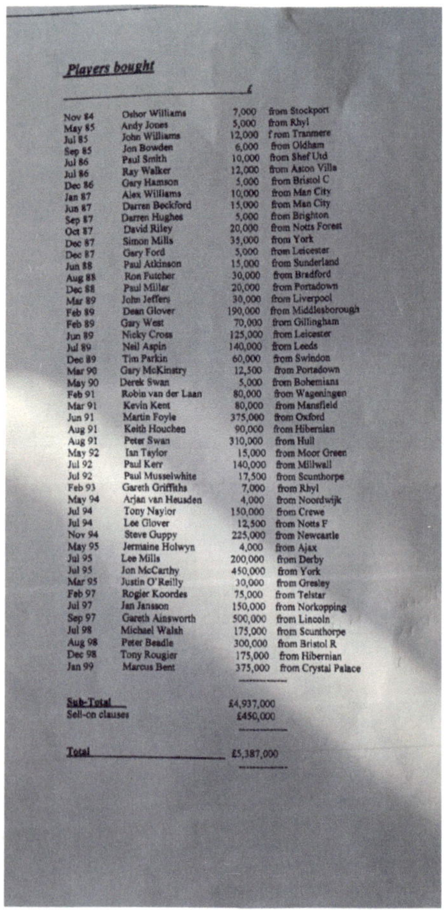

Players bought

		£	
Nov 84	Oshor Williams	7,000	from Stockport
May 85	Andy Jones	5,000	from Rhyl
Jul 85	John Williams	12,000	from Tranmere
Sep 85	Jon Bowden	6,000	from Oldham
Jul 86	Paul Smith	10,000	from Shef Utd
Jul 86	Ray Walker	12,000	from Aston Villa
Dec 86	Gary Hamson	5,000	from Bristol C
Jan 87	Alex Williams	10,000	from Man City
Jun 87	Darren Beckford	15,000	from Man City
Sep 87	Darren Hughes	5,000	from Brighton
Oct 87	David Riley	20,000	from Notts Forest
Dec 87	Simon Mills	35,000	from York
Dec 87	Gary Ford	5,000	from Leicester
Jun 88	Paul Atkinson	15,000	from Sunderland
Aug 88	Ron Futcher	30,000	from Bradford
Dec 88	Paul Millar	20,000	from Portadown
Mar 89	John Jeffers	30,000	from Liverpool
Feb 89	Dean Glover	190,000	from Middlesborough
Feb 89	Gary West	70,000	from Gillingham
Jun 89	Nicky Cross	125,000	from Leicester
Jul 89	Neil Aspin	140,000	from Leeds
Dec 89	Tim Parkin	60,000	from Swindon
Mar 90	Gary McKinstry	12,500	from Portadown
May 90	Derek Swan	5,000	from Bohemians
Feb 91	Robin van der Laan	80,000	from Wageningen
Mar 91	Kevin Kent	80,000	from Mansfield
Jun 91	Martin Foyle	375,000	from Oxford
Aug 91	Keith Houchen	90,000	from Hibernian
Aug 91	Peter Swan	310,000	from Hull
May 92	Ian Taylor	15,000	from Moor Green
Jul 92	Paul Kerr	140,000	from Millwall
Jul 92	Paul Musselwhite	17,500	from Scunthorpe
Feb 93	Gareth Griffiths	7,000	from Rhyl
May 94	Arjan van Heusden	4,000	from Noordwijk
Jul 94	Tony Naylor	150,000	from Crewe
Jul 94	Lee Glover	12,500	from Notts F
Nov 94	Steve Guppy	225,000	from Newcastle
May 95	Jermaine Holwyn	4,000	from Ajax
Jul 95	Lee Mills	200,000	from Derby
Jul 95	Jon McCarthy	450,000	from York
Mar 95	Justin O'Reilly	30,000	from Gresley
Feb 97	Rogier Koordes	75,000	from Telstar
Jul 97	Jan Jansson	150,000	from Norkopping
Sep 97	Gareth Ainsworth	500,000	from Lincoln
Jul 98	Michael Walsh	175,000	from Scunthorpe
Aug 98	Peter Beadle	300,000	from Bristol R
Dec 98	Tony Rougier	175,000	from Hibernian
Jan 99	Marcus Bent	375,000	from Crystal Palace
Sub-Total		£4,937,000	
Sell-on clauses		£450,000	
Total		£5,387,000	

The evidence I presented to the tribunal of the players I had bought and sold for Port Vale and the circa £5 million profit I had made for the club.

The 'flat cap march' before the home game after my sacking in January 1999. I'd managed Port Vale for 843 matches.

Saying thank you to the incredible Port Vale fans at the surprise tribute night at Trentham in May 1999; just the tonic I needed after a tough few months. Wonderful memories.

…ER REFLECTS ON THE SPECIAL RELATIONSHIP BETWEEN CLUB AND MANAGER

It must have been a heatwave at Vale Park – John in the dugout without his flat cap.

…ale... a happy heaven!

Vale of cheers – John takes the crowd's applause at his testimonial match against Aston Villa.

problems. But that was John Rudge. Once described as a "nuts and bolts manager" by Ron Atkinson, he was head coach, chief scout, public relations officer, chief fundraiser and poet rolled into one.

He was canny, too, in courting the supporters who, in turn, helped to keep him in a job and how genuinely sad John was not to reach that milestone of 20 years with the club.

Loyalty was the name of his game and the greatest pity of his departure was that he was, in many ways, tailor-made for the role that was on offer of Director of Football that would have accommodated all his qualities.

Unfortunately, John felt the "circumstances" were not right for him to continue at the club and Port Vale lost rather more than just a manager on that sad morning of January 18, 1999.

Man of the people – John is congratulated by Vale fans.

The brochure from that emotional night which became something of a This is Your Life moment, with colleagues and friends throughout my career showing up. I'd like to thank them all.

A whole new chapter in my footballing life begins; at rivals Stoke City, with manager Gary Megson (right) and coach Nigel Pearson.

Discussing the impending Icelandic takeover with chief executive Jez Moxey.

Icelandic manager Gudjon Thordarson could be fun, abrasive or sombre. His mood swings became a huge issue as he became more and more obsessed with promotion and fell further into dispute with his own board. I got on very well with Gudjon and was caught in the middle.

Far left: Celebrating clinching promotion at the Millennium Stadium in 2002. Wonderful days, but they proved to be Gudjon's last at Stoke.

Left: My granddaughter Danielle gets an early feel for lifting silverware.

New manager Steve Cotterill arrived in summer 2002 with a reputation after his success at Cheltenham Town and appointed coaches David Kevan and Ronnie Sinclair (right), but would only last 13 games before he too fell out with the Icelandic board and quit for Sunderland.

On scouting duty, pen and notepad at the ready. By this stage using the cap to go incognito really was a non-starter.

Johan Boskamp arrives for a madcap year in charge. Chairman Gunnar Gislason (centre) already looks wearied and Boskamp hasn't even fallen out with anyone yet.

Long-standing source of fantastic Dutch players, Jan de Koning, who then came to Stoke as assistant manager before we both fell out so spectacularly with Boskamp.

The return of Tony Pulis, coupled with that of Peter Coates and his new Bet365 company, galvanised Stoke City towards the Premier League within a couple of seasons. Here, Tony is being my ballboy. I never miss an opportunity to remind him he was once my apprentice at Bristol Rovers!

While here, Tony is laughing at another of my hilarious pranks.

At the 2011 FA Cup Final with Gerry Francis, who acted as a consultant throughout our time in the Premier League.

Stoke City chairman Peter Coates rejuvenated the club and bankrolled our march to the Premier League.

Our grandchildren Cameron, Hollie, Danielle and Emma were all born in the Stoke City era.

On certificate-awarding duties with a youthful Ryan Shawcross, pre-legend days.

Returning to Port Vale to support chairman Norman Smurthwaite … and my former captain Neil Aspin, now manager, in 2017. Neil managed to turn the club's fortunes around from a seemingly hopeless position to avoid relegation from the Football League.

Being the figurehead at Port Vale once again meant photo opportunities and media interviews.

Posing with a Potteries legend (Boomer the Vale mascot) and 'Nello'. Neil probably won't thank me for including a photograph of him at Vale Park in this book, but then he really shouldn't have kidnapped George Andrews before the final Potteries derby at the Victoria Ground now, should he?

Receiving a replica of the Autoglass Trophy 25 years on from our Wembley victory.

Del has always been at my side.

Dining with Kevin and Carol Shanahan (left), the new owners of Port Vale, with Del, Lisa and Deb.

Being announced as Port Vale club president …

… and made an honorary member of the Port Vale Supporters' Club in 2019; chairman Mark Porter doing the honours.

Honoured to be given the EFL Lifetime Achievement award in 2021, especially, as Rick Parry told me, it was voted for by managers.

The statue fundraising committee with sculptor Michael Talbot seated at the table with me.

On the pitch at the Etihad Stadium before Vale's FA Cup third round tie there in January 2020. Tom Pope's equaliser was a wonderful moment.

Being back involved as club president at Port Vale allowed me to be on the balcony as Darrell Clarke (left) and Andy Crosby celebrated winning the 2022 League Two play-off final.

Winning promotion is the least the wonderful Vale owner Carol Shanahan deserves for her incredible work, alongside husband Kevin, at the club since they took over in May 2019.

A crowd-pleaser into my late-70s … even young people want my autograph!

Our wonderful family; (from the left) our eldest Lisa, her husband Darren and their two children Danielle and Hollie, then myself and Del, accompanied by (from the right) Deb, her husband Andy and their two children Cameron and Emma.

The banner featuring Alex Ferguson's kind quote about me on the staircase in the main stand at Vale Park; ironically the Lorne Street stand which Bill Bell became so obsessed with but never finished.

Raising funds for the statue. Mugs with my mug on.

Two views of the maquettes made by wonderful sculptor Michael Talbot.

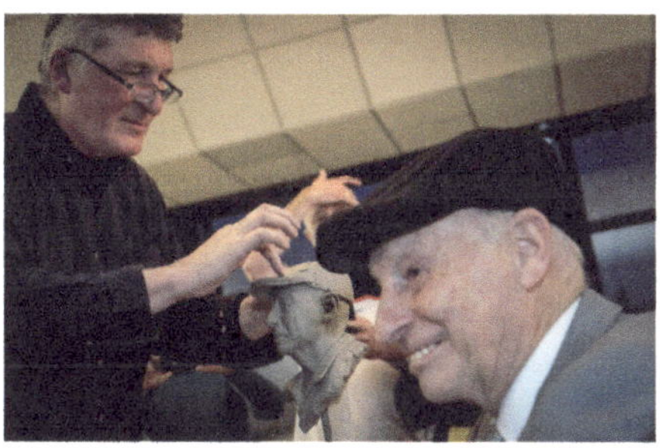

And here is Michael hard at work trying to make me look good, very difficult.

Our family all together; Del, Deb, Lisa, John and myself.

Robbie Earle very kindly gave me his Jamaica 1998 World Cup shirt which I have hung on the wall in my home office. He wrote 'To the "Gaffer", thanks for all your help all those years ago, Robbie'.

My bust in my study at home is where I keep my 2002 play-off winning medal, my Kangol 'JR 843' cap and the thank you medal I received from the 'Dougie Mac' for the funds raised at my farewell dinner at Trentham in 1999.

Hard at work finishing the book.

'Hold your nerve, Gerry,' I urged him. Eventually, I managed to persuade the likes of Marlon Broomes, Peter Sweeney, Bruce Dyer and Luke Chadwick to join us, while Johan used his Belgian and Dutch connections to sign Belgian midfielder Junior and Czech winger Martin Kolar, who Boskamp eulogised over; Junior was 'one of the most talented players in Belgium' and about the Czech star Boskamp said, 'People will be as crazy about Kolar as they were about Hoekstra, he has the same magic.'

Neither cut the mustard.

He did also bring in Belgian right-back Carl Hoefkens, a genuine talent who would be voted as Player of the Season, impressing with his technical ability and attacking flair.

At this point Johan was also complimentary about me in the media, for example, saying, 'John knows the game here in a way I don't. Also, I don't have the patience to sit in an office. John spoke for seven hours to the agent of Carl Hoefkens. I was saying, "stop it, let him go", but he went on and we got him.' In fact, I got on quite well with Johan at that stage. I got him fixed up with my friend Hugh Gallagher's empty apartment, so he could settle into the area. He had recently lost his wife at a young age and kindly invited me to meet his family in his country, so I flew over to Holland with him and enjoyed their wonderful hospitality. I then invited Johan round for dinner with my family. Things felt on track.

Even more so when I managed to bag Paul Gallagher on loan from Premier League Blackburn. At this stage my influence was very high and I was enjoying being involved in securing the signatures of some fantastic talent. Gallagher was a particularly good player and a great signing, I felt. I would still argue that the British players proved to be better value than most who arrived from overseas. As examples, I'd give you Hannes Sigurdsson (the last Icelander to join the club) and another Boskamp signing, Peter Kopteff. Their arrivals may have kept the board happy that the foreign market was being exploited, but they contributed little over the season.

* * *

Unexpectedly, this ragtag, rebuilt team started brightly and fans, especially those wearied by the more regimented tactics under the previous manager, delighted in the freer football Boskamp frequently delivered. Gone was the rigid defensive training and the four centre-halves across the back. Instead, we had old-style full-backs bombing down the wing.

However, defensively we became a slow-motion car crash. Supporters simply weren't used to losing 11 league games over a season at the Brit, including 3-0 drubbings by Watford, Cardiff and Hull, although, on the flip side, nor were they accustomed to winning 4-1 at Ipswich and 5-1 at Brighton. This was the up and down nature of that season.

It was tough and unrelenting and, when he realised what the job of managing in England entailed, Johan quickly tired of the demands. He was, without doubt, a strange manager, who arrived at 10.15am, just as the players were going out training, while he sat in reception having a cup of tea on the couch before going out – he became very attached to that couch. I ended up taking some of the sessions in that first part of the season, returning to find that Johan had left at 2.30pm. At one point I sat him down and asked him if he understood that the English way was for the manager to do everything.

'No, no, I just come in and do training. That's what we do on the continent.'

'You're in England now,' I told him, leaving aside the factual inaccuracy of him 'doing' training.

But Johan just said, 'No, I'm leaving now,' and headed off.

He may have had a very good record managing in Belgium, but Johan just couldn't fathom the work ethic demands of English management after a lifetime of coaching in the morning and putting his feet up in the afternoon on the continent.

Where he excelled was in press conferences, though not always for the right reasons. His media appearances remain legendary in the Potteries. Right from the start they were off the wall. The first league game of the season was against Sheffield Wednesday and, after Johan attended a pre-season friendly to scout the opposition, a BBC Radio Stoke reporter asked how his trip to watch them had gone. The reporter was probably expecting a conventional answer about Wednesday's style of play or potential threats, but instead Boskamp replied, 'I found a great chip shop 200 yards from the ground.'

If that was surprising, shortly afterwards, in an interview aimed at discovering more about this relatively unknown new manager, Johan was asked to tell BBC Radio Stoke's listeners something they wouldn't know about him. 'I'm not really a man,' exclaimed Johan, before bursting out laughing. On another occasion, he once asked legendary commentator Nigel Johnson live on air if he was in love with defender John Halls.

But his *piece de resistance* came in another live radio interview when Johan was asked to comment on a Polish player who should have been signing for Stoke but had messed us around, changing his mind at the 11th hour; 'Ahh, he's a shit guy,' was the manager's frank verdict. Forthright as ever.

Johan's grasp of English was not always the best and he then misheard a Nigel Johnson question about the problems Stoke had with players' agents. 'Nah man, I have no problem with Asians,' came the confused reply. He also once misinterpreted the terrace chant 'Boskamp, Boskamp give us a wave' as meaning the fans wanted him to leave, until I persuaded him otherwise.

* * *

To bring more players in we needed money. Frankly, we were utterly desperate, but that summer had seen me pull off one of the best transfer deals I've ever managed to complete; the sale of rookie goalkeeper Ben Foster to Manchester United. Fergie had helped me a lot when I needed players; however, on this occasion, it was the other way round: I sold him one.

We had picked up Ben from non-league Racing Club Warwick for £15,000 in 2001 after I had been put on to the 18-year-old by my old friend Colin Dobson. Ben was a talented young lad, but we already had two experienced goalkeepers at Stoke, so he wasn't getting near the first team at this early stage and I loaned him out regularly. In early 2005, Denis Smith, the legendary Stoke centre-back, was manager at Wrexham, who were struggling and in administration so he couldn't buy players, only sign loanees. He rang to see if he could borrow a goalkeeper and I told him the only one I had was a youngster. Denis wanted a more experienced keeper, but I encouraged him to take Foster and have a look at him. When Denis saw Ben train, he put him straight into the first team, then rang me back to say how happy he was with my suggestion. With Ben between the sticks, Wrexham made it to Wembley and beat Southend 2-0 to lift the Football League Trophy. In Wrexham's midfield happened to be Darren Ferguson, Alex's son. So, Fergie went to watch the final and saw Foster playing out of his skin. The next Monday I had a phone call from a Manchester United scout who I knew.

'Rudgie,' he said.

'What?'

'Who is this Ben Foster lad you've loaned to Wrexham? Fergie is going mad at us giving us a right bollocking because he has never appeared in any of our scouting reports. We've no idea who he is.'

The next thing I know, I'm being summoned to United's training ground. You have to get there very early for Alex because he gets in at the crack of dawn, so I arrived before eight o'clock in the morning for a summit.

'I want to buy your keeper,' Alex says.

I went in high. 'Alex, he's going to be an England international, so he's going to cost you a million pounds.'

'A million! What do you mean? He hasn't even played a game for you yet!'

I kept my cool. 'Alex, he really is going to be good.'

'Jesus, Rudgie, you're a pain in the arse, you are.'

But I stood my ground. If you don't ask you don't get.

In the end Alex agreed, plus I negotiated various add-ons and sell-on clauses which would see Stoke receive a further £2 million in the future if Ben played for England and won trophies whilst at Old Trafford.

Ben signed and did indeed go on to play for England and appeared countless times in the Premier League for West Brom and Watford. He couldn't quite make it at Old Trafford because I think he was just that bit too young to be a success there when he signed. The demands are so great playing in front of 75,000 fans with the likes of Beckham, Scholes and Giggs. It came a bit too soon for him, but he has had a wonderful career, topped off by returning to Wrexham to help them win promotion back into the Football League in fairy-tale fashion in April 2023.

Whenever Alex sees me now, he claims I robbed him of a million pounds for Foster, but, to be fair, Alex sold him to Birmingham for £4 million, so I think United did OK out of Ben.

Deal done, when I returned to Stoke, chief executive Tony Scholes asked me how much I'd got for Ben. When I told him £1 million, he nearly fell off his chair.

'A million pounds?! I thought you'd get £700,000 at best! That's a miracle, John.'

* * *

Ben's sale enabled Johan to finally land the player he'd been hankering after since he had joined the club. Sambegou (Sammy) Bangoura had scored 22 goals in 59 appearances for Standard Liège in Belgium in the previous two seasons and, before that, 41 goals in 74 games for Lokeren. Those were good stats in a league comparable to the Championship and, following my success with Hoefkens, I was sent to negotiate the deal, armed with approval to spend up to the £1 million Foster's sale had brought in.

I travelled to Liège in late August and negotiated them down from an initial asking price of £1.25m to £900,000, although that was still a club record fee. Bangoura was tall, lithe and had a great spring. His heading ability was excellent and he knew where the net was. Sammy took a little time to adjust, but then went on a great scoring spree, netting eight goals in nine matches, including six in a row in one productive spell during November and December. Johan was being proved right from what I could see.

The problem was, the Guinea striker arrived with so much baggage to carry – both literally and figuratively – he often missed flights; usually those bringing him back to Stoke. We'd had to battle hard to win a Home Office appeal to get him a visa in the first place and the fight to get him into the country was hard won. Except he didn't enter Britain; on the first occasion he turned up at Manchester airport, he was turned away due to problems with his documentation.

Then, after he finally entered the country, just three days later he was arrested and detained in a police cell overnight over an alleged attempt to assist an illegal immigrant – apparently some relation or other – enter the UK through East Midlands airport. That was dropped a week later and he could finally get down to some training.

Controversy, however, was never far away.

Just as he was in that rich vein of scoring form, in early January 2006 Sammy had to go and play for his country in the 2006 Africa Cup of Nations. After scoring one goal in the group stages as Guinea won their section, once they had got knocked out in the quarter-finals by Senegal, Bangoura should have been back in the UK again in time to play against Preston on 4 February, but he did not turn up until 12 February. Nightmare. There were no messages, so we had no idea where he was. He was utterly AWOL, although not necessarily in Africa. Johan drove past Bangoura's house one night and the lights were on, so none of us understood why he didn't appear for training. At this point the manager's patience ran out and he told a *Sentinel* reporter, 'I have no respect for the guy and want to kick him in the balls.'

When Sammy finally appeared, he offered an apology, but only a vague explanation and was fined two weeks' wages. More importantly, the team had not scored in the league since Bangoura's final game before jetting off as the season went to pot. However, Bangoura would only score once more in a further 15 outings in a Stoke shirt, in a 4-1 win at Ipswich. His head had gone. Simple as that.

It's fair to say Johan had a love-hate relationship with Sammy and the increasingly exasperated Boskamp pinned the reluctant striker up against the wall on at least one occasion. Bangoura once turned up with a cast on his arm, saying he'd broken it. We never found out how.

Around this time, Bangoura was apparently the subject of a £2.75m bid from an unnamed Russian club, which the Icelanders surprisingly turned down. It was a huge mistake, although even after everything, Johan wanted to keep him as he thought he could turn the wayward striker around.

In August 2006, Bangoura returned to pre-season training 37 days late. I was sent to meet him at the airport when he finally arrived and he claimed the reason for his late return was that he could not get a passport for his four-month-old daughter, who had to remain in Guinea. He limped off after just 43 minutes of his first appearance of that campaign and was farmed out on loan to FC Brussels, then Boavista in Portugal, for whom he eventually signed permanently for a fee of £270,000 that August after I persuaded Bangoura's agent, who I now knew well, that he had to go. We were well rid of him, although I understand he still owes former friend and strike partner Mama Sidibe £2,000.

* * *

Despite dealing with our wayward striker as a team, together in one sense, by the time all that happened, Johan and I were actually not speaking. Our cordial working relationship ended when everything went spectacularly up in flames at Coventry on the night of Wednesday, 2 November 2005. Having been in the Ricoh Arena dressing room before the game discussing tactics, as was usual, I was sitting in the stands with the English directors (there were no Icelandic directors at the game) as Coventry took an early lead. They were all over us before Taggart hammered a spectacular equaliser home from around 25 yards and then, just after half-time, Gallagher curled in a beauty to put us ahead. We had won just once in seven games, losing the other six and were desperate to win, but the home side were putting us under immense pressure. With around 20 minutes to go, from where I was sitting, I could see our left-back, who was the inexperienced Lewis Buxton as our usual left-back, Marlon Broomes, had been sent off the previous Saturday at Southampton, was in trouble, being far too far infield, giving Coventry's right-winger room to burst forwards, supported by their right-back, so they were double-teaming us. Wanting to help, I walked down to the front of the stand intent on chatting with Johan about the problem I'd identified, but found he was out on the edge of the technical area giving instructions, so turned to Jan de Koning, telling him to stop the right-winger getting forward as he was causing us so many problems. Jan got up and told Buxton directly, rather than Johan, but I didn't think anything of it as we nullified the threat and hung on to win the game for a vital three points; job done.

Or so I thought.

Dutch substitute goalkeeper Ed de Goey had observed what went on between Jan and I from his position on the bench and, after the game, told the manager what had happened; effectively that I had come down and told players what to do. To say Boskamp took exception to this is putting it mildly. He went ballistic when I arrived down in the dressing room after the match, shouting about how he had been undermined. What I had no idea about was that Johan had witnessed the same thing happen in Holland where it did actually damage the manager in question, who lost his authority and then his job. Boskamp said he wouldn't stand for it and we had a furious row.

Wanting to clear the air as I could see how Johan thought I was interfering, the next day in his office I apologised to him for over-stepping the mark, explaining I didn't do it to undermine or embarrass him, but to help. We won after all. But Johan wouldn't accept it and carried on creating issues over the incident. I feel he actually wanted to use this as a way out; making it them or me, hoping the board would choose us over him and pay him up as he was finding it very difficult. The board wanted to smooth it over, but Johan simply wouldn't let it lie, using every opportunity to have a dig at both Jan and I. On one occasion, Boskamp publicly said, 'I'm not Adolf Hitler, but Jan knows I will never work with him again.'

I was astonished and shocked at how the manager turned on us in the media throughout that period. He once said, 'If Jesus Christ came downstairs to say "do this", I wouldn't care. I knew then it was over. If I had said nothing, I would have lost all the respect of my players. Everybody says forgive; I can forgive, that is no problem. But I can't forget. Some people are disappointed, but it's got nothing to do with the club. It's between me, John and Jan. I told the board, "If you want John to stay with me or Jan then it's not possible." If the club say John Rudge is more important than me then I have no problem.'

It's clear his version of events wasn't consistent with the actual facts, but once Boskamp had made his mind up that was that. The die was cast, the feud became bitter and, after a few months of the board attempting to keep the peace, hoping it would blow over, Boskamp finally issued them with an ultimatum – either they go or I do. Jan and I were put on gardening leave in March 2006 as the board, tired of his antics, called his bluff, with owner Magnus Kristinsson apparently telling Boskamp, 'You will finish what you have started.' At that point, I had no idea whether I was going to have a job and Johan and I never spoke another word once I was cast out.

Whether it was because of Boskamp or in spite of him, let's not forget that, following that victory at Coventry putting us on a run of six wins in eight games, we were as high as fifth in the league table on Christmas Day. With all this nonsense going on behind the scenes, the club found themselves 16th by mid-February, after winning just one match in ten and scoring a mere six goals in that time due to Bangoura's unplanned absence.

Although Johan promoted Taggart and Noel Blake to be his assistants, the team remained utterly inconsistent throughout the remainder of the season as the manager took a back seat, although how he could have done much less than when I was working with him, I'm not sure. Meanwhile, he kept himself busy by taking every possible opportunity to rubbish me in the media. He frequently made a joke of not knowing my name and when Radio Stoke asked him what his worst moment in football was for an on-air profile he said simply, 'Coventry.'

In response, I diligently kept my mouth shut, aside from one occasion when, as Luke Chadwick was signed permanently, I pointed out in *The Sentinel* that it was I who had brought him to the club on loan in the first place.

As the season neared its end with no chance of promotion, it became clear Boskamp would be leaving, but I had no clarity over whether I still had a job, although Jan was formally sacked in April 2006, moving to work first at Celtic as head scout before joining Liverpool's academy. I still speak with Jan now as he is a scout for Portsmouth, operating across northern Europe.

Resigned to a managerial future elsewhere, Boskamp continued his media outbursts, some of which were far less ridiculous than the feud between us, which only existed in his head. He once publicly commented on the split in the boardroom, 'You cannot work with two groups. Either the Icelandics stay, or the English buy the club. Otherwise you destroy it.' He fired one final parting shot before departing by warning the two factions, 'This club ain't big enough for the both of you.'

Johan Boskamp may have been manager for a few months, but Stoke City fans will not forget him in a hurry.

Neither will I.

Chapter 17

Getting their Coates

'It was my birthday, so where else was he going but watching the reserves?!'

Debbie Rudge

WHILE I was on gardening leave, I kept in touch with the Coates family, who couldn't believe the fuss, but were coming under increasing pressure to save their club from this loose cannon with too much ammunition in Boskamp on the one hand and a listless, cashless board on the other. The Icelanders were £5 million in debt and marooned in mid-table. Their investment had not paid off; they needed to sell.

Those golden shares meant only Peter Coates and Keith Humphreys could realistically buy the club now Phil Rawlins had set himself up in the USA and it was only a matter of time until a deal was done. A lot of people thought Peter was completely crazy wanting to put himself back into the firing line, but it really showed his love for Stoke City and his desire to right what he saw as the wrongs of his first tenure as chairman. When I met him on 6 June, as the sale went through and he laid out his vision for the club to me, Peter also told me he thought it would be important for the area if the football club were doing well. Stoke-on-Trent was having a difficult time, having lost the pot banks and the mining industry. He thought that if Stoke could get in the Premier League it would give the city a lift.

Peter wasn't the only one with unfinished business, though; he brought back Tony Pulis as manager, which I felt was the right move, while I was also playing Lazarus, having been resurrected from my gardening leave. Back in business, once again alongside Tony, it was like we'd never been apart. The future looked a lot less bleak than it had at the turn of the year, but I had no idea of the adventure that awaited us.

* * *

Despite the club's financial situation being dire, what no one really realised was how wealthy the Coates family now were. Bet365 had become a global phenomenon and multi-billion-pound business thanks to Peter and his daughter Denise, so Peter was in a very different position to when he had sold control of Stoke in 1999. He now bankrolled a push for the Premier League, giving Tony his full backing and allowing him to effectively run the club from top to bottom. Given that so many of Boskamp's signings had been failures, Tony and I set about a huge recruitment programme, but these things take a bit of time and early on, because of a run of only one win in the first nine games, there was quite a bit of fan dissent, a lot of it due to supporters being very split on his playing style following that binary season. On 29 September 2006 a 'Red Card' protest was planned by a disaffected group of fans calling themselves the 1972 Committee, led by a Richard Grisdale. They had around 10,000 cards printed with 'Give Pulis his cards' on one side and 'Time to get rolling, Tone' on the other and were planning to hand them out before the game against Preston. In reality, despite a lot of publicity, hardly any supporters wanted to get involved. Many of those fans who once castigated Pulis could now see the merits of his more disciplined approach after the white-knuckle ride of Boskamp's tenure.

Ironically, we signed Lee Hendrie (on loan from Aston Villa) that morning, plus fellow loanees Rory Delap (Sunderland) and Salif Diao (Liverpool) a week or so later and results changed almost instantly. Danny Higginbotham had signed from Southampton for a knockdown £225,000 the previous month and Andy Griffin returned to the club he started out at, on loan at first, but then permanently for £300,000 in January 2008. Tony was back with a vengeance, hell-bent on delivering promotion for Peter.

The money Bet365 pumped in meant construction of the new training ground and facilities began, which served to attract stars over the coming seasons. Another benefit was that all the behind-the-scenes politics had been removed. Peter and Tony were very close and Tony knew that if he sold a player that money would be available to be reinvested in new players, not be taken out of the club as it had been before, which made a huge difference. My role was no longer to be a buffer between a manager and board at war, which was a mighty relief, so so I could concentrate on helping to recruit the players Tony wanted.

The day of that protest, we drew 1-1 with Preston with Ricardo Fuller, a new £500,000 signing from Southampton who everyone believed had dodgy knees but Tony was desperate to sign, scoring his first goal for the club and Hendrie hitting the bar with a cheeky free kick. We didn't look back. The following week we won 4-0 at Leeds, with Fuller scoring again, cutting in off the left wing and curling into the far corner right-footed, then 2-1 at home to Sunderland, the red-hot promotion favourites who would eventually go up as champions. We won eight of the next ten. The game was afoot.

* * *

Tony wanted to create a spirit and togetherness, which the players bought into and, to kick this off, he took this new squad away in the first week of October for a week's bootcamp in Devon; mud runs, assault courses, cross country running, swimming and target practice. They loved it and it worked brilliantly.

We used that time to sign Liam Lawrence from Sunderland, on loan initially and then permanently for £500,000 when the January transfer window opened, as it was clear Luke Chadwick's back wasn't going to allow him to play a full part and we sold him to Norwich for £220,000. Liam had been cast aside by Roy Keane after falling out with his manager. To say he was a character is putting it mildly. He was always getting himself into trouble, although mostly in ways I can't publish. Suffice to say, dogs, staircases, ladies and video cameras were involved (at differing times) and we were ceaselessly entertained, if sometimes frustrated when he made himself unavailable through his antics by injuring himself. He proved an excellent signing overall, scoring some cracking goals from distance and running himself into the ground for the club after buying into the new culture Tony had set.

That was typical of that squad of players. For example, Fuller actually took a reduction in wages to join because Tony sold the club to him on the basis of him leading the line, playing every week and winning promotion to the Premier League. This group became the heart of the team which won promotion and established itself in the Premier League, so I suppose you can say we did great business from August 2006 to January 2007.

One horrible incident occurred when Rory Delap, who had joined on loan from Sunderland but was due to sign permanently in the January transfer window, broke his leg in his first home game, as it happened against Sunderland, in a tackle with his former team-mate Robbie Elliott. Peter Coates said immediately that we would keep faith with Rory and sign him, as we had promised, which showed the commitment to the players the owners had and that we would not abandon them as soon as there was a problem. It served to endear the entire squad to the club.

Despite that setback, we had some great results – a 3-1 win at the Hawthorns sticks in the mind for how Fuller ripped the West Brom defence apart, but all of those signings came just too late in the season for us to put together a run good enough to get us into the play-offs and we finished eighth. However, I felt the faith that the chairman had shown in the manager and myself to pull together a squad was being repaid in spades. The fans were beginning to believe, too; even those red cards got dumped into some chap's garage. I wonder if they are still there now.

* * *

As we felt we had the core of a promotion-winning squad we were very judicious about who we now brought in. In summer 2007, Tony signed Richard Cresswell from relegated Leeds for £500,000 and Jon Parkin from Hull for £275,000. Tony used Cresswell a lot on the left side of midfield and he would score 12 vital goals for us that campaign. Cresser was an immaculate professional, Parkin left a little more to be desired. On the pre-season training camp in Austria, Jon managed to gash his leg badly on a runaway golf cart, the first of his many pranks. You always had to be on the lookout when he was around; later that week, just before a prestigious friendly against Real Madrid, he kidded our fitness coach that he was taking a tray full of cakes to his room for his pre-match warm up. Jon liked his food. He was a big lad, with a penchant for kebabs, and I also remember that pre-season running up Trentham Hills beside him, egging him on as he was at the back of the group. I urged him to make it to the top for so long that I actually did the whole hill, beating Jon to the top, feeling fairly fresh myself, while Parky was a blubbering heap. Bear in mind I was at this point 63 and he was a professional athlete, and you'll understand that he wasn't a 90-minute all-action running machine. However, Jon had a great eye for goal and was great fun to have around.

That and the signings helped earn myself a new three-year contract, not bad for an old feller. It came at a time when the manager's chair was vacant at Vale Park following Martin Foyle's departure, so I suppose Peter Coates was ensuring I didn't head anywhere else. As part of that, I actually moved in to share an office with Tony Pulis, although neither of us were sure who was supposed to keep an eye on who.

It's fair to say that there were certain players that Boskamp had signed that just did not fit the mould of a Tony Pulis player. One such was Carl Hoefkens, who wasn't in the manager's plans, so we accepted a £750,000 bid for him from West Brom in August 2007. We also moved young striker Martin Patterson on to Scunthorpe as he was never going to play ahead of the forwards we now had on our books. Scunthorpe manager Nigel Adkins didn't want to pay us anything as Martin had reached the end of his contract, but I made our case to the tribunal which agreed with us that the club had played a significant part in his development so I got us some compensation.

Rather more reluctantly, we had to part with Danny Higginbotham, who moved to Premier League Sunderland for £2.5 million, saying he had received an offer too good to refuse and wanted to go back to the top flight.

In his place, we brought in young centre-back, Ryan Shawcross, from Manchester United. We'd had his fellow fledgling Lee Martin on loan, who knew Ryan as he'd also been on loan with him at Royal Antwerp earlier that year. The problem was that Shawcross had already agreed to join Norwich on loan for the season. This was where my relationship with Alex Ferguson was really useful, as I helped Tony persuade him to loan Shawcross to us, which Alex agreed to as long as we could convince Ryan we were the better option. That was down to Tony. As Ryan had been told by Fergie he wouldn't get into the first team at Old Trafford as Rio Ferdinand and Nemanja Vidić were the first-choice centre-halves, his line to the youngster was: 'Come to our place and you'll play.' He then also locked Shawcross in his car until he signed the contract, a tactic I applauded.

Even at 19, Ryan was tall, dominant in the air and also scored the odd goal. He was still growing at that point, but did brilliantly for us and, the following January, we persuaded Fergie to sell him to us for just £1 million, the same amount I'd got from him for Ben Foster who had never played in Stoke's first team; a steal. That only happened because Ryan went to see Fergie to say, look,

I can't get in your team and I want to play, please can you let me go. That was very mature for a 19-year-old. I am so grateful for all the help Fergie gave us then, as he didn't particularly want to let Shawcross go.

To partner Ryan, we brought in Leon Cort from Crystal Palace, initially on loan, but then permanently for a club record £1.2 million in the January transfer window. That pair proved very adept at getting their heads on to the end of our new not-so-secret weapon, both bagging eight goals that season. The devastating source of their bucketful of goals? Rory Delap's long throw. It has become entrenched into football folklore now, but back in 2007, no one knew what a potent weapon it would prove to be. The story goes that one day the players were messing around after training and Rory, now recovered from that broken leg, was hurling these long throws into the penalty area, which coach Mark O'Connor brought to Tony's attention. Tony felt it could help us and so it proved. Rory's throw catapulted us to success. It came in fast and flat and just needed the merest of flicks to send it goalwards and we scored bundles of goals that way during the promotion season via the likes of Shawcross, Cort, Fuller and Sidibe. Rory could reach the penalty area from almost anywhere in the opposition half too and it put immense pressure on defences, such that we also benefitted from five own goals scored from Delap's howitzers.

One of the other implications of Bet365 being more involved in Stoke City was that data analysis, which was so critical to the success of their betting business, became more important to the recruitment process at Stoke. This has since become very much the modern way, but it had started even back in the late 2000s. Tony and I still placed just as much emphasis on watching a player ourselves and then meeting with them to find out more about what makes them tick, and assess their character, commitment and work ethic because that was going to be crucial if we were to be successful. These days some clubs recruit on raw data alone, even the controversial Expected Goals (xG) data, which does the rounds. Important though that is, it can never give you a complete picture. You don't get any feel for the character of a player, how they socialise with the group, that kind of thing. Consequently, Tony and I would be out on the road together a lot, often to the most random of games. I remember one occasion we headed out to watch the reserves at Barnsley and, as we drove, we saw someone lying on the pavement on Weston Road, so stopped to see if we could help, only to discover that his friend who was with him thought he was having a heart attack and needed CPR. Tony and I dived in, giving first aid. It turned out the young man (he was only 20) was actually having an epileptic fit, so we made sure the lad was in the right position, did not swallow his tongue and kept his airways clear until the paramedics arrived. He made a full recovery, I'm delighted to say.

When I got home and relayed the tale to Del, she said she didn't even know I was a first-aider! But, of course, as qualified FA coaches, Tony and I are trained to know what to do in these situations.

I should also point out that my youngest, Deb, when she read about the incident in the paper, said, 'It was my birthday, so where else was he going but watching the reserves?!'

* * *

Ryan Shawcross made a memorable debut on the opening day of the 2007/08 season at Cardiff, scoring the only goal of the game, although we also had to thank keeper Steve Simonsen for saving an 88th-minute penalty, getting up to stop the rebound too. That was a great start to the campaign and it gave the players huge faith as the manager gelled them together, making them a stronger unit than the previous near-miss campaign, especially as Delap was back fit and the long throw had been discovered. They really were brilliant times and we had a purple patch in November and December, winning five of six games, culminating in another world-class display by Fuller against West Brom. Ric bagged a hat-trick in a 3-1 victory which knocked Albion off the top of the table, although they would end up as champions. The question was whether we could outlast Phil Brown's Hull City for the second automatic promotion spot or end up in the dreaded play-offs.

Salif Diao signed later in the autumn after having his contract cancelled by Liverpool and becoming a free agent. Once he had joined, we used the January 2008 transfer window to let John Eustace go to Watford for £250,000 due to his injury record, whilst bringing in young Danny Pugh for £500,000 from Preston as a back-up to Cresswell on the left side of midfield. We really felt our squad was giving us what we needed at that point, so the only additional bit of business we did on deadline day was to bring in young midfielder Glen Whelan from Sheffield Wednesday for £500,000. We had a problem getting the deal over the line, though, as his agent wasn't actually correctly qualified, as by this time agents had to hold formal licences with UEFA, so at the last minute we had to get another agent to stand in and act for Glen, who turned out to be an incredible servant. His role was to sit in front of the back four, winning the ball back and playing it on. He was so consistent. Every time Tony thought he could get in an upgrade player, such as Dean Whitehead, and Glen got dropped, within a month or so he had forced his way back into the team, so vital was he to us.

One story I remember about Glen came a few years later when we were on a pre-season tour in Florida and he lost his passport. I had to escort him to the Irish embassy to get him a replacement and we drove all the way up from the south to Washington to get him a replacement so he could get back into the UK. I can think of a few players I'd have left behind. Not Glen.

* * *

As the season built to a climax, we found ourselves faced with a horribly familiar scenario; our star striker had failed to return from international duty, shades of Sammy Bangoura. Ricardo Fuller had jetted off to play for Jamaica, but, far from returning as arranged the day before our crucial game at fellow promotion contenders

Wolves, there was no sign of him. Tony was furious, especially when it turned out Jamaica hadn't actually played any games …

There was still no sign of Fuller as the players reported to the Brit ahead of travelling down the M6 to Molineux. The now incandescent Pulis was ready to rip him to shreds, but in Ric walked, shades on, smile beaming, Reggae-Boyz style as if nothing was amiss. Tony gave him a fearful bollocking and told him he was lucky to even be on the bench. However, Tony knew exactly what he was doing as Fuller knew he had to make amends and, when he was brought on with around half an hour remaining, he made all the difference. Deep into injury time, we were hanging on to a 3-2 lead under intense pressure, when Ric picked the ball up on the edge of our own penalty area, ran the whole length of the pitch, turned two Wolves defenders inside out and lashed the ball past Wayne Hennessey to secure a famous 4-2 victory, the second in a run of five consecutive wins which propelled us into second place.

Tony tolerated Fuller and his foibles because he was one of those special players who could be truly devastating on his day. But he was also a nightmare to manage at times and, to ensure nothing untoward happened again, I was once sent to accompany him to Jamaica when he flew off to play for the national team. I remember getting on the plane and persuading the stewardess to allow me to upgrade to first class, while Ric stayed with his team-mates in club. I had a ball! The hotel was lovely too and I met his national team manager, Rene Simoes. Ostensibly this trip was to see if there were any of Ric's Jamaican team-mates we might be interested in signing, but really I was (barely) undercover to simply ensure he got back to Stoke on time.

In contrast, Fuller's striker partner Mama Sidibe had been utterly reliable during the season, unfortunately being consistent in not finding the back of the net. Mama had scored twice in 32 games up until that point, although both had proved to be winning goals in crucial victories over Southampton and Norwich as the season came to boiling point. A disappointing home defeat to Crystal Palace was followed by a brilliant come-from-behind win at Coventry. We now had three games remaining and if we won them all we knew we would be up.

The first of those crucial matches was against fellow promotion contenders Bristol City, in the late Sky TV game, buoyed by the news that Hull had lost at Sheffield United earlier that afternoon. Sidibe was in inspired form, heading home a free kick to put us in the lead and then racing clear on to a Fuller pass to charge from the halfway line and slot home from the edge of the box. Like Ric, Mama often disappeared overseas to play for his country and we had lost him for most of January as Mali played in the 2008 African Nations Cup, but in qualifying for that tournament he, and striking partner Freddie Kanouté, had been attacked by fans as they left the field in Togo at the end of the 2-0 victory which secured their place. Thankfully Mama was only superficially hurt, despite being stabbed, but there was blood everywhere, he told me on his return, and the players had had to barricade themselves in their dressing room once they'd managed to make it off the pitch amidst the riot. Credit to Mama, he was back playing, putting that incident behind him, very quickly.

After defeating Colchester in the last ever match at Layer Road, thanks to a Cresswell goal, we now faced a final home game against relegation-threatened Leicester, managed by none other than Ian Holloway, a big friend of Tony and I. All we needed was a point to confirm promotion, while Leicester had to equal Southampton's result to stay up. It was incredibly tense and, sitting in the stands, I felt utterly helpless. As director of football all my work that season had been done. I had to leave the manager, coaches and players to it. Foxes keeper Paul Henderson made two brilliant saves from Fuller before Gareth McAuley headed against our post. As news filtered through that Southampton had taken a 3-2 lead against Sheffield United, Leicester piled forward and we concentrated merely on defending that crucial draw. Our keeper Carlo Nash, who we brought in on loan from Wigan and I still see now as he is the goalkeeping coach at Port Vale, made a superb double save. We were clinging on.

As we moved into what promised to be a nail-biting period of extra time, the news filtered through that Ipswich had beaten Hull and our nearest challengers had fallen at the final hurdle. We were up no matter what happened now, but the lads had pride not to lose and repelled Leicester's attacks. When the final whistle came we were up, they were down and the pitch was invaded by thousands of ecstatic Stoke fans, jubilant that 23 years in the wilderness had come to an end; an incredible achievement by Tony and the squad. The celebrations were joyous and walking around the pitch to the noise of 'Delilah' being sung was fantastic; a truly unforgettable experience and it fully justified Peter Coates' decision to return two years earlier.

After 49 years in the game, I had finally reached the Premier League.

Chapter 18

Let's All Do the Wenger

'Arsène Wenger despised Stoke City.'

John Rudge

SO, APPROACHING 64 years of age, I would be working in the top flight for the first time. We were now fishing in a very different talent pool and I was sent to the 2008 European Championships in Austria and Switzerland in order to identify transfer targets. Nice work if you can get it. Good trip though it was, it did not yield any signings. Partly that was because those made in the first half of the summer and after tournaments always cost more as it gives the buying club certainty in having the player at the club for pre-season training camps, plus for the August games. Later signings aren't necessarily any cheaper, however, as their fees can be inflated due to the closeness of the deadline, but there is a golden period between those two periods in which we did our business.

As soon as promotion was confirmed, I started to be contacted by agents thinking we had millions of pounds to spend. We did, making four signings for more than the previous club record of £1.2 million. The new record fee of £5.5 million went on recruiting Dave Kitson, who was Tony's signing, a proven Premier League goalscorer from relegated Reading. Our next-costliest signing was midfielder Seyi Olofinjana from Wolves for £3 million, then there was centre-half Abdoulaye Faye, who cost £2.25 million from

Newcastle, which, considering he became Player of the Season after a stunning string of performances, was cheap at twice the price. We also spent the same £2.5 million fee we had sold Danny Higginbotham for to bring him back from Sunderland after he too fell out with Roy Keane.

Tony always liked a quality goalkeeper and here we got a bit of luck. Initially he wanted to sign Scott Carson from Liverpool, but Carson messed us around and chose newly promoted West Brom instead. So, we picked up Thomas Sorensen on a free transfer. Thomas was an experienced keeper, still Denmark's first choice, who had been let go by Aston Villa manager Martin O'Neill in favour of Brad Friedel, who he had signed from Liverpool, who was actually five years older. I believe we got the better end of that piece of 'luck' as Carson let in the vast majority of the 67 goals West Brom conceded in finishing bottom of the Premier League, while Thomas was solid behind our revamped defence, letting in just 13 goals in 14 games as we picked up 24 points from an end-of-season run to finish 12th. Late in the campaign, Sorro kept a clean sheet while Carson let an early Fuller shot from outside the area bobble past him as we won 2-0 at the Hawthorns. I managed to convince Sorensen to sign using my usual methods of persuasion, with Tony Pulis telling *The Sentinel*, 'Rudgie stuck him in an attic somewhere for two days until he signed.'

Despite all these arrivals, we were overwhelming favourites to go straight back down or 'do a Derby' as it had become known, as the previous season County had set a record low points total for the top flight of just 11, recording one sole victory. In fact, after our opening game saw us 0-3 down by half-time to Bolton, bookmaker Paddy Power paid out on all bets which had Stoke to be relegated, earning themselves huge publicity in doing so as it became a massive talking point in the media. However, that was manna from heaven for Tony, who used it to unite the squad and then the city behind us, going on a one-man publicity campaign to rouse the supporters, who responded by making the Britannia Stadium the most intimidating and loudest ground in the Premier League. Opponents crumbled, starting with the first visitors, Martin O'Neill's top-four challenging Aston Villa, who had qualified for the UEFA Cup that season, so they were a very good team. A fantastic game was tied at 2-2 when, late on, Rory Delap wound up for a throw-in at the Boothen End. The penalty area was packed, but rising above the rest was big Mama Sidibe, the man I'd persuaded to sign for us when Tony left the first time, to flick a header into the bottom corner and send the stadium into overdrive. It really was hairs on the back of your neck stuff and set the tone for the rest of the season. I believe that Paddy Power stunt helped us massively as it got every Stoke fan thinking, 'Let's get behind the team and show them.' We should actually have paid the bookmaker back.

Rory's throw took centre stage as opponent after opponent failed to deal with it. I don't think even Tony and Rory realised what a weapon it was going to be in the top flight as each time it became a theatrical set piece, with the fans in the stands holding their hands out anticipating the ball being flung in with an 'oooooooooooo', then, as it was released, it turned into 'whoooooosh'.

It became so intimidating that it was better than a free kick or a corner, so much so that Hull goalkeeper Boaz Myhill dithered over whether to put a long through ball out for a throw and actually chose to concede a corner instead of facing another Delap howitzer. David Moyes described Rory as 'the human sling' after we scored twice from his long throws in an early season 2-3 home defeat to his Everton side and Athletics Ireland got in touch to ask if Rory would like to represent them in the London 2012 Olympics, while sports journalists were tracking down Steve Backley, former British javelin thrower, to ask if he was helping to coach Rory. He wasn't. Meanwhile, Stoke fans took to taunting visiting fans by singing 'You've only come for the throw-ins!'

Tottenham's goalkeeper Heurelho Gomes ended up crying, being caught on the TV cameras, such was the intensity of the bombardment he suffered as we beat them 2-1 in October, while, when Arsenal visited in November, we opened the scoring when Ricardo Fuller flicked in another Delap bomb, while Gunners centre-half Kolo Touré raised his arm to appeal for offside ... although, of course, you cannot be offside from a throw-in.

That game, which we also won 2-1, was the start of a decade-long feud between the two clubs, although on that particular day there was no sign of that at all. Afterwards, Arsène Wenger, the Arsenal manager, shook hands politely and congratulated us, even being humble and respectful in his post-match press conference.

As soon as he got back to London, his tune changed, accusing us of being overly physical and aggressive, although there was only one player sent off in that game; Arsenal's Robin van Persie for an assault on Thomas Sorensen, while Emmanuel Adebayor kicked Ryan Shawcross in the throat, which went unpunished by the referee.

Arsène didn't see those, apparently.

A lot was made by Wenger of us making the Britannia pitch smaller, both width- and length-ways in readiness for the Premier League. Well, why wouldn't we? It made Rory's throw a more potent weapon and gave far less room for the best players in the world to ply their trade. In any case, the pitch was still the same size as those at Craven Cottage and Fratton Park. He also railed about the towels around the ground which Rory used to dry the ball on and the fact the throw took time out of the game. Talk about sour grapes.

Early the next season, Wenger made ridiculous comments about us being a 'rugby team', while commenting on the forthcoming north London derby. So, the next time his team turned up at the Britannia, the crowd treated him to several renditions of 'Swing Low, Sweet Chariot', the England rugby team's song, as we sent them packing from the FA Cup 3-1. Late on in that game, Arsenal actually tried their own version of the long throw. It didn't work. Hilariously. Stoke fans derisively informed the visiting manager that he 'didn't see that'; they liked nothing more than to bait Wenger.

I honestly don't think Arsène could stomach our brand of up and at 'em football triumphing at all, let alone so regularly, over his version of the beautiful game. He just couldn't get his head round it. Supporters used to tell me we were living rent free in his head. I suppose you could say we still are given he is still trying to ban the throw and replace it with a kick-in all these years later in his current role as FIFA's chief of global football development.

Back then, Wenger kept wittering on about us constantly, often when Arsenal weren't even due to play Stoke. It was remarkable. We loved it.

When they did visit, the fans would absolutely murder him. In April 2011, Wenger jumped out of his dugout after Dean Whitehead went down like the proverbial sack of spuds under no challenge at all to win a free kick late in the game, waving his hands around in frustration. Before he knew it, the entire stadium copied him, singing 'Let's All Do the Wenger'.

He didn't take it well, especially when it was featured heavily on that night's *Match of the Day*, with Gary Lineker giggling away.

Over the years, Arsène was the only opposing manager who didn't invite us in for a drink post-game. Wenger also never accepted our invitation for a drink, although his assistant Steve Bould (a former Stoke player) always did. Arsène despised Stoke City, but his pathological hatred of Rory's long throw helped us become famous across the globe.

Thanks, Arsène.

* * *

Arguably more important than occasionally upsetting some of the bigger clubs was the need to defeat those in and around us at the foot of the table. We beat both Sunderland and West Brom 1-0 and drew with Hull 1-1 in a run of games which saw us hit 20 points by Christmas. All those positive results were at home, though, and our away form showed just three points on our travels before the turn of the year, although one of those was in a battling draw at Anfield. The last away game of 2008 proved a disaster. After taking an early lead at West Ham, when the Hammers scored an equaliser,

Ricardo Fuller and Andy Griffin had a verbal spat, which quickly turned physical as Ric clipped Griff round the ear, getting sent off for violent conduct ... against his own captain. We ended up losing 1-2 and lost Fuller through suspension, although Tony told me the pair had kissed and made up within a day or so. He still fined Ricardo the maximum two weeks' wages, bemoaning the fact that, just a few days earlier at the Christmas party, Ric and Andy had been best pals, even swapping silly shirts with each other.

At that stage we were in the bottom three, had one striker suspended for three games and Dave Kitson hadn't yet scored a goal for the club. Our chances of Premier League survival didn't look good.

We held a council of war as we knew we needed to strengthen and identified two key targets; striker James Beattie and left-winger Matthew Etherington, spending £5.5 million to secure the pair. Beattie, a proven Premier League goalscorer, arrived from Championship side Sheffield United, while Etherington had been languishing in West Ham's reserves, despite his obvious talent.

Looking for waifs and strays had been something I had spent my entire career doing and Tony now christened us the Kennel Club, as we were a dogs' home (Battersea, not Crufts as Tony would claim) for rehabilitating ageing old pros with various ailments and injuries. In Etherington's case it was a gambling habit, so it was noted that he was joining a club owned by the largest bookmaker in the country. Matty owed around £800,000 in debts, which the club worked with him to settle over time. That faith was repaid in spades as he proved a wonderful signing.

Beattie and Etherington made the world of difference to our attacking play and connected brilliantly from the off, with Beattie scoring five in his first six league games, several from Ethers' passes. One of those came in a remarkable win against Mark Hughes' Manchester City side, who had just been taken over by the Abu Dhabi oil tycoons and boasted £32.5 million signing Robinho in their ranks. I remember when the team sheets came in and working out that our starting 11 cost around £10m, which was £2m less than Hughes had paid for left-back Wayne Bridge.

To make matters worse, we had our talisman Delap sent off in the first half when, after being fouled, he booted the ball at close-quarters into Shaun Wright-Phillips' unmentionables. Wright-Phillips should also have gone for retaliation and was later suspended retrospectively, but it left our ten facing the gazillionaires' 11.

However, the injustice only served to turn up the volume from fevered to volcanic as wave upon wave of sky blue attacks pelted our penalty area. Then suddenly, at the other end, Whelan won a tackle and set Etherington free to cross for Beattie to run Bridge under the ball, back off and head home beautifully at the far post; a classic centre-forward's goal. We went into half-time 1-0 up and, despite having ten men, Tony orchestrated a masterful defensive display in the second half as we were completely under the cosh. Our box looked like the Alamo at times, but try as they might Manchester City could not breach our defence. Urged on by an incredible Stoke crowd, whose visceral chanting lifted our wearying players time and time again, we held on for a famous victory. *The Sentinel* dubbed Tony the 'shell-suited Rommel' in a piece venerating the tactical masterclass which had sunk the billionaires.

That performance showed the spirit and togetherness that bonded our team and fans. The metaphorical litmus test for top players and clubs around the world had now become 'Can he do it on a cold, wet Wednesday night at Stoke?' £32.5 million Robinho clearly couldn't. My favourite was when people began to ask that question about Lionel Messi around 2011 and 2012. I knew we'd made some impact when that nonsense was getting bandied around!

From that point onwards, with the crowd's backing, we didn't look back and survived comfortably. The noise after the two goals which defeated Wigan in our final home game at the end of the season was measured at a record 120 decibels as the party broke out.

Stuff that in your pipe and smoke it, Paddy Power.

* * *

Close season was always one of my busiest periods. That summer of 2009 we looked at players such as Kevin Phillips, Marlon Harewood, Lee McCulloch, Brian Howard and Maik Taylor to strengthen the squad. None of them quite came off and it shows how many irons in the fire are needed to land the occasional signing as there is so much competition for good players when you are in the Premier League. We also missed out on Cardiff's Joe Ledley, who Tony really wanted to sign. We offered £6 million, but Celtic swooped to offer Ledley £25,000 a week, which our board refused to match.

Those we did get over the line included Sunderland's midfielder Dean Whitehead and defender Danny Collins, youthful Uruguayan midfielder Diego Arismendi from Nacional and relegated Middlesbrough's Turkish playmaker Tuncay, plus his clubmate, the giant centre-half Robert Huth. Over £20 million spent. When you consider our entire budget for the promotion season had been just £11 million it showed the different league we were now operating in.

Perhaps the archetypal Stoke player of that era was Huth, the big German youth, as the Stokies called him. I remember he came to sign along with his agent, who was also German, and the chap came in, handed chief executive Tony Scholes and myself a piece of paper with a number written on it and said, 'That's the amount we want for his wages, take it or leave it.' I tried to negotiate and said, 'Well, how about if we do …', but I never got to finish the sentence as the agent simply tapped the piece of paper and said, 'No, no, that is his wages. He signs now or not at all.' Negotiation, German style.

Tony Scholes and I looked at each other. It was the quickest signing I've ever made.

These days, of course, agents have become far more prevalent, but I have to say the scariest agent I faced in my time across my desk as manager of Port Vale was Andy Porter's mother! She drove a very hard bargain.

Huth and Tuncay couldn't have been more different as players or people. Robert got into the team as right-back initially as he couldn't displace Abdoulaye Faye. With Danny Higginbotham at left-back, Tony had four centre-halves across the back four once again. There was less dissent from fans this time as the 2009/10 season saw us comfortably in mid-table.

We also grew the backroom staff to include scouts and coaches, then groundsmen and a full catering team once the new training ground was completed. Over the years Tony had as his assistant or coach, Mark O'Connor, Lindsay Parsons, David Kemp, Dave Kevan, Sam Ellis and Peter Reid, while Gerry Francis, a long-term friend of Tony, again from Bristol Rovers, joined as a consultant, who sat alongside me in the stands at games and advised Tony on tactics. As opinions around him grew, Tony began to develop his methods of play and my influence on the first team lessened. I focussed more on recruiting players identified by the manager and was involved far less frequently in any coaching or tactical tweaks. As things developed, I was travelling all over the place; America, Africa and the Caribbean.

* * *

We had by now become a well-established Premier League club, but there were two incidents which blighted our progress.

The first occurred in early December at Arsenal's Emirates stadium, although it had nothing to do with Arsène Wenger, for once. We lost the game 0-2, but had put in a decent performance. In the dressing room afterwards, the players were buzzing about going out for their Christmas party which they had arranged for that night and the following one. However, as Tony Pulis finished his post-match briefing with the players, he said, 'See you for training on Monday,' before disappearing into the manager's room to disrobe in readiness for a quick shower before his press conference.

The players were nonplussed, as they thought they had an agreement to have the extra day off and their unofficial spokesman, James Beattie, started telling them that Pulis must have forgotten what he'd agreed. As Tony emerged with a towel around his waist and bottle of shower gel in hand, he thought Beattie was talking behind his back and fronted up to him angrily, which led to a fracas, the towel going flying, and Peter Reid and I having to insert ourselves between the angry pair. I avoided getting a right hook for my troubles as tempers quickly cooled and we kept Tony and James apart. Player/manager upsets are commonplace in football and this one was no different. Both of them could be a bit fiery and we prevented a more serious incident occurring.

The lads were in for training on the Monday as the manager required, having had a good night out in London, but Tony decided to make an example of James, who ended up training with the under-23s and was sold to Rangers shortly afterwards. When news of the confrontation leaked it made some lurid headlines. We made sure no one made any comment, which has meant there have been some pretty graphic imaginings written about how the incident occurred. All in all, it really was just a flashpoint, the type of which happens at every club during the course of a season.

The second incident occurred during the home game against the Gunners, after Danny Pugh had headed in another Delap long throw to give us an early lead before Nicklas Bendtner equalised. With about 20 minutes to go, Ryan Shawcross went into a tackle with Gunners midfielder Aaron Ramsey, resulting in the young Welshman breaking his leg. In the aftermath, much was made of the ferocity of Ryan's challenge, which saw him sent off, but the reality was shown on Sky Sports that he was only 0.15 of a second late in the tackle. Things can be that quick in football. He was also shown to have been fouled by Bendtner as he ran towards Ramsey, which could easily have accounted for that split-second delay. Knowing Ryan, I knew there was nothing intentional about the tackle, but that wasn't how Wenger and many of the press corps reported the incident, which still rumbles on, being brought up from time to time today. Thankfully, Aaron made a full recovery and went on to have a superb career, although I understand he never accepted Ryan's apology, which is a shame.

* * *

It wasn't just the red side of north London we regularly annoyed, I remember there was one occasion when the Tottenham chairman Daniel Levy got pretty angry with us too.

Portsmouth's 22-year-old goalkeeper Asmir Begović was a wanted man in the January 2010 transfer window. Of the clubs in for him, Spurs were the most glamorous, while we were probably the least. The difference was, it was very unlikely Asmir would play at Tottenham, while we were looking for a successor to Thomas Sorensen and could promise Asmir he would play in the cups. At the time Portsmouth were a club in crisis and were clearly going to get relegated. Their controversial chairman Milan Mandaric was selling off his prize assets, including centre-half Younes Kaboul, who Levy signed for Spurs. Begović underwent a three-part, in-depth medical at Tottenham, but we had got wind of this and wanted to pitch our offering to him before he signed. Because he was friends with our coach Mark O'Connor, we knew Asmir had been on a fairly low wage, was regularly getting paid late by his current club, and had just had his first child, so he needed security. We offered to quadruple his wages and told him how we saw him as the next big thing, whereas for Tottenham at best he would be their third-choice keeper behind Gomes and Carlo Cudicini and anyway he was only the makeweight to ensure they signed the £8 million Kaboul, while at Stoke he could play behind Shawcross and Huth. No matter how debatable the veracity of some of that may have been, it worked. Asmir decided the Potteries were going to be better for him than north London. We finally agreed a £3.25 million fee with Portsmouth just before the 5pm deadline once Asmir told them he would not sign for Spurs. Apparently, when Levy found out he was on the phone to Asmir's agent demanding the money back for the medical he had paid for!

Another player we signed in 2010, this time that summer, was Jon Walters. Jon would prove to be a classic Tony Pulis signing. He had fallen out with Roy Keane, who was his manager at

Ipswich, over Keane's refusal to allow him to move to the Premier League, famously going literally head-to-head with Keane in one disagreement. Three of us went to watch him on separate occasions, but we were divided about him, with Peter Reid being less than impressed. But Tony believed in his work rate up front and, no doubt, his obvious bravery in facing down Keane, and we paid £2.75 million for him. Jon would go on to score 62 goals in 271 games and win 54 caps for the Republic of Ireland as he proved the perfect workaholic foil for a bigger striker such as Kenwyne Jones or Peter Crouch.

Speaking of Kenwyne, we signed him for a club record £8 million in that same transfer window to totally freshen up the strike force, with Beattie gone and Fuller and Sidibe ageing. Kenwyne was a very laid-back man-mountain. On his day he could be devastating as he was a physical beast of a striker and he was great in the air, but he was also tentative at times and difficult to rile up to perform if he wasn't in the mood.

Another thing Tony chose to do was make Ryan Shawcross club captain, even though he was only 22. It proved a wonderful decision, although Tony did occasionally like to pick out his skipper for a half-time dressing down to make a point. I remember one game at Blackburn in which we were 2-0 up and comfortable by half-time, but Tony didn't want the players to relax in the second half, so he picked Ryan out, battering him for playing dreadfully (he hadn't) just to keep them all on their toes. Jonathan Woodgate was one of the subs and as the team trooped out for the second 45, he turned to the manager and said, 'Gaffer, please don't bring me on, I can't play as well as Ryan and I don't want you to crucify me like that!'

Again, we were very solid in the Premier League, finishing 13th, but only three points off eighth place. However, the story of that season was not in the league, but in the FA Cup.

* * *

Walters bagged two extra-time goals to finally see off Championship Cardiff in a third round replay to avoid an early exit and we then sneaked past Wolves thanks to a Huth header and late Sorensen penalty save. Sorro saved more than his fair share of spot kicks and that one saw us through to face Championship Brighton in the fifth round at home. That tie was over by half-time as we went 3-0 up to make it through to a home quarter-final against Avram Grant's West Ham. We actually lost a league game the weekend beforehand 0-3 at Upton Park, but this team were a different kettle of fish at the Britannia and, roared on by a fervent crowd once again, took an early lead when Huth headed another Delap Exocet powerfully home.

The Hammers controversially equalised when Freddie Piquionne appeared to bring a pass down with his arm before slotting home. These were the days well before VAR, so the referee awarded the goal despite the protests. That just served to whip up even more of a fervour and we won a penalty early in the second half, only for Fuller's shot to be saved by Robert Green. The winner arrived, however, a few minutes later when we won a free kick 30 yards out. The first effort hit the wall, but referee Mike Jones saw it as a handball and awarded another, even closer, free kick. This time, instead of Jermaine Pennant hitting it with his right foot, Danny Higginbotham took a run up and lashed it with his left, beating the wall. Green got down to his left, but the strike had too much power for him and sneaked over the line. We held on fairly comfortably to reach a first semi-final since 1972. Wembley glory awaited.

Pennant had signed from Real Zaragoza in August 2010, two years after he had rejected us to try his luck in Spain when leaving Liverpool. He was a fabulous footballer, but something of a maverick and I remember, when he travelled back to the UK, he left his Porsche Cayenne at Zaragoza train station whilst en route to Madrid to fly into Manchester to sign and then promptly forgot all about it. He'd even left the keys in the glove compartment! Players' attitudes to cars had changed since my excitement about my Lada in 1980.

We now had two flying wingers and were one of the most attractive sides to watch in the Premier League on our day, despite what Monsieur Wenger might have been trying to tell everyone. In fact, the week before the cup final we hammered Arsenal 3-1, scoring one beautiful goal, when Pennant hammered home from distance against his former employers, and two very scrappy ones, including yet another from a long throw, which saw Kenwyne allow the ball to hit him in the midriff three yards out and catapult into the net.

We reached that final by absolutely pummelling Bolton at Wembley on a gloriously sunny day on which everything went perfectly. Those twin wingers caused mayhem, with Etherington lashing in the first goal from around 25 yards and Pennant setting up the third for Jones to sidefoot home when clean through. His joy at scoring was a wonderful thing, as was his somersault celebration, not bad for an enormous feller. In between, Huth scored his third goal of the cup run, smashing in a right-footed half-volley. I'm not sure who was more surprised with that peach of a strike, Bolton's goalkeeper, his team-mates or Huthy himself! We were 3-0 up at half-time and the Bolton end was bordering on empty by the time Walters scored a brace in the second half.

The final 5-0 scoreline was the biggest win at Wembley by a domestic club since before the Second World War and a brilliant day out for our 40,000 or so jubilant supporters. I just sat in the stands muttering incredulously to myself as I watched it all unfold, reflecting on the long road I'd travelled since joining Port Vale as coach 31 years earlier. At half-time I turned to Del and said in utter disbelief, 'We're going to be in the bloody final here!' All those giant-killings had never seen me get so far in the world's greatest cup competition before, so to reach the showpiece event was a huge thrill and exemplified the turnaround brought about by Peter Coates since his return to the club five years earlier.

Before that game, Ricardo Fuller, who was injured, gave an inspirational team talk which really fired the lads up. It really was as good as anything I've ever heard any manager say, including myself and Tony, and, as I climbed up to my seat in the stand, I felt we were as prepared for the game as we could be. Little could I have known what awaited.

* * *

Who should we face in the final, but Manchester City, the team we had humbled, not only back in January 2009, but also knocked out of the cup in 2010. One of the key differences was they now had superstars like Vincent Kompany and Mario Balotelli in their ranks, so were becoming more like the force we know them as today. They still hadn't won anything since 1976, though, so were desperate to lift the trophy. Meanwhile, in the month between winning the semi-final and walking out again at Wembley we picked up a series of injuries which threatened to put a huge dent in our chances.

Huth and Etherington picked up knee injuries, but battled back to be just about fit for the big day, while Higginbotham and Fuller both missed out. Had the final been scheduled for the weekend after the league season ended we may have had more of a chance, but for some reason it was on the penultimate league weekend, so the players had a fortnight's less recuperation time.

Despite the injuries, we kept the game tight, with Sorensen making a couple of unbelievable saves, one from Balotelli with the end of his fingertips to stop a shot flying into the top corner. The game was a total contrast to the semi-final as we carried very little attacking threat and eventually we succumbed in the 74th minute when a loose ball at a corner fell to Yaya Touré, the giant Senegalese midfielder, who lashed it home with his left foot from ten yards.

Try as they might, the players couldn't rouse a grandstand finish, although Jones did find himself clear and bearing down on Joe Hart, but the ball just wouldn't sit down for him to get a clean strike on and the chance went begging. It was the classic game too far. Full credit to the players who battled and weathered the Manchester City storm, though, they fought like titans.

The 27,000 Stoke fans in attendance all stayed to see the cup being lifted and applaud the victors, a sign of the class of the people of the Potteries that I have come to know and love. Not for them, emptying the stadium as soon as the final whistle sounds, or, as Bolton fans did at the semi-final, at half-time. They were proud and so was I. It was a fantastic achievement to reach the first FA Cup Final in Stoke's history. I am delighted and honoured to have played a part in one of the club's greatest seasons.

Chapter 19

It's Thursday, it Must Be Switzerland

'I settled into a comfy outdoor armchair by the pool,
shades on and, as the glorious southern
French sun beat down on my head, turned
to Jonathan and said, "I think I may have
made a bit of a cock-up ... "'

John Rudge to agent Jonathan Barnett

AS THE delirious Stoke fans left Wembley in their happy thousands after the 5-0 demolition of Bolton in the FA Cup semi-final on that balmy spring afternoon, they sang, 'We're all going on a European tour,' because simply reaching the final meant, under the rules at that time that, as Manchester City finished in the Champions League places, we, as runners-up in the FA Cup, would enter the new UEFA Europa League. This was only the third time Stoke had qualified for Europe in their history and the first for 37 years. The draw paired us with Croatian veterans of European competition Hajduk Split; from Burslem to the Balkans, my career kept on astonishing me.

The rigours of a season playing Thursday and Sunday in both European and Premier League competition meant we needed a much larger squad, so we signed defenders Matthew Upson and Jonathan Woodgate to bolster the side and nearly secured striker

Craig Bellamy, but he opted for Liverpool not Stoke, when leaving Manchester City.

Then came deadline day and perhaps one the most entertaining ones in a long line. We had often become the focus, after making three signings on our first deadline day in the Premier League, and Sky TV's Rob Dorsett was a permanent fixture outside our Clayton Woods training ground and then the Britannia Stadium as the day wore on, with hundreds of fans joining him to get their faces on television. Meanwhile, the two Tonys and I would be beavering away trying to make last-ditch signings.

31 August 2011 was a bonanza for those supporters as news broke that striker Cameron Jerome had signed from Birmingham City for £4 million. But then came the big one, literally; Peter Crouch was on our radar. Crouch had been an established England international and was one of the most recognisable players in the country. For him to join Stoke would set a new standard. Tony Pulis was desperate to sign him, partly because he'd missed out on him all those years before, and badgered Jonathan Woodgate into ringing his former team-mate every hour for the two days leading up to the deadline in order to persuade him. It helped that the Spurs manager was our old mate Harry Redknapp, although we still weren't in Daniel Levy's good books, which may be why things unfolded as they did.

Levy insisted that if we wanted Crouch we also sign Honduras midfielder Wilson Palacios, who wasn't a player we were really interested in and complicated things, with Tony Scholes being against the £15 million package deal. In order to secure one of England's most talismanic strikers, Pulis was happy to take the risk and persuaded Peter Coates by telling him, 'Crouch will guarantee you Premier League football for years, Peter.'

No matter what Scholes' representations may have been, the chairman agreed. It was perhaps the greatest example of how Bet365 made a massive difference and we were able to buy players we would never have been able to dream about before.

We still tried getting out of signing Palacios, as he had been injured, but Levy wasn't having any of it. It was both or we didn't get Crouch. An additional complication at the time was that we were trying to keep wages to around £40,000 a week, but Crouch was on a lot more than that and we had to manipulate a few things like bonuses and a signing-on fee to get the deal done to keep the formal wages within the structure if anyone asked. But it did mean that within the dressing room there were some players on significantly different money to others. It put me in mind of the dispute when I was a player when we found out at Carlisle that Hughie McIlmoyle was on £7.50 a week more than us; except by 2011 the differential could be tens of thousands, rather than under a tenner.

On deadline day, Levy called Crouch to tell him in no uncertain terms that a move to Stoke had been lined up as Spurs were buying Emmanuel Adebayor and excitement bubbled up around the place as Dorsett gave regular updates on Crouchy's progress, none of which were accurate. At one point Peter was said to be in a helicopter flying up to Stoke. He wasn't; he was tucking into a burger at the McDonald's on the Target roundabout on the A40 out of London, awaiting notification the deal had been agreed by the clubs before travelling up for his medical.

As part of brokering the deal, Scholes and I had to meet with Crouch's agent, Jonathan Barnett, earlier that week. I had known Jonathan for years since recommending him to my Vale protégé Anthony Gardner, who needed an agent as a young lad when signing for Spurs. Anthony had only played a few games for Vale, but was obviously going to be a fantastic player and he'd had agents contacting him to try and sign him up as the next big thing. Just after I had left Vale, Jonathan came to my house, wanting to be recommended to Gardner. After spending some time with him, I knew he would look after this 18-year-old starlet and indeed he got him a good deal when he signed for Tottenham the following year. I met with Anthony and his mum, who was a nurse, I believe, and advised them to choose Barnett over the two or three others.

In return, as I was a free agent at that point, Jonathan asked me if I would like to go and work for him as I had a lot of experience of buying and selling players, but I turned him down as I wanted to continue in management, saying, 'I'm sorry, Jonathan, I don't think it's for me.'

Cut to August 2011 and Jonathan was now a super-agent and a millionaire many times over. To agree personal terms for Crouch, he invited Scholes and I to his pad in Cannes and we flew out to be picked up by Jonathan in his chauffeur-driven, top-down sports car. We drove up to his villa overlooking the harbour, my hair flying all over the place, both of them. On arrival, we took in the view of millionaires whizzing around in their speedboats and yachts as we walked from the car to the poolside, where all his family and friends were gathered around to welcome us. I settled into a comfy outdoor armchair, shades on, was handed a cocktail and a fruit platter to die for prepared by his personal chef and, as the glorious southern French sun beat down on my head, I turned to Jonathan and said, 'I think I may have made a bit of a cock-up when I turned you down a decade or so ago! I've missed the bloody boat here!'

Crouch was a huge success for us, both as a goalscorer and off the pitch, creating a wonderful dressing room atmosphere. He also brought brilliant publicity to the club, partly via his high-profile wife Abbey, who won the BBC's *Strictly Come Dancing* in 2013. Around that time, Stoke City were big news and we had visits from the likes of Sugar Ray Leonard, Diego Maradona, Pele and even Archbishop Desmond Tutu.

Palacios was less successful, with Tony Pulis once telling the press he couldn't pick him because it was 'too windy' at the Brit, making just 13 league starts in two seasons. I'd still argue that having to sign him to secure Crouch made sense, however.

We nearly didn't sign Crouch for another reason. Another contact of mine recommended Senegalese striker Demba Ba, but he failed his medical in January 2011 due to an ongoing knee issue, after we had agreed a fee of £7 million with Hoffenheim and the player and his agent had agreed personal terms. Before we knew it, Ba had been signed by West Ham, then moved to Newcastle and Chelsea, for combined fees of £12.3 million without his knee being a problem. Had Ba signed, who knows if we would have been given the money for Crouch later that year?

* * *

There was a massive buzz around the city for Stoke's first European adventure since 1974. Joining the competition in the third qualifying round meant we began competitive football on 28 July, defeating our Croatian visitors 1-0 thanks to a second-minute Walters header. Stoke had never won a European tie before, so the pressure to complete the job in Split was huge. The stadium was incredibly intimidating, packed to the gills with Hajduk fans, flags and coloured smoke everywhere. But the lads stood up to the task brilliantly and nicked a 1-0 victory on the night, 2-0 on aggregate, thanks to a last-minute own goal.

Next stop on our European tour was Switzerland as we drew little-known FC Thun, from a town near the beautiful lakes in the Bernese Oberland, not far from Interlaken. The first leg took place on a balmy August evening in the shadow of the central Swiss Alps and Stoke fans celebrated Danny Pugh putting us in the lead by singing 'Doe a Deer' from *The Sound of Music*, whilst doing a conga around the away end. It went on for about half an hour! These were heady days indeed. We took that one-goal lead back to the Brit, hammering Thun 4-1 to reach the group stage. It was at that point that the button was pressed on the signings of Crouch, Palacios and Jerome as, not only would we need the bodies, but we would have the money generated from six matches against Israel's Maccabi Tel Aviv, Turkish side Besiktas and European heavyweights Dynamo Kyiv from Ukraine.

To prepare, we weren't sent round Europe to scout – instead we watched videos and phoned our contacts around the continent to find out more about our opponents. But that whole period was a wonderful experience, which tested us both at home and abroad as a club and particularly as backroom staff supporting the manager.

We opened our group stage campaign in Kyiv, although Tony Pulis got himself into trouble for querying whether Ukraine was even in Europe. We were football managers, not Brains of Britain, let's be honest. Actually, the point he was making was that all three of the clubs we were facing were thousands of miles away, but he certainly earned himself some headlines and stiff questions with that comment.

When we arrived in the Ukrainian capital, Tony appeased the local press, who were gunning for him, by taking us all to see the memorial to the infamous 'Death Match' on the outskirts of the city. This commemorated a game between a team made up of players from Dynamo Kyiv and Lokomotiv Kyiv which defeated a team of Nazi soldiers in August 1942, while Ukraine was under occupation. Several of the victors' players were then hunted down and murdered by the Nazis. It was a sobering visit that brought home how lucky we are to work in football in the era we do.

The following night we drew 1-1 thanks to a first goal for Jerome against a team which included the likes of Andriy Shevchenko and Andriy Yarmalenko. That was a superb start and defeating Besiktas 2-1 in the next game at the Brit, coming from behind to do so, set us up brilliantly.

Then came two matches against the weakest side in the pool, Maccabi Tel Aviv. We were three up within half an hour in the first match at the Brit when Jerome got himself sent off by a fussy Greek referee for two yellow cards. Just after half-time, Tel Aviv were also reduced to ten when their midfielder Ziv lost his boot in a challenge with Shotton, got annoyed he hadn't been given a free kick and ended up firing his boot, which had remained on the end of his foot, into the nearby linesman's face in a fit of pique; one of the more bizarre red cards.

We also won in Tel Aviv, 2-1 thanks to a rare goal from Dean Whitehead amidst a deluge of a rainstorm, but then came the crucial return game with Kyiv, who had only drawn at home with Tel Aviv and so needed to beat us at the Brit to have any chance of progressing. We went behind to an early Upson own goal, but pressed hard and equalised with just ten minutes left when Kenwyne Jones soared to head home a Pennant cross. Asmir Begović fingertipped a late shot round the post to keep us level and we were through to the last 32, a truly tremendous achievement.

Having already qualified, we experienced how British sides have had to cope with the kinds of shenanigans which go on behind the scenes in European competition before our last match. Firstly, we were delayed taking off from Manchester because of supposed congestion in Turkish airspace. Then, when our pilot made up time so we arrived at Istanbul slightly early, we were redirected to Sabiha Gekcen airport, 60km from our initial destination of Ataturk airport, and in fact on the wrong continent as it was on the Asian side of the Bosphorus. We were then held there for three hours before being allowed to take off for the hop to Ataturk. Besiktas had to win to go through, so it was a clear attempt to tire us out by delaying us for over four hours in total and showed us the remarkable lengths countries will go to in order to win.

It worked. We lost that match at Besiktas, after taking the lead through a wonderful Fuller strike, but then having Upson sent off when conceding a penalty, and that defeat meant we finished second and would face one of the group winners or one of the third-placed teams from the Champions League group stages who didn't qualify for the last 16 of that competition, which turned out to be the case when we came out of the hat against Valencia.

* * *

As is common with clubs playing in Europe on an occasional basis, our Premier League form was affected by playing the additional matches and all the European travel, as it was tough playing midweek and then Premier League on a Sunday on a regular basis. After winning in Thun, for example, we flew directly to Norwich, instead of going back home to Stoke, to prepare for our away game there. That made a lot of difference as we nicked a late 1-1 draw. It didn't always go so well; after that famous draw in Kyiv, we were hammered in the Sunday away game 0-4 at Sunderland and after winning in Tel Aviv we collapsed 0-5 at Bolton. Those results were what shaped Tony's decision to take a vastly reduced squad to Valencia for the round of 32 second leg. Valencia at the time were one of the best teams in Europe, managed by Unai Emery. Despite fielding arguably our full-strength team at home, Valencia had dominated and won 0-1, so the chances of us getting through were minimal. Despite this, thousands of Stokies travelled to Spain and celebrated in the town centre, before heading out to the Mestalla where the 'reserves', which actually included ten internationals, put up a far better showing than the first team had in the home leg, although they couldn't summon a goal and also lost 0-1 to go out 0-2 on aggregate.

Tony came in for a lot of criticism for that and it was one of the first indications that fans were unhappy with some of his decisions. In fact, there were three former international captains on the field that night and all of the starting 11 had played in previous European ties that season. We had won one in nine league games and had a must-win home match against Swansea the following Sunday in what was already our 44th game of the season, despite it being February still. We won 2-0, with the rested players to the fore, so I felt Tony was justified in making that decision, but understand why some supporters who had spent their hard-earned cash to travel out to Valencia only to find that he had left behind six players, plus three who were injured, felt aggrieved.

That wasn't the only way Tony was finding himself embattled at that time. Tony Scholes' influence had grown stronger as the years went on and, eventually, he became a board member and director, before leaving to join the Premier League in 2022. The chief executive has to be the board's ally as it is their job to manage money closely, and that's understandable, but it led to tension between himself and the manager, especially over the Crouch deal.

Being between the two Tonys wasn't easy and whenever I sided with one or other over transfer decisions, then the other wasn't pleased. I was always doing it for football reasons, but I wasn't always convinced either of the Tonys were, as it felt like more of a contest with me as piggy in the middle, taking on that Bill Lodey role of the go-between. I would go to Scholes to tell him that Pulis wanted a particular player, but Scholes would say 'no' or allow him to spend less money than he knew it would take to sign him and I felt the relationship became detrimental. It didn't help that Scholes said something in the paper that Pulis didn't like and that led to more in-fighting and the underlying friction was always there, despite the success we had in establishing Stoke as the longest-serving club in the Premier League outside the big six.

* * *

One of my matchday jobs was to make my way up to the Waddington Suite around 2pm each home game and reveal the team selection to the guests in the hospitality area, hosted by Stoke legend Terry Conroy. Terry and I always used to have great banter to keep the hordes entertained as we went through the side and I explained how we were going to play. However, this one day, Tony Pulis colluded with Terry and made sure I got given completely the wrong line-up, so there I was going through a totally fictitious team, with Tony and Terry doing me up like a kipper. Naturally, I got my own back on him, but that story isn't one for publication.

My last big signing was England star Michael Owen, who had become a free agent, having left Manchester United in summer 2012. Michael lived in north Wales, about an hour's drive from Stoke and Tony rang me to tell me that he had spoken with Michael's agent and agreed in principle to sign him, so Michael was driving down to put pen to paper. As I was the only member of the management team at the ground, I would have to negotiate the contract. 'No problem,' I said, 'leave it to me.'

The agent soon turned up to discuss terms, but this was actually the day of the deadline for submitting the players in your squad for the first half of the 2012/13 season to the FA and the cut-off point was 4pm. It was by now 3pm and no Michael. Eventually, the agent received a call from a clearly flustered Owen telling him that he had missed the turn-off at junction 15 of the M6 and was heading further south to Stafford where he'd have to turn round. We were coming right up to the deadline and it was now touch and go whether we'd be able to sign him.

I used the time to get Peter Coates to sign off Michael's wages and then rang the FA to inform them that the deal had been done and that the squad list would be following as soon as the star reached the ground (we couldn't submit a player in the squad who we didn't actually have a contract for). They weren't happy, pointing out that we had more than the allowed 25 players on our books already, but I persuaded them to allow us to submit late under the circumstances and we then had to wait with bated breath for an FA review panel to approve things.

Given that Michael is a trained helicopter pilot, the irony of him not being able to navigate roads was not lost on me. At least he never flew to training – lads like Glen Whelan would have eaten him alive. Owen eventually arrived at the ground just after the deadline had passed to sign his one-year contract and the FA panel accepted our squad as valid after a hairy couple of days' wait.

After all that, Michael's time at Stoke was a huge disappointment as he scored only once in the nine appearances he made. Injuries had taken their toll and he retired, receiving a standing ovation from both sets of supporters as he came on as a substitute at Southampton. A nice touch from Tony.

Owen had replaced Ricardo Fuller, who had left at the end of the 2011/12 season. A club legend, who scored 50 goals in 208 games for Stoke, Ric now has a bar named after him at the Bet365 Stadium, a well-deserved honour, despite the many 'moments' he gave us and is undoubtedly one of our best signings at Stoke.

Geoff Cameron, Michael Kightly, Charlie Adam and Steven N'Zonzi also all signed in summer 2012 and we went ten matches unbeaten, conceding just four goals, leading up to a fantastic 3-1 comeback win over Liverpool on Boxing Day, which left us in seventh place. Was this the best team Tony had built?

But then form fell away. In fact, the second half of that campaign felt like creeping relegation as we were very poor, winning just one in the next 13 league games, and the supporters started to revolt against the manager, especially after a terrible 1-3 home defeat by Aston Villa. We eventually rallied to finish 13th thanks to wins at QPR and at home to Norwich. It had felt like a long two years since that FA Cup glory.

The final home game of the 2012/13 season against Spurs saw a celebration of Stoke City's 150th anniversary, as, at that time, we were the second-oldest league club after Notts County, who were one year older. It was a wonderful day with players from every era returning for a pre-match parade, but they, like my heart alert which had now been put to rest, merely served to remind me that I was getting old.

Chapter 20

Dad's Army

'It's got a bit like Dad's Army.'

Stoke chairman, Peter Coates

NOTHING LASTS forever.

In October 2012 I was called to a meeting at the Britannia Stadium and put on notice by Tony Scholes that, come the end of that season, my contract would not be renewed. Disappointed, I rang Peter Coates and asked to see him. Peter thanked me for all my work over the years, but said the place was getting 'a bit like Dad's Army'. He clearly wanted to change things and, at 68, my time was up at Stoke City. The board, of course, has the right to make decisions like that and, although I was disappointed, I am grateful for the Coates family enabling me to finally make it into the Premier League, reach the FA Cup Final and compete in Europe in the twilight of my career.

The remainder of that campaign saw Mark Cartwright brought in as technical director, as John Coates, Peter's son, took over more direct running of affairs from his father. So, I lost almost all of my influence and became disassociated with the club as the board put together the team to move them forward. In fact, I didn't even travel to the final game of the 2012/13 campaign at Southampton, as I just drifted away; yesterday's man after 14 years at the club, although they did present me with some parting gifts, which I really appreciated. I must say Peter Coates and his family were good to me. All you need to know about them is that season ticket prices remain at 2007 levels, fixed by the board to support fans who would otherwise not be able to afford them. Then, they added free away travel too. Full respect to them.

I had worked with five different managers, spent around £50m in transfer fees and broken the transfer record several times to bring Premier League football back to Stoke. I look back at my time there with equal fondness as at Port Vale, although, of course, I was never the main man.

Would I have done anything differently? Not personally. When it was announced that Tony Pulis and many of his backroom team would also be leaving once the 2012/13 season ended, it was clear that a whole, new broom approach was being taken by the board and you have to say that, for many years, the Mark Hughes era brought wonderful players and a different brand of football to Stoke City.

Could Tony have done anything to keep that from happening? Well, sometimes you have just run your course, but I do think Tony did not encourage the young players as much as Peter Coates wanted him to at the end, an accusation which had been levelled at him during his spell under the Icelandics too. On that occasion I really didn't agree as the likes of Gareth Owen, Lewis Buxton, Karl Henry and Lewis Neal all graduated from the academy or reserves to play regularly, while Kris Commons, a tricky winger who had an eye for goal, went on to star for Nottingham Forest and Celtic, winning several trophies and playing regularly in Europe. Then there were two mainstays of the promotion-winning squad; Andy Wilkinson and Carl Dickinson, the full-backs, who were given their first chances by Tony, with Wilko becoming a bona fide club legend who played in the cup final and Europe.

In any case, as a manager of a football club, you are in one of the most precarious professions on the planet, so you want players who can do a job for you now, not risk too many youngsters who are in the process of developing, especially the higher up the leagues you go.

When I started at Vale in Division Four, we could take a punt on the likes of Robbie Earle, Mark Bright and Mark Chamberlain and allow their talents to blossom over time. There just isn't any patience in the modern game at Premier League level and, perhaps not surprisingly, under Hughes, I don't think Stoke went down that route in any case.

It is true that Tony preferred to sign mature, experienced players, often who he already knew, but that is entirely understandable, especially when the chances of taking more than 10 per cent of academy graduates are pretty negligible as such a huge percentage fall by the wayside for various reasons. That is why I always ensure kids in any academy complete their education and tell them about how I went to night school and studied for O levels and other practical courses until I was well into my 20s.

In my opinion, Tony Pulis turned out to be exactly the right manager for Stoke City, across both his spells, and we worked extremely well together. We had a wonderful time and used to have all sorts of practical jokes going on. I'm sure that's what has kept me looking so young ... hairline excepting, but then I have the cap to disguise that.

* * *

I found it strange not being involved in football as I had been for 50 years or more. That didn't last long, though, as I still wanted to work and, as I'd never had what my mates called a 'proper job', it had to be in the game.

I'd actually been for a chat at my boyhood club, Wolves, in early 2013 to see if I could help them as they were struggling to stay in the Championship and had just sacked manager Stale Solbakken, replacing him with Dean Saunders. They wanted me to scout for them, but that didn't work out and, once I left the Britannia Stadium, for a while I helped out Beswick's football solicitors; a Potteries-based firm who had been acting as agents for a range of players I'd had a lot of dealings with as director of football at Stoke. I enjoyed my time working with them to try and sign up young players as clients. One that sticks in my mind is a youthful Aleksandar Mitrovic, who you will know as Fulham's Serbian striker who bangs in goals for fun. In 2014, he had played a season at Anderlecht and Newcastle were in the hunt to bring him over to the Premier League, which they eventually did a year later. I travelled over with a chap (who shall remain anonymous) from Beswick's, who, it turned out, had booked the flight to an airport over 100 miles from Brussels and I had to phone one of my contacts to drive across to pick us up so we could negotiate with our target. The triumph of experience over youth.

Before I could complete that deal, Stan Ternent, who I had played with at Carlisle, got in touch and I moved on. Stan had joined Steve Bruce at Hull as chief scout and I worked with them to look at players in the west and Midlands, returning to my roots of travelling around the country watching games and writing reports.

In May 2014 Hull reached the FA Cup Final, which I got to attend at Wembley, although it ended sadly as Arsenal came back from an early two-goal deficit to win 3-2. That, though, qualified the Tigers for the Europa League, so I was back in Europe again, three years after that epic campaign with Stoke, although on this occasion, after defeating Slovakians Trencin 2-1 in the third qualifying round, Hull missed out on the group stage, going out on away goals to Belgian side Lokeren.

I enjoyed my time working for Hull as there was very little direct pressure, but then, in early October 2017, I received a phone call from my former player Neil Aspin, who told me he had just been appointed as Port Vale's manager under new owner Norman Smurthwaite and wanted me to assist him. Neil and Norman sealed the deal by coming to my house to discuss how we could keep Vale in League Two as the club had just five points from 11 games at the time. It was a scenario reminiscent of that in which I took over from John McGrath at the club in January 1984. As Neil had been such an outstanding player for me, I jumped at the chance as I was desperate to ensure Vale did not drop out of the league and was appointed football advisor. Neil and assistant Gary Brabin did a great job, winning four of the next six games and then having another run of four wins and a draw in five matches in December to get them out of trouble. I don't want to take any credit for that, but it was great being back involved. It was him, his coaches, and the players who turned things around, staying up despite a long run without a win in the second half of the campaign.

The next season, things didn't improve and Neil, feeling very overwhelmed with the job, came to me and said Norman was going to fire him. I phoned Norman, but he denied this and said that Neil had simply had enough. He wanted the sack. So, inevitably, it came. Neil could sometimes be a strange boy as a player. It carried on whilst he was manager, it seemed. I tried to ring Neil back three times, but he never answered and I haven't really spoken to him since, aside from at the odd former players' get-together. He is, though, now head coach at National Conference South club Dover Athletic.

John Askey took over and asked me to stay and help. He also had Dave Kevan to assist him, who I had worked with at Stoke. Initially, John had a good run of results and Vale were vying for the play-offs, but then a poor run followed and, in 2021, John was relieved of his position, being replaced by Darrell Clarke who would win promotion for the club through the play-offs in 2022, before being relieved of his duties as I was finishing writing this book.

By that time, Carol and Kevin Shanahan had bought Port Vale from Norman Smurthwaite (in May 2019) and the club has been transformed by them. They are wonderful owners, who have the community at heart, with enormous focus on the supporters. Vale is now in very good hands.

For me, any football club lives at the heart of its community. It often gives folk an outlet, something to cling on to in times that are challenging in their own lives. So, throughout my career, I have always made a point of ensuring I met and supported as many local people and businesses as I could. I suppose it goes back to my days on my family's market stalls. There was such a sense of community at Wolverhampton market, and we helped each other. I've just carried that on because I am aware of how important football clubs are in people's lives. Our success gives them a lift, puts a spring in their step. And that gives you a lasting impact as great as any victory.

Consequently, I was always happy to attend supporter events, attend community photoshoots or give out prizes, as I did that fateful night in 1997 when I bottled out of handing in my resignation to Bill Bell.

I also liked my players to make community visits and appearances. Tony Pulis shared this ethos and he and some of the Stoke players, notably Rory Delap, raised thousands of pounds for the local children's hospice, the Donna Louise Trust. Tony even climbed Mount Kilimanjaro, although that only counts as his second-most difficult life experience, after marking me.

Obviously one such difficult time in everyone's life was the Covid-19 pandemic. Vale were brilliant for the community during that period, producing hundreds of meals and distributing them to the surrounding area every day. They even got the restaurants and hotels from around the city which were closed during the lockdown period to move their fridges and stoves to Vale Park to increase capacity and I believe they produced around 350,000 meals during the pandemic for the local community. Outstanding.

In November 2019, I was named as Port Vale's president and am extremely proud and grateful to the Shanahans for honouring me with that position. They have also hung a big banner up on the wall at Vale Park, which you will see in the photo section of the book. It has me and Pej on it, with Alex Ferguson's quote about me printed on it. Speaking of Sir Alex, I am so honoured he has written a foreword for me – thanks to him for his kind(ish) words.

I now watch every Vale game, home and away, travelling with Carol and Kevin. This meant I was in attendance when we returned to Wembley for the play-off final in May 2022 and defeated Mansfield Town 3-0 to return to League One. That was a wonderful occasion and fantastic result for both the manager, his team and the Shanahans, who deserve every possible success.

* * *

How do you measure success in football? Is it winning trophies or is it spending 19 years at Port Vale and having to sell your best players? Or even feeding your local community in difficult times?

Personally, I have had no bigger tribute than from my friend Sir Alex Ferguson who (for once) put aside all those pestering phone calls he received from me to kindly say, 'Port Vale fans should get down on their knees and thank God for John Rudge.' That, and the continuing smiles and handshakes I receive at Vale Park or on the occasions I pop in to watch a game at the Bet365 Stadium, are everything to me.

Sometimes I look back and think there should have been other things in life than the game. My family has always been of paramount importance to me. We are now settled in a beautiful area of Stoke-on-Trent down at the south end of the city. When we arrived from Torquay in that bleak winter of early 1980, we were lucky to find a house on a good estate, but then ended up buying some nearby land and building our house and then, later, Lisa and Deb built their own houses in our back garden, so now the entire Rudge family live a minute's walk from each other. It is bliss as far as Del and I are concerned. Deb jokes we could build a tunnel between the houses.

Our eldest, Lisa, who is married to Darren, a mechanic who owns his own garage, has worked her way up within NatWest Bank after I got her an interview when she was 16 because the manager of the Burslem branch was a Vale fan. She is now very senior in her role, covering Staffordshire and Cheshire, with 37 years of service.

Deb is married to Andy, who works in IT. She would have been a professional footballer if she had been born into this modern era as the women's game has come on so strongly over the past few years and she was mad crazy on football. Still is. Instead, she trained to be a PE teacher, but, after several years of teaching, moved to work for Stoke City, after I had left the club, working in the community department, where part of her role is training primary teachers to teach PE if it isn't their specialism.

Del and I are so very proud of our grandchildren; Lisa's two Danielle and Hollie, and Deb's pair, Cameron and Emma. They are stepping on their own life-ladder now, taking exams, starting university and entering the world of work. They mean everything to Del and I and we are so fortunate to have them so close, although we are also fortunate that, unlike so many other children and grandchildren, they aren't a pain in the backside! We love going on holiday together and we are involved in all the things they do. We are truly blessed and Del and I thank our lucky stars every day for what we have. I am also very close to my sister Pat, her children Robert and Julie and their families.

* * *

To play professional football is the dream of many lads and now many girls who kick a ball. I knew from the age of seven that it was all I wanted to do. I've been so lucky. Football, it is often said, is but a short career, so I was proud and fortunate to have spent some 60 years in the game. As I write I am coming up on 79 years old. I have lived all over the country, won promotions, lifted trophies at Wembley, suffered relegation and coped with all sorts of professional hardships, including sorting out difficult chairmen and broken washing machines, moving players' furniture, acting as a hotel concierge, becoming an immigration expert, marriage guidance counsellor and international diplomat, delivering first aid and had a heart scare myself; occasionally my career has broken out into actual football.

After the pandemic, my children told me they would like to take me to see where we used to live when we moved around the country. So, we've now been to Huddersfield where I met Del and saw our old haunts, plus visited the church where we got married and the site of Leeds Road, Huddersfield's old ground.

Then, after Port Vale played at Swindon in the 2022 play-offs, we travelled on down to Bournemouth and I rang Tony Pulis and met up in Sandbanks where he and his wife live, just seconds from the beach. When you get there, you have to wait for the gates to open; he's Lord Pulis now, you know. We went out for coffee and, as we drove into this harbour full of yachts, all of a sudden a car pulled up alongside us and who gets out of it but Harry Redknapp. The kids had rung him up and arranged for him to meet us. It was wonderful to catch up.

I've also had time for the first period in my life to reflect on what the game has done for my peers. We all had wonderful careers, don't get me wrong, but in 2021, when Denis Law, the man whose bed I slept in as a youth and whose shoes I gave to my father, announced publicly that he had dementia, it really hit me.

Heading the ball was one of my biggest assets as a player. I could jump much higher than might be expected for someone with a small frame, making my 5ft 10in stretch above much larger defenders. So, I am grateful that I haven't been affected as so many others have. I remember back in the early 1960s, working with my mate Allan Gilliver to throw the ball against a wall in the gym at Huddersfield and head it as powerfully as we could over and over. Allan now has Alzheimer's and is very unwell, residing in a care home. Denis and Allan are still with us as I write, but many aren't. You may know of the case of Jeff Astle, the West Brom and England striker, whose family have campaigned so vigorously to bring to the fore the link between heading a football and dementia since his early death, but there are many more who have been affected.

My managerial mentor John McGrath died aged 60, while Chris Balderstone died suddenly at his home in Carlisle in 2000 and Peter Clark, my own brother-in-law, died of a heart attack in 2008 when exercising in the gym. Even more sadly, my former player John Jeffers died after a long illness in 2021, aged just 52. John fought his illness in the way he played his football, ferociously.

Far too many have been taken or afflicted too soon and nothing has brought this home to me more than my long-standing friends and colleagues of 50-odd years Don Megson and Colin Dobson both dying during the writing of this book.

I also attended the funerals of both Sir Stanley Matthews, in 2000, and Gordon Banks, in 2019, legends of the game and heroes in the Potteries.

I met Stan quite a few times, each a privilege and an honour. He was the Stoke president when I joined, but passed on in February 2000, not long after his beloved wife Mila. It is incredible to think that he was still playing in the First Division aged 50! And, of course, Stan managed Port Vale, so we had something to talk about there. Stan's daughter Jean Gough still attends the odd Vale game as a guest of Carol Shanahan.

I attended Stan's funeral at St Peter's Church in Stoke and then the reception back at the Britannia Stadium and remember the roads being lined ten deep all the way round the city, with thousands gathering outside the church to celebrate an amazing life.

Gordon Banks was a member of the Trentham golf club, like myself, and we played a few games together. I thought he was a really nice man and we enjoyed our rounds, before he too passed on in 2019.

All this has made me so grateful for the living the game has given me and the opportunities it has presented to my family. I had 843 games as Port Vale manager and served another 14 years at Stoke, but not as manager, so I don't quite qualify for the official 1,000 club which features the likes of Alex Ferguson, Neil Warnock, Denis Smith and Tony Pulis. However, I was the director of football for 707 competitive games at the Potters, so I'm claiming honorary membership.

After being inducted into the Stoke-on-Trent sporting Hall of Fame in 2014, being an honorary son of the Potteries now, I was then recognised by the Football League, being awarded the EFL Contribution to League Football Lifetime Achievement Award for outstanding service and dedication to football in 2021. That came as a total surprise, although everyone else seemed to know about it, apart from me.

Initially, my children had been involved in organising the event in 2020, but then Covid struck and everything got delayed, so they had to keep quiet for a year. They managed to persuade me to attend the ceremony in April 2021, which was held at Vale Park and televised on Sky Sports, so I could be presented with the award. However, as it was the tail end of the pandemic, the girls got more involved than they thought because, as they were in my Covid 'bubble', they had to hand me the plaque. They were lucky I was still there as, during the ceremony, I got a bit fed up as it was dragging on as these dos can. Then, the presenter started banging on about this final award which was being given to some old feller who'd begun life in Wolverhampton, debuted at Huddersfield and played for a load of clubs before ending up as manager at Port Vale and director of football at Stoke City. It took me a while to realise, but I suddenly turned to Del and said, 'Hey, they're talking about me!'

She smiled and replied, 'Yes, love.'

The next day, I rang Rick Parry, the chief executive of the Football League, to say thank you for the award and he told me it had been voted for by the managers on the EFL committee and they had almost unanimously chosen me. What a great honour.

* * *

Port Vale's fans always supported me throughout my time as manager of their club. Now they have given me the ultimate accolade of setting about raising around £100,000 in order to have a statue cast of me which will stand outside the ground. Not surprisingly I'll be wearing a flat cap. I am deeply honoured and grateful and have tried to help in every way I can, including in promoting the sale of mugs and attending fundraising dinners. Thanks go to the likes of Mark Porter, Matt Jackson, Paul Dixon, Kirsty Rollings, Dave Thorley and Phil Potts, treasurer, in particular, but there are so many more to thank who have given their time and effort.

The statue, sculpted by renowned local artist Michael Talbot, who also created both the Sproson statue outside Vale Park and the statue of Arnold Bennett which is outside the museum in Hanley, is going to be sited at the entrance to Vale Park, behind the Hamil Road End and just off the main road opposite the pub the Williams family ran, which I am delighted with. The aim is to unveil it on my 80th birthday in October 2024.

I've seen a mock-up, which is called a maquette, and have included photos of it in the photo section, so you can see what you are helping to fund. The statue is apparently going to be 7ft 6in high. I always said I was bigger than I looked, so I'm claiming it's life-size.

Despite my girls pestering me to complete the book I began all those years ago, and often being asked by others too, it has never felt right until now. I'm delighted that the proceeds from it will be going to the statue fund. It's the least I can do to say thank you to those wonderful supporters. Thanks go to you for buying and reading this copy too. It really does cap it all.